SIMPLE & EASY KETO DIET

SIMPLE & EASY KETO DIET

Essential Recipes to Lose Weight and Achieve Optimal Health

JEN FISCH

founder of KetoInTheCity.com

ROCKRIDGE
PRESS

For general information on our other products and services or to obtain technical support, please contact our Customer Care Department within the United States at (866) 744-2665, or outside the United States at (510) 253-0500.

Rockridge Press publishes its books in a variety of electronic and print formats. Some content that appears in print may not be available in electronic books, and vice versa.

The contents of this book were previously published in *The Easy 5-Ingredient Ketogenic Diet Cookbook: Low-Carb, High-Fat Recipes for Busy People on the Keto Diet* by Jen Fisch (2018) and *The Complete Ketogenic Diet For Beginners: Your Essential Guide to Living the Keto Lifestyle* by Amy Ramos (2016).

Cover photography, clockwise from left: Nadine Greeff/Stocksy; Yellow Cat/Shutterstock; Aksana Yasiuchenia/Shutterstock; Nadine Greeff; TheCrimsonMonkey/istockphoto.com
Interior photography: © Nadine Greeff, 2017; photographs p.98 and p.170 © Shannon Douglas, 2018
Author photograph © Suzanne Strong

Printed in China

ISBN: 978-1-64152-277-9

CONTENTS

INTRODUCTION

I'M SO HAPPY you've decided to explore the ketogenic way of eating with me.

Following a keto diet has helped so many people. My journey with low-carbohydrate eating began over a decade ago, at the recommendation of a doctor I was seeing for acupuncture. When I was 18 and 19 years old, I was diagnosed with two autoimmune disorders: psoriatic arthritis and psoriasis. I was looking for ways to alleviate pain and inflammation, and the doctor recommended that I cut sugar out of my diet. This was the first time I had thought about the connection between food and autoimmune disorders.

I followed his advice, started on a low-carb diet, cut out sugar, and saw relief within weeks. I noticed a definite decrease in the inflammation in my joints as well as in my skin, which had been angry and red. This started me on a path of discovery, learning more about how my body reacts to various foods and finally finding an eating plan that could help me feel like my best self.

For many years I followed a mostly low-carbohydrate eating plan, but I also went through periods where I "fell off the wagon." Then, a few years ago, I started having more autoimmune issues again. My doctors thought perhaps I had Crohn's disease, but they weren't sure. After many tests and few answers, I decided to go back to experimenting with food to see if I could help heal myself. I started by eating high-quality foods (organic, grass-fed, etc.) but with gluten-free carbs. I saw some improvement with my issues, but I just felt sluggish, and after six months of following that plan, I had gained weight thanks to those tasty gluten-free treats that are so readily available these days.

Then I came across the ketogenic diet. At first, it seemed like the induction phase to the Atkins diet, but I liked the idea of eating real foods, lower in protein, with a focus on healthy fats. I had never heard of "keto" at the time, and like many people, I felt a little confused and overwhelmed by the new keto terms. What on

Earth is ketosis? What is a macro, and how do I measure it? But I decided to try the keto diet, and I am so glad I did.

Immediately I loved the challenge of creating keto-friendly meals that were quick and easy, and also delicious. I am a single mom, and I work full time. I also have an extremely busy teenage daughter, so I like to keep recipes (and everything else in my life) as simple as humanly possible. In my experience, you do not need a lot of exotic ingredients and a cupboard full of special oils to whip up amazing keto meals.

The recipes in this book will help satisfy cravings you will have for those high-carb favorites you used to eat pre-keto. Having those cravings is normal. Most people have eaten a high-carbohydrate diet their entire lives, so it is definitely an adjustment to go keto. But I encourage you to stick with it.

For this book, I created as many recipes as I could that could be considered quick or easy or both. You'll find a variety of meals in here that have just 5 ingredients or fewer, and many others that won't even take 30 minutes from start to finish. Who has the time these days to spend hours preparing a meal? The recipes are full of flavor and healthy fats. You'll be cooking with natural, wholesome ingredients that are affordable and easy to find. There is no need to go to five different grocery stores just to hunt down a bunch of unfamiliar ingredients. My recipes make keto easy!

Come along as I guide you on your keto journey. I know you can do it!

CHAPTER ONE

GETTING STARTED WITH KETO

Low-fat, low-calorie, gluten-free, Atkins, Weight Watchers, South Beach . . . the list of diets goes on. If you're trying to choose, how do you decide? Will you have to starve yourself; eat bland, uninspiring food; strictly count calories; or go through various induction phases? Which diets are nutritionally sound? Which ones are both safe and satisfying? And maybe most importantly, which ones can you follow long term and make part of your lifestyle?

What the more successful diets have in common is the reduction of foods rich in carbohydrates. Studies show that people who eat low-carb diets without reducing their calorie intake lose more weight than people who eat low-fat, lower-calorie diets. In addition, low-carb dieters generally show more improvement in important health indicators such as triglyceride, blood sugar, and insulin levels.

Why are low-carb diets more effective than low-fat, low-calorie diets? It comes down to how your body works.

The Science Behind It All

When you eat a diet high in carbohydrates, your body is in a metabolic state of *glycolysis*, which simply means that most of the energy your body uses comes from blood glucose. In this state, eating a meal causes your blood glucose to spike. This in turn causes your body to produce higher levels of insulin, which promotes storage of body fat and blocks the release of fat from your adipose (fat storage) tissues.

The keto approach stops this cycle. Consuming a low-carb, high-fat diet puts your body into a metabolic state called *ketosis*. That's where the term *ketogenic* comes from. Your body breaks down fat into ketone bodies (ketones) for fuel as its primary source of energy. In ketosis, your body readily burns fat for energy, and fat reserves are constantly released and consumed. It's a normal state—whenever you're low on carbs for a few days, your body will naturally go into a state of ketosis.

Why Go Keto?

When you eat a ketogenic diet, your body becomes efficient at burning fat for fuel. Your body more readily burns the fat it has stored (the fat you're trying to get rid of), resulting in more weight loss. In a keto diet, most of the calories come from fat. Fats are the most efficient source of energy; using fat for fuel provides consistent energy levels, and it does not spike your blood glucose, so you don't experience the highs and lows that result when you eat large amounts of carbs. A consistent energy level throughout your day means you can get more done and feel less tired doing so.

Moreover, fats are very slow to digest and are calorically dense. Keto dieters commonly consume fewer total calories because they're satiated longer and don't feel the need to eat as much or as often.

The keto diet promotes fresh whole foods—meat, fish, veggies, and healthy fats and oils—and greatly reduces processed, chemically treated foods. It's a diet that you can sustain and enjoy long term. What's not to enjoy about a diet that encourages eating bacon and eggs for breakfast!

NOT JUST FOR WEIGHT LOSS

In addition to the benefits for weight loss, an increasing number of studies show that the keto diet helps reduce risk factors for diabetes, heart disease, stroke, Alzheimer's disease, epilepsy, and more. Eating a keto diet in the long term has been proven to:

- Result in more weight loss (specifically, loss of body fat)
- Reduce blood sugar and insulin resistance (commonly reversing prediabetes and type 2 diabetes)
- Reduce triglyceride levels
- Reduce blood pressure
- Improve levels of HDL ("good") and LDL ("bad") cholesterol
- Improve brain function

IF YOU HAVE DIABETES

When you eat carbs, your body breaks them down into glucose, a simple sugar, which quickly and significantly raises your blood sugar levels. Then you produce insulin to reduce this spike in blood sugar. After years and years of this cycle, your body will need to produce more insulin at once to achieve the same results, a state called *insulin resistance*. Very commonly, insulin resistance turns into prediabetes, metabolic syndrome, and, eventually, type 2 diabetes.

If you have diabetes, the keto diet can still work for you. For type 2 diabetics, it can begin to reverse the condition; for type 1 diabetics, it can greatly improve blood sugar control.

KETO OR PALEO?

Keto and Paleo are often referred to interchangeably, but they are different eating plans.

Paleo is all about eating the way humans did several thousand years ago, when there were no processed foods and people were limited to foods they could hunt (meats) and gather (nuts, seeds, and plants). A typical Paleo diet is not as high in fat or as low in carbs as the keto diet, and you can eat sweet potatoes and other high-carb vegetables. There are many types of Paleo diets, but typically the macros tend to be closer to 65 percent fat, 15 percent protein, and 20 percent carbs.

The keto diet excludes high-carb vegetables and starches because they raise glucose levels and kick you out of ketosis. To successfully follow a ketogenic diet, you must keep your body in a state of ketosis; otherwise, you are simply following a low-carb eating plan.

Dairy is another differentiator. On keto, full-fat dairy can be a great source of healthy fats, although you're not required to eat dairy. The most traditional form of Paleo diet avoids dairy completely, although some types of Paleo plans do allow dairy products.

It is possible to follow the keto diet while also following some Paleo principles—particularly the focus on natural, high-quality foods. In addition, you can swap out some ingredients for more Paleo-friendly alternatives. For example, you can replace heavy whipping cream with coconut milk.

Always consult with your doctor before beginning the keto diet, especially if you have type 1 diabetes. If you take medications, you may have to immediately decrease your doses. Your doctor may recommend doing a trial under supervision to monitor your blood glucose levels and insulin doses.

Living in Ratios

The keto diet is built on ratios. It's important to get the right balance of macronutrients so your body has the energy it needs. Macronutrients, or macros, are the major nutritional elements that make up the caloric content of your food— carbohydrates, protein, and fat. According to the Centers for Disease Control and Prevention, the typical American diet is about 50 percent carbohydrates, 15 percent protein, and 35 percent fat. A typical keto diet, in contrast, flips those proportions. On the keto diet, 65 to 75 percent of the calories you consume should come from fat. About 20 to 25 percent should come from protein, and the remaining 5 to 10 percent from carbohydrates.

Each type of macronutrient provides a certain amount of energy (calories) per gram consumed.

- Fat provides about 9 calories per gram.
- Protein and carbohydrates each provide about 4 calories per gram.

Here are the same numbers broken down into an average 2,000-calorie daily diet by grams and percentages:

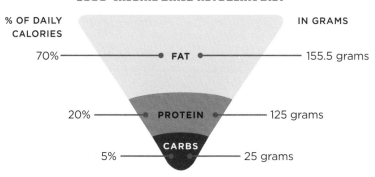

2000-CALORIE DAILY KETOGENIC DIET

% OF DAILY CALORIES		IN GRAMS
70%	FAT	155.5 grams
20%	PROTEIN	125 grams
5%	CARBS	25 grams

Keep in mind that 2,000 calories is just an example—the number of calories you consume daily should be tailored to your body, activity levels, and goals.

ALL THAT FAT?

Is that much fat good for you? Eating 70 to 75 percent fat on the keto diet probably seems a little crazy if you are used to a typical high-carb, low-fat diet. In fact, when starting on the keto diet, many people find that it's relatively easy to quit carbs but much more difficult to hit their recommended fat intake every day. The most important thing to remember is that not all fats are created equal! You want to eat high-quality fats: grass-fed butter, ghee (clarified butter), grass-fed meats, organic full-fat dairy, avocados, macadamia nuts, and salmon. You should avoid low-quality fats, such as vegetable or canola oils. You will notice that on the keto plan, you won't be hungry as often because the high-quality fats will keep you satisfied and feeling full.

CALCULATING YOUR CALORIES AND YOUR MACROS

How do you determine the total calorie intake and macronutrient percentages that are right for you? There are many ketogenic-based macro calculators available online from sites such as ruled.me, tasteaholics.com, and ketointhecity.com. You can also find plenty of others through a quick Google search for "keto calculator."

With a macro calculator, you'll be able to easily and quickly plug in your numbers and get an immediate estimation of your body's caloric needs. The macro calculator will ask you to enter information (height, weight, activity level, goals, etc.), and based on that information, it will suggest your keto macros. The macros represent the upper limit of your ideal nutritional intake for each day. Macros will be broken down into calories, fat, protein, and carbohydrates. If weight loss is your goal, it is often recommended that you stay under 20 net carbs per day. You can also use an app, such as Carb Manager, to track your carb consumption.

One of the great things about the keto diet is that it doesn't require you to track each and every number to hit your goals. But if you want to do so, tracking is a great way to speed up your progress, and it will give you a visual reminder to stay on course every day.

TOTAL CARBS AND NET CARBS

"Net carbs" refers to the number you get when you take the total grams of carbohydrates in a certain amount of food and subtract the number of grams of fiber included in that amount. The rationale is that fiber is a carbohydrate that your body cannot digest. For example, ½ cup of cauliflower has 2.65 grams of carbohydrates and 1.2 grams of fiber. So you subtract the fiber from the total carbohydrates, and the net carb content of that serving is 1.45 grams. Some people monitor their total carbohydrates while on the keto diet, and some follow net carbs; it is a personal decision. In this book both total carbs and net carbs are noted in recipe nutritional calculations.

BECOMING KETO-ADAPTED

Once they begin sticking to their ketogenic macros, most people reach a state of ketosis within a couple of weeks, but becoming keto-adapted takes a little longer. Becoming keto-adapted means that your body has switched over from using glucose as its main source of energy to using fat for energy. This process can take anywhere from four to eight weeks.

Once you become keto-adapted, glycogen (the glucose stored in your muscles and liver) decreases, you carry less water weight, your muscle endurance increases, and your overall energy levels are higher than before. Also, if you kick yourself out of ketosis by eating too many carbs, you return to ketosis much sooner than when you were not keto-adapted. Additionally, once you are keto-adapted, you can generally eat up to 50 grams of carbs per day and still maintain ketosis.

Preparing for the Keto Lifestyle

Switching your body from glucose burning to fat burning is a big change. And with change comes a period of adjustment—it's a time of healing for your body. When you first begin a ketogenic diet, it is important to focus on nutrient-dense foods, get plenty of rest, and monitor your electrolytes. Electrolytes are certain chemicals in the body, such as sodium and potassium, that have many important functions, including stimulating muscles and nerves and maintaining cellular function, regulating your heartbeat, and more.

MANAGING THE "KETO FLU"

The keto flu is avoidable, and you can reduce its duration simply by adding more sodium to your diet. Here are some of the easiest ways to do it:

- Add more salt to your meals.
- Drink soup broths, such as beef and chicken.
- Eat saltier foods, such as pickled vegetables and bacon.

To replace other electrolytes, try to eat more of the foods listed below:

ELECTROLYTE	FOODS CONTAINING ELECTROLYTE
Potassium	Avocados, nuts, dark leafy greens such as spinach and kale, salmon, plain yogurt, mushrooms
Magnesium	Nuts, dark chocolate, artichokes, spinach, fish
Calcium	Cheeses, leafy greens, broccoli, seafood, almonds
Phosphorus	Meats, cheeses, nuts, seeds, dark chocolate
Chloride	Most vegetables, olives, salt, seaweed

Remember that if you don't feel better right away, the "keto flu" will pass within a couple of days, and you'll emerge a fat-burning machine!

Starting a ketogenic diet involves cutting out most processed foods—and that can cause a drop in your consumption of electrolytes. Processed foods have a lot of added sodium, for example, so when you stop eating them, your overall sodium intake can drop. Additionally, the reduction in carbs reduces insulin levels, which in turn tells your kidneys to release excess stored sodium. Between the reduction in sodium intake and flushing of excess stored sodium, your body begins to excrete much more water than usual, and you end up low on sodium and other electrolytes.

When this happens, you may experience symptoms such as fatigue, headaches, coughing, sniffles, irritability, and/or nausea. This state is generally known as the "keto flu." It's very important to know that this is not the actual influenza virus. It's called the "keto flu" only because the symptoms are similar, but it's neither contagious nor a real virus.

Many people who experience these symptoms believe the keto diet made them sick and immediately go back to eating carbs. But the keto flu phase actually means your body is withdrawing from sugar, high carbs, and processed foods and is readjusting so it can use fat as its fuel. The keto flu usually lasts just a few days while the body readjusts.

Keep these guidelines in mind as you prepare to "go keto":

Drink a lot of water. You will need to drink more water than you are currently drinking. In the beginning stages of the diet, you will be shedding a lot of water. The carbs in your body tend to hold on to water, and when you stop eating them, your body will begin to release that water, so you need to replenish it. A good guide is to make sure you get at least half your body weight in ounces of water daily. For example, if you weigh 200 pounds, you should drink at least 100 ounces of water (a bit more than 3 quarts) every day.

Get plenty of salt. People who eat a standard American diet typically consume foods that have a lot of added salt: bread, for example. When you're on keto, you are cutting out a lot of processed foods in favor of whole, natural foods. So don't be afraid to salt your food (using high-quality salt), and if you feel like you still need more salt, sip some meat-based vegetable broth. Consider sea salt or pink Himalayan salt, which typically contain trace amounts of other minerals: potassium, magnesium, copper, and iron.

Keep in mind that pink Himalayan salt is not the same thing as pink curing salt. Both are sometimes referred to as "pink salt," but there's a world of difference between the two. Pink Himalayan salt is an unrefined salt used to flavor food, and its characteristic pink color comes from the trace elements it contains. Pink curing salt is a mixture of table salt and sodium nitrite, dyed pink to distinguish it from regular table salt. It is commonly used as a preservative in curing meats—for example, for making corned beef or sausage. You do *not* want to use this in your recipes or sprinkle it on your food!

Find easy ways to get your fat in. It may sound daunting to consume 65 to 75 percent of your daily diet in fat, but there are lots of easy ways to take it in throughout the day. The easiest way is to add butter and/or healthy oils to almost everything you eat.

Do your research before eating out. You can find something keto-friendly on almost any restaurant menu, but it does take some practice! If you can, before you go out, look online at the restaurant's menu to figure out the good keto options. Meat and vegetables are usually a great place to start. Be careful with sauces, dressings, and marinades; they can have lots of hidden carbohydrates. When in doubt, ask your server for the ingredients in the sauces, and if he or she doesn't know, ask to have the sauce left off. Restaurants are used to special requests, so don't be afraid to ask for exactly what you do and don't want.

Read labels. Pay attention to the ingredients listed on the packaged products you buy. The best products have just a few ingredients with recognizable names, meaning they're made with fewer additives and preservatives. Also, read the nutrition information to see how high the carb count is. Many companies love to add sugar to their products, so be on the lookout. Over time, you'll get to know which products are good and which are not as you look at nutritional labels.

INTERMITTENT FASTING

Many people incorporate intermittent fasting (IF) as part of a ketogenic lifestyle. Briefly, IF involves eating all of your food for the day within an "eating window" typically lasting 8 hours. For example, you might choose to eat only between 10 a.m. and 6 p.m. During the time outside the eating window, some people opt to drink Bulletproof Coffee (page 46) and water, but no solid food. The Bulletproof Coffee can curb your appetite because of its high fat content (grass-fed butter and Brain Octane Oil). The general idea is that the longer you are on the ketogenic diet, the less hungry you will become, because the higher amount of fat you are eating will satiate you.

Cleaning Out Your Pantry

Out with the old, in with the new. Having tempting, unhealthy foods in your home is one of the biggest contributors to failure when you start any diet. To succeed, you need to minimize any triggers to maximize your chances. Unless you have an iron will, you should not keep addictive foods such as bread, desserts, and other non-keto-friendly snacks around. Below is a list of items that you will want to remove from your kitchen and pantry.

Starches and grains: cereal, pasta, rice, potatoes, corn, oats, quinoa, flour, bread, bagels, wraps, rolls, and croissants.

Sugary foods and drinks: refined sugar, fountain drinks, fruit juices, milk, desserts, pastries, milk chocolate, candy bars, etc.

Beans and legumes: beans, peas, and lentils. A one-cup serving of beans alone contains more than three times the amount of carbs you want to consume in a day.

Processed polyunsaturated fats and oils: vegetable oils and most seed oils, including sunflower, safflower, canola, soybean, grapeseed, and corn oil. Also eliminate products containing trans fats, such as shortening and margarine—anything that says "hydrogenated" or "partially hydrogenated."

Fruits: bananas, dates, grapes, mangoes, apples, and other high-carb fruits. Be sure to give away any dried fruits, such as raisins and prunes, as well. Dried fruit contains as much sugar as regular fruit but more concentrated, making it easy to eat a lot of sugar in a small serving. For comparison, a cup of raisins has over 100 grams of carbs, whereas a cup of grapes has only 15 grams of carbs.

Keep in mind that these now unwanted foods in your pantry can feed many others. Please don't throw them away! Find a local food bank or homeless youth shelter to donate them to.

KETO-FRIENDLY ALTERNATIVES

Here is a chart showing keto-friendly alternatives to some high-carb foods—enjoy them at any time.

Note: Net carbs are the total carbs minus dietary fiber (soluble and insoluble) and sugar alcohols. Fiber and sugar alcohols are not counted toward net carbs because the human body cannot digest and break them down into glucose, so they do not spike blood sugar.

NOT SO FRIENDLY	NET CARBS	QUANTITY	KETO-FRIENDLY ALTERNATIVE	NET CARBS
Milk	12 grams	1 cup	Unsweetened almond milk	0 grams
Pasta	41 grams	1 cup	Zucchini noodles	3 grams
Wraps or tortillas	18 grams	1 medium	Low-carb tortillas	6 grams
Sugar	25 grams	2 tablespoons	Stevia or erythritol	0 grams
Rice	44 grams	1 cup	Shirataki rice	0 grams
Mashed potatoes	22 grams	½ cup	Mashed cauliflower	4 grams
Bread crumbs	36 grams	½ cup	Almond flour	6 grams
Soda	39 grams	12 ounces	Water, tea, or coffee	0 grams
French fries	44 grams	4 ounces	Zucchini fries	3 grams
Potato chips	46 grams	3½ ounces	Mixed nuts	14 grams

Restocking Your Pantry and Refrigerator

Below are suggestions for restocking your pantry, refrigerator, and freezer with easy-to-find, delicious, keto-friendly foods and ingredients that will help you lose weight, become healthy, and feel great!

THE BASICS

- Water, coffee, and tea
- Sea salt and/or pink Himalayan salt
- All spices and herbs
- Sweeteners, including stevia and erythritol
- Lemon juice or lime juice
- Low-carb condiments: mayonnaise, mustard, pesto, and Sriracha
- Broths (chicken, beef, bone)
- Pickled and fermented foods, such as pickles, kimchi, and sauerkraut
- Nuts and seeds, including macadamia nuts, pecans, almonds, walnuts, hazelnuts, pine nuts, flaxseed, chia seeds, and pumpkin seeds

MEATS, FISH, AND EGGS

- Any type of meat is fine for the keto diet, including chicken, beef, lamb, pork, turkey, game, etc. It's preferable to use grass-fed and/or organic meats if they're available and your budget permits. You can and should eat the fat on the meat and skin on the chicken.
- All wild-caught fish and seafood slide into the keto diet nicely. Try to avoid farm-raised fish.
- Go crazy with the eggs! Use organic eggs from free-range chickens, if possible.

VEGETABLES

- You can eat all nonstarchy veggies, including broccoli, asparagus, mushrooms, cucumbers, lettuce, onions, peppers, tomatoes, garlic (in small quantities—each clove contains about 1 gram of carbs), Brussels sprouts, eggplant, olives, zucchini, yellow squash, and cauliflower.
- Avoid all types of potatoes, yams and sweet potatoes, corn, and legumes like beans, lentils, and peas.

ABOUT THOSE SWEETENERS . . .

Stevia and erythritol may sound strange if you haven't heard of them before. They both come from natural sources and are safe to use in any quantity.

Stevia is extracted from the leaves of a plant called *Stevia rebaudiana*. Stevia has zero calories and contains some beneficial micronutrients such as magnesium, potassium, and zinc. It's readily available in liquid or powder form online and in most supermarkets. It's much sweeter than sugar, so containers are usually very small—you won't need nearly as much.

Erythritol is a sugar alcohol that is low in calories, about 70 percent as sweet as sugar, and can be found naturally in some fruits and vegetables. Sugar alcohols are indigestible by the human body, so erythritol cannot raise your blood sugar or insulin levels. Several studies have proven it to be safe. Sugar alcohols can sometimes cause temporary digestive discomfort, but among the available sugar alcohols—which also include xylitol, maltitol, and sorbitol—erythritol is considered to be the most forgiving and best for everyday use. Erythritol is the main ingredient in the Swerve brand of granulated sweetener. Several recipes in this book call for Swerve.

FRUITS

- You can eat a small amount of berries every day, such as strawberries, raspberries, blackberries, and blueberries. Lemon juice and lime juice are great for adding flavor to your meals. Avocados are also low in carbs and full of healthy fat.
- Avoid other fruits, as they're loaded with sugar. A single banana, for example, can contain around 24 grams of net carbs.

DAIRY

- Enjoy full-fat dairy products—milk, butter, sour cream, heavy (whipping) cream, cheese, cream cheese, and unsweetened yogurt. Although not technically dairy products, unsweetened almond and coconut milks are great as well.
- Avoid low-fat milk and skim milk, as well as sweetened yogurt, as it contains a lot of sugar. Avoid any flavored, low-fat, or fat-free dairy products.

FATS AND OILS

- Avocado, coconut, and olive oil, as well as butter, lard, and bacon fat are great for cooking and consuming. Avocado oil has a high smoke point (it does not burn or smoke until it reaches 520°F), which is ideal for searing meats and frying in a wok.
- Make sure to avoid oils labeled "blend"; they commonly contain only small amounts of the healthy oil and large amounts of unhealthy oils.

Favorite Keto Products

The following are products that can be particularly helpful as you follow your new keto lifestyle. Some are staples, and some are snacks or sweet treats.

Pasture-Raised Eggs: Buying pasture-raised eggs makes a difference; the yolks tend to be a deeper orange color, and the eggs are delicious. Vital Farms is the brand I buy; alternatively, you may be able to get pasture-raised eggs at your local farmers' market.

Grass-fed Butter: Grass-fed butter just tastes better; once you switch, you will never go back. My go-to brands are Kerrygold and Vital Farms. Kerrygold is widely available at Whole Foods, Costco, Trader Joe's, Walmart, and Safeway. Both Kerrygold and Vital Farms offer unsalted and salted options.

Bulletproof Brain Octane Oil: Bulletproof is a brand that makes a variety of high-quality keto products, including coffee, ghee, and Brain Octane Oil. The Brain Octane Oil is a very easy way to add high-quality fats to anything you eat. One tablespoon of the oil has 14 grams of fat, no flavor, and no smell. Brain Octane Oil is used in Bulletproof Coffee (page 46), often called "butter coffee." There are many other ways to use it.

Ghee: Ghee is clarified butter, meaning that it has no milk solids. It has a high smoke point, so it is great to use for cooking. Just as with butter, grass-fed ghee is preferable. Many people who follow the keto diet avoid dairy products, so ghee is a perfect replacement for butter in cooking, as well as a tasty addition to Bulletproof Coffee.

Spice Mixes: Seasoning can really enhance a dish and a meal. You can make your own seasoning mixes so that you know exactly what is in them, or you can look for brands that make Paleo or keto-approved mixes.

Perfect Keto MCT Oil Powder: This product is wonderful for adding high-quality fats in dishes and drinks. Oils can be messy and, of course, can add an oily texture to drinks. MCT oil powder adds fats, but it has a nice creamy texture that works perfectly in beverages such as coffee and smoothies. You can also use it in baking because it adds no other flavors, just healthy fats.

Perfect Keto Protein Collagen MCT Oil Powder: Also by Perfect Keto, this dairy-free protein powder contains collagen. Collagen is beneficial for the joints, hair, skin, and nails, among other things. The production of collagen in our bodies slows down as we age, so consuming products like this one with added collagen can help combat some of the collagen loss.

Nui Cookies: Nui was created by two friends who lost weight on a ketogenic diet and decided to launch their own brand. Their cookies come in delicious flavors, and the texture is moist and chewy.

Marcona Almonds: Marcona almonds are an oilier almond with a flatter shape and a delicate taste. I have bought them at Costco and Trader Joe's. Trader Joe's sells a couple of varieties, including ones flavored with rosemary and truffle oil.

Shirataki Noodles and Rice: Made from the root of an Asian yam, shirataki products consist primarily of glucomannan, a type of dietary fiber. Shirataki-based noodles and rice are gluten-free, soy-free, and calorie-free and have zero net carbs. The brand Miracle Noodle offers a variety of noodle styles, as well as rice, so you can make all your favorite dishes in a keto-friendly way. These two products really expand what you can do with keto cooking.

Primal Kitchen Products: If you aren't going to make your own mayonnaise and salad dressings, this is one keto-friendly brand you can rely on. Their mayo is made with avocado oil and is sugar-free.

Equipping Your Kitchen

You don't need to have a bunch of fancy equipment to cook the recipes in this book, but the right tools can make the difference between feeling frustrated in the kitchen and having fun in the kitchen. Below are listed the "must-have" items as well as some "nice-to-have" items.

MUST-HAVE KITCHEN EQUIPMENT

Any home cook will need a basic collection of knives (including one or two chef's knives), cutting boards, measuring cups and spoons, spatulas and whisks, and mixing bowls. The following items are also used frequently in this book and will be good to make sure you have on hand.

8-by-8-inch and 9-by-13 inch baking dishes: These can be used for roasting vegetables and meat, and for baking everything from egg frittatas to lemony fish to cheesecake.

9-by-5-inch loaf pan: This is a standard-size loaf pan used for baking Keto Bread (page 97).

10- and 12-inch skillets with lids (one of each): One great choice is cast iron. Cast iron skillets have been used for centuries and were one of the first modern cooking devices. They don't wear out, are healthier to use than nonstick skillets (they have no chemical treatment of any kind), retain heat very well, and can be used both on the stove and in the oven.

Baking sheet: You will want to have two large baking sheets for one-pan meals and for baking.

Blender: A blender is great for making smoothies, coffee drinks, soups, and sauces. If you don't have a blender, a food processor can take care of the job. Both the food processor and blender are extremely useful, and each has its relative strengths for certain applications. But if budget or space considerations require that you choose only one, go for either a food processor or one of the newer appliances that claim to do the job of both. One food processor / blender brand is NutriBullet. The blending containers come with lids or drink spouts so you can take them to go or use them as storage. They're also easy to clean, making the whole system extremely convenient.

Colander: A colander is important for washing fresh fruits and vegetables. A medium-size colander should be adequate unless you are cooking for a crowd.

Electric hand mixer: If you've ever had to whisk an egg white by hand until you get stiff peaks, then you know just how difficult it is. Electric hand mixers save your arm muscles and massive amounts of time, especially when mixing heavy ingredients. If your budget permits, a countertop stand mixer is even more powerful.

Fine-mesh sieve: This is indispensable for straining solids from the liquid when you're making stock, such as Rich Beef Stock (page 22) and Herbed Chicken Stock (page 23).

Food processor: A food processor is a powerful tool, ideal for blending certain foods or processing foods together into sauces and shakes. Most blenders are simply not powerful enough to handle many foods, especially tough vegetables such as cauliflower.

Grater and zester: In addition to grating cheese (it's less expensive to grate your own than to buy it preshredded), this tool is also a must for shredding vegetables. Some graters even have storage containers attached to them for convenience. A citrus zester can also be handy: Several recipes in this book call for zesting of citrus.

Ice pop molds: There are a lot of fun ice pop molds out there, and you can choose any shape to make the delicious keto-friendly ice pop recipes included in this book.

Muffin tin: You'll need a standard muffin tin for several of the recipes. The BLTA Cups (page 202) call for a jumbo muffin tin, but a standard tin will work, too.

Saucepans: A small (2-quart) and a large (4.5-quart) saucepan will work for most recipes.

Slow cooker: A slow cooker, such as the original Crock-Pot and other brands, is very handy for making easy one-dish meals, especially in the winter. Some are very simple, while others have timers and other fancy mechanisms. A 6-quart slow cooker is a good size for the recipes in this book.

NICE-TO-HAVE KITCHEN EQUIPMENT

The kitchen section of any store can be a wonderland—there are so many intriguing gadgets to be found! Although they aren't absolutely necessary, you may find that the following items can make a big difference to your speed, efficiency, and enjoyment in the kitchen.

Basting brush: A basting brush can help you apply oils without making a mess. If you don't have one, you can also use a leafy green or paper towel instead.

Cooling rack: Several of the recipes call for transferring a finished dish from the oven to a cooling rack. If you don't have one, setting your hot dishes on trivets or potholders will work, too.

Immersion blender: This tool is very handy for quickly blending soups and sauces right in the pan or bowl, instead of in a food processor or countertop blender.

Instant cooking thermometer: Cooking steak and chicken is much easier when you can easily prod the meat and find out whether it's at the level of doneness you're shooting for.

Rolling pin: If you have a rolling pin, it will come in handy for making dishes like pinwheels. If you don't have one, a wine bottle will work just fine.

Spiralizer: Spiralizers make vegetables into noodles or ribbons within seconds. They make cooking a lot faster and easier—noodles have much more surface area and take a fraction of the time to cook. For example, a spiralizer turns a zucchini into zoodles, and with some Alfredo or marinara sauce, you can't tell you aren't eating pasta.

Support for Your New Lifestyle

When starting the keto diet, let your closest friends and family members know you're serious about it and which foods you're trying to avoid. This will help during gatherings or outings. You may face some resistance in the beginning, and that's absolutely normal. The high-carb, low-fat diet has been the standard in most people's lives, and keto is a complete turnaround. Just focus on yourself and your progress. Soon enough, your high energy, weight loss, and overall positive outlook will make even naysayers curious.

If you don't live alone, be sure to discuss with your housemates—whether they're significant others, family, or roommates—your plan to remove non-keto-friendly foods from the kitchen and pantry. If some items must be kept, try to agree on a special location to keep them out of sight. This will also help them understand that you are serious about starting your diet, and it will lead to a better experience for you at home overall (people love to tempt anyone on a diet at first, but it will get old and they'll tire quickly).

Sticking to your diet in the beginning can prove difficult when close friends and family aren't eating the same as you. Even worse, they are eating all the things you're trying not to eat. Every person is different, and you likely know who will support you and who will not. For those who support you, explain that you're avoiding carbs and request politely that they not offer you anything when you're eating together.

A great place for initial support is reddit.com's keto subreddit: www.reddit.com/r/keto. You'll find hundreds of thousands of other keto-ers from around the world posting their experiences and progress and supporting each other throughout their journeys.

About the Recipes

In this book you will find easy, flavorful recipes for every meal. Many of the recipes can be prepared in 30 minutes or less. To make the keto lifestyle easy for you to stick to, each recipe includes nutrition information that reflects macronutrient ratios for succeeding on keto. Note that nutrition information reflects the ingredients called for in the main recipe, not any variations or ingredient substitution suggestions.

The recipes also include helpful labels: No Cook, 30 Minutes or Less (from start to finish), One Pot, and One Pan (for recipes that require just a single skillet, baking dish, or sheet pan).

Most recipes also include at least one of the following types of tips: prep tip, ingredient tip, cooking tip, substitution tip, serving tip, and storage tip. In addition, a large number of recipes include variation suggestions for other flavor or ingredient combinations you can use to keep recipes fresh and interesting.

You're about to discover all the delicious ways you can make easy, keto-friendly recipes. Let's start cooking.

BASICS & STAPLES

◄ Avocado-Lime Crema, page 32

RICH BEEF STOCK

Makes 8 to 10 cups / Prep time: 15 minutes / Cook time: 12½ hours, plus 30 minutes to cool

If you have never attempted beef stock before, you might be wondering where to find beef bones for this recipe. Beef bones are actually quite common in many grocery store meat sections, usually a little out of the way next to the tongues and kidneys, but they are often prepackaged and displayed. If your store does not have beef bones in the cooler or freezer, ask your butcher—there may be some in the back, or you can ask them to save the bones from the next meat order.

2 to 3 pounds beef bones
   (beef marrow, knuckle bones,
   ribs, and other bones)
8 black peppercorns
5 thyme sprigs
3 garlic cloves, peeled and crushed
2 bay leaves

1 carrot, chopped into 2-inch pieces
1 celery stalk, chopped into big chunks
½ onion, peeled and quartered
1 gallon water (enough to cover the
   bones and vegetables)
1 teaspoon extra-virgin olive oil

1. Preheat the oven to 350°F.

2. Place the beef bones in a deep baking pan and roast them in the oven for about 30 minutes.

3. Transfer the roasted bones to a large stockpot and add the peppercorns, thyme, garlic, bay leaves, carrot, celery, and onion.

4. Add the water, making sure the bones are completely covered.

5. Place the pot on high heat and bring to a boil, then reduce the heat to low so that the stock gently simmers.

6. Check the stock every hour, at least for the first 3 hours, and skim off any foam that forms on the top.

7. Simmer for 12 hours total, then remove the pot from the heat. Cool the stock for about 30 minutes.

8. Remove any large bones with tongs, and strain the stock through a fine-mesh sieve. Discard the leftover vegetables and bones.

9. Pour the stock into containers with tight-fitting lids and cool completely before storing in the refrigerator for up to 5 days or in the freezer for up to 2 months.

PER SERVING (1 CUP) Calories: 65; Fat: 5g; Carbs: 1g; Net Carbs: 1g; Fiber: 0g; Protein: 4g

HERBED CHICKEN STOCK

Makes 8 cups / Prep time: 15 minutes / Cook time: 12 hours, plus 30 minutes to cool

Chicken stock works well with many veggies and herb flavors. However, try to always include onions—they contain quercetin, a flavonoid that remains in the stock after the solids are strained out. Quercetin can help prevent diabetes, fight cancer, and promote a very healthy cardiovascular system.

2 chicken carcasses (see Prep Tip)

6 black peppercorns

4 thyme sprigs

3 bay leaves

2 celery stalks, cut into quarters

1 carrot, washed and chopped roughly

1 sweet onion, peeled and quartered

1 gallon cold water (enough to cover the carcasses and vegetables)

1. Place the chicken carcasses in a large stockpot with the peppercorns, thyme, bay leaves, celery, carrot, and onion.

2. Add the water, making sure the carcasses and vegetables are completely covered, and place the pot on high heat. Bring to a boil, then reduce the heat to low and gently simmer, stirring every few hours, for 12 hours.

3. Remove the pot from the heat and let the stock cool for 30 minutes. Remove any large bones with tongs, then strain the stock through a fine-mesh sieve. Discard the solid bits.

4. Pour the stock into containers with tight-fitting lids and cool completely. Store in the refrigerator for up to 5 days, or freeze the stock for up to 3 months.

PREP TIP Chicken carcasses can be frozen in zip-top bags. When you have two or three, make this lovely stock by putting the frozen carcasses right in the pot.

PER SERVING (1 CUP) Calories: 73; Fat: 5g; Carbs: 2g; Net Carbs: 2g; Fiber: 0g; Protein: 5g

AVOCADO-HERB COMPOUND BUTTER

Makes 2 cups / Prep time: 25 minutes, plus 4 hours to chill

Avocado shows up a fair bit in keto recipes because it is a spectacular source of monounsaturated fats, oleic acid, and omega-3 fatty acids. This high-fat profile makes reaching your keto macros easier and can increase absorption of beta-carotene in other ingredients by as much as 400 percent. Avocado is also high in fiber and lutein.

¼ cup butter, at room temperature

1 avocado, peeled, pitted,
  and quartered

Juice of ½ lemon

2 teaspoons chopped fresh cilantro

1 teaspoon chopped fresh basil

1 teaspoon minced garlic

Pink Himalayan salt

Freshly ground black pepper

1. Place the butter, avocado, lemon juice, cilantro, basil, and garlic in a food processor and process until smooth.

2. Season the butter with salt and pepper.

3. Transfer the mixture to a sheet of parchment paper and shape it into a log.

4. Place the parchment butter log in the refrigerator until it is firm, about 4 hours.

5. Serve slices of this butter with fish or chicken.

6. Store unused butter wrapped tightly in the freezer for up to 1 week.

PREP TIP The best avocados for this butter are ripe, soft fruit. Place unripe avocados in a paper bag for a few days to speed up the ripening process.

PER SERVING (1 TABLESPOON) Calories: 22; Fat: 2g; Carbs: 1g; Net Carbs: 1g; Fiber: 0g; Protein: 0g

STRAWBERRY BUTTER

Makes 3 cups / Prep time: 25 minutes

If you have ever picked your own strawberries, you might remember the sweet fragrance of ripe berries in the field and intense flavor of a berry warm from the sun. Fresh berries make this butter absolutely delicious. Let the butter soften a bit outside of the refrigerator, then spoon some of it over chicken or fish before serving.

2 cups shredded unsweetened coconut

1 tablespoon coconut oil

¾ cup fresh strawberries

½ tablespoon freshly squeezed lemon juice

1 teaspoon alcohol-free vanilla extract

1. Put the coconut in a food processor and purée it until it is buttery and smooth, about 15 minutes.

2. Add the coconut oil, strawberries, lemon juice, and vanilla to the coconut butter and process until very smooth, scraping down the sides of the bowl.

3. Pass the butter through a fine sieve to remove the strawberry seeds, using the back of a spoon to press the butter through.

4. Store the strawberry butter in an airtight container in the refrigerator for up to 2 weeks.

PER SERVING (1 TABLESPOON) Calories: 23; Fat: 2g; Carbs: 1g; Net Carbs: 1g; Fiber: 0g; Protein: 0g

PEANUT SAUCE

Serves 4 / Prep time: 5 minutes

Peanut sauce will bring your chicken dishes to another level. You can also toss zoodles with it and use it with any dish where you want to bring in some Asian-style flavor.

½ cup natural creamy peanut butter
  (such as Justin's)

2 tablespoons soy sauce
  (or coconut aminos)

1 teaspoon Sriracha sauce

1 teaspoon toasted sesame oil

1 teaspoon garlic powder

1. In a food processor (or blender), blend the peanut butter, soy sauce, Sriracha sauce, sesame oil, and garlic powder until thoroughly mixed.

2. Pour into an airtight glass container and keep in the refrigerator for up to 1 week.

INGREDIENT TIP For added texture, use chunky peanut butter.

PER SERVING Calories: 185; Fat: 15g; Carbs: 8g; Net Carbs: 6g; Fiber: 2g; Protein: 7g

TZATZIKI

Serves 4 / Prep time: 10 minutes, plus 30 minutes to chill

Tzatziki sauce is a delicious accompaniment to a variety of dishes, especially those with a Mediterranean flavor. The key to making it is getting all the water out of the cucumber. That aside, tzatziki is super easy to make.

½ large English cucumber, unpeeled

1½ cups Greek yogurt (such as Fage)

2 tablespoons extra-virgin olive oil

Large pinch pink Himalayan salt

Large pinch freshly ground
   black pepper

Juice of ½ lemon

2 garlic cloves, finely minced

1 tablespoon fresh dill

1. Halve the cucumber lengthwise, and use a spoon to scoop out and discard the seeds.

2. Grate the cucumber with a zester or grater onto a large plate lined with a few layers of paper towels. Close the paper towels around the grated cucumber, and squeeze as much water out of it as you can. (This can take a while and can require multiple paper towels. You can also allow the cucumber to drain overnight in a strainer or wrapped in a few layers of cheesecloth in the refrigerator if you have the time.)

3. In a food processor (or blender), blend the yogurt, olive oil, salt, pepper, lemon juice, and garlic until fully combined.

4. Transfer the mixture to a medium bowl, and mix in the fresh dill and grated cucumber.

5. Chill this sauce for at least 30 minutes before serving. Keep in a sealed glass container in the refrigerator for up to 1 week.

INGREDIENT TIP Mince the garlic cloves as finely as possible for best results.

SUBSTITUTION TIP You can use sour cream instead of Greek yogurt.

PER SERVING Calories: 149; Fat: 11g; Carbs: 5g; Net Carbs: 5g; Fiber: 1g; Protein: 8g

HOLLANDAISE

Makes 2 cups / Prep time: 20 minutes / Cook time: 10 minutes, plus 20 minutes to stand and cool

You might think this sauce looks like a great deal of work, and you wouldn't be entirely wrong—but the luscious, spoon-coating creation at the end of the process is more than worth the effort. Hollandaise does not keep longer than about 2 hours, and only that long if the temperature in your kitchen is not too hot, so don't make more than you can use in one meal.

1½ cups unsalted butter

4 large egg yolks

2 teaspoons cold water

Juice of 1 small lemon (about 4 teaspoons)

Pinch pink Himalayan salt

1. Place a medium heavy-bottomed saucepan over very low heat, and melt the butter.
2. Remove the saucepan from the heat and let the melted butter stand for 5 minutes.
3. Carefully skim the foam from the top of the melted butter.
4. Very slowly pour the clarified part of the butter (it should be a clear yellow color) into a container, leaving the milky solids in the bottom of the saucepan.
5. Discard the milky solids and let the clarified butter cool in the container until it is just warm, about 15 minutes.
6. Set a medium saucepan with about 3 inches of water in it over medium heat until the water simmers gently.
7. In a large stainless steel bowl, whisk the egg yolks and the cold water until they are foamy and light, about 3 minutes.
8. Add 3 or 4 drops of the lemon juice to the yolks and whisk for about 1 minute.
9. Place the bowl onto the mouth of the saucepan, making sure the bottom of the bowl does not touch the simmering water.
10. Whisk the yolks until they thicken a little, about 1 to 2 minutes, then remove the bowl from the simmering water.

11. In a very thin stream, add the clarified butter to the yolk mixture, whisking continuously, until you have used up all the butter and your sauce is thick and smooth. If you add the butter too quickly, the sauce will break.

12. Whisk in the remaining lemon juice and the salt.

13. This sauce should be used right away or held for only an hour or so. Throw away any unused sauce.

INGREDIENT TIP Add some chopped tarragon to the hollandaise if you want to make a béarnaise sauce instead.

PER SERVING (1 TABLESPOON) Calories: 173; Fat: 17g; Carbs: 1g; Net Carbs: 1g; Fiber: 0g; Protein: 5g

HERB-KALE PESTO

Makes 1½ cups / Prep time: 15 minutes

Nutritional yeast adds a lovely, almost cheesy taste to this pesto as well as a hearty amount of protein and fiber. Nutritional yeast is also a fabulous source of vitamin B12, which is one of the most prevalent nutritional deficiencies in the world. Vitamin B12 is crucial for many metabolic functions and for maintaining both a healthy cardiovascular system and nervous system.

1 cup chopped kale

1 cup fresh basil leaves

3 garlic cloves

2 teaspoons nutritional yeast

¼ cup extra-virgin olive oil

1. Place the kale, basil, garlic, and yeast in a food processor and pulse until the mixture is finely chopped, about 3 minutes.
2. With the food processor running, drizzle the olive oil into the pesto until a thick paste forms, scraping down the sides of the bowl at least once.
3. Add a little water if the pesto is too thick.
4. Store the pesto in an airtight container in the refrigerator for up to 1 week.

SUBSTITUTION TIP Try spinach or any other dark leafy green in place of the kale for interesting variations. You can also use any of an assortment of different herbs in the same quantity as the basil in this recipe.

PER SERVING (2 TABLESPOONS) Calories: 44; Fat: 4g; Carbs: 1g; Net Carbs: 1g; Fiber: 0g; Protein: 1g

ALFREDO SAUCE

Serves 2 / Prep time: 5 minutes / Cook time: 10 minutes

There is nothing like a warm bowl of fettuccine Alfredo with its rich, buttery, creamy sauce. Use this sauce to top Miracle Noodles of the fettuccine variety, served with some grilled chicken cooked with fresh herbs. The sauce is simple to pull together, and chances are you'll have the ingredients on hand.

4 tablespoons butter

2 ounces cream cheese

1 cup heavy (whipping) cream

½ cup grated Parmesan cheese

1 garlic clove, finely minced

1 teaspoon dried Italian seasoning

Pink Himalayan salt

Freshly ground black pepper

1. In a heavy medium saucepan over medium heat, combine the butter, cream cheese, and heavy cream. Whisk slowly and constantly until the butter and cream cheese melt.

2. Add the Parmesan, garlic, and Italian seasoning. Continue to whisk until everything is well blended. Turn the heat to medium-low and simmer, stirring occasionally, for 5 to 8 minutes to allow the sauce to blend and thicken.

3. Season with salt and pepper, and stir to combine.

4. Toss with your favorite hot, precooked, keto-friendly noodles and serve.

5. Keep this sauce in a sealed glass container in the refrigerator for up to 4 days.

INGREDIENT TIP You can also use a delicious grated cheese mixture that combines Parmesan, Asiago, and Romano.

PER SERVING Calories: 294; Fat: 30g; Carbs: 2g; Net Carbs: 2g; Fiber: 0g; Protein: 5g

AVOCADO-LIME CREMA

Serves 4 / Prep time: 5 minutes

Think of this crema as a smoother guacamole that can also be used to top many different dishes. Try it on anything from salads to meaty entrées.

½ cup sour cream

½ avocado

1 garlic clove, finely minced

¼ cup fresh cilantro leaves

Juice of ½ lime

Pinch pink Himalayan salt

Pinch freshly ground black pepper

1. In a food processor (or blender), mix the sour cream, avocado, garlic, cilantro, lime juice, salt, and pepper until smooth and fully combined.

2. Spoon the sauce into an airtight glass jar and keep in the refrigerator for up to 3 days.

3. Ingredient tip For an elegant presentation, put the crema in a zip-top bag and cut off a small corner to create a piping bag. The crema looks beautiful piped over tacos, meat, deviled eggs, and more.

PER SERVING Calories: 87; Fat: 8g; Carbs: 4g; Net Carbs: 2g; Fiber: 2g; Protein: 1g

CREAMY MAYONNAISE

Makes 4 cups / Prep time: 10 minutes

Homemade mayonnaise is a truly decadent condiment, and you can control the ingredients that go into the recipe. It's not difficult to make, especially with an immersion blender or food processor, but whisking up a batch by hand can be satisfying. It is fun to watch the ingredients emulsify before your eyes. Keep the mayonnaise in the refrigerator in an airtight container for up to 4 days.

2 large eggs

2 tablespoons Dijon mustard

1½ cups extra-virgin olive oil

¼ cup freshly squeezed lemon juice

Pink Himalayan salt

Freshly ground black pepper

TO MAKE BY HAND

1. In a heavy, large bowl, crack the eggs. Whisk the eggs and mustard together until very well combined, about 2 minutes.

2. Add the oil in a continuous thin stream, whisking constantly, until the mayonnaise is thick and completely emulsified.

3. Add the lemon juice and whisk until well blended.

4. Season with salt and pepper.

TO MAKE IN A FOOD PROCESSOR

1. Crack the eggs in the processor bowl. Add the mustard and blend until very smooth.

2. While the processor is running, slowly add the oil in a thin stream until the mayonnaise is thick and completely emulsified.

3. Add the lemon juice and process until smooth.

4. Season with salt and pepper.

PER SERVING Calories: 61; Fat: 7g; Carbs: 0g; Net Carbs: 0g; Fiber: 0g; Protein: 0g

SRIRACHA MAYO

Serves 4 / Prep time: 5 minutes

This spicy mayo is a sauce that makes any food better. Creamy with a kick, it is perfect for dipping chicken, veggies, and anything else you can grab.

½ cup Creamy Mayonnaise (page 33) or store-bought

2 tablespoons Sriracha sauce

½ teaspoon garlic powder

½ teaspoon onion powder

¼ teaspoon paprika

1. In a small bowl, whisk together the mayonnaise, Sriracha, garlic powder, onion powder, and paprika until well mixed.

2. Pour into an airtight glass container, and keep in the refrigerator for up to 1 week.

INGREDIENT TIP You can adjust the amount of Sriracha sauce to increase or decrease the spice level.

PER SERVING Calories: 201; Fat: 22g; Carbs: 2g; Net Carbs: 1g; Fiber: 0g; Protein: 1g

AVOCADO MAYO

Serves 4 / Prep time: 5 minutes

You can easily make your own mayonnaise using avocado. Maybe you're out of mayo, or maybe you just like making your own. Avocado makes a great mayo that is delicious mixed into dishes or used to top a keto-friendly burger or sandwich.

1 medium avocado, cut into chunks
½ teaspoon ground cayenne pepper
Juice of ½ lime

2 tablespoons fresh cilantro leaves
   (optional)
Pinch pink Himalayan salt
¼ cup extra-virgin olive oil

1. In a food processor (or blender), blend the avocado, cayenne pepper, lime juice, cilantro, and salt until all the ingredients are well combined and smooth.

2. Slowly incorporate the olive oil, adding 1 tablespoon at a time, pulsing the food processor in between.

3. Keep in a sealed glass container in the refrigerator for up to 1 week.

INGREDIENT TIP You want your avocado to be ripe: not too hard, but not too soft. A perfectly ripe avocado should just yield to light thumb pressure next to the stem. Unlike other methods for checking ripeness, this doesn't bruise the avocado.

PER SERVING Calories: 58; Fat: 5g; Carbs: 4g; Net Carbs: 1g; Fiber: 3g; Protein: 1g

GARLIC AIOLI

Serves 4 / Prep time: 5 minutes, plus 30 minutes to chill

Garlic aioli always sounds so fancy when it is on a restaurant menu, but it really couldn't be easier to make. The chives and parsley are not mandatory, but the fresh herbs are a great addition to this sauce.

½ cup Creamy Mayonnaise (page 33)
  or store-bought
2 garlic cloves, minced
Juice of 1 lemon

1 tablespoon chopped fresh flat-leaf
  Italian parsley
1 teaspoon chopped chives
Pink Himalayan salt
Freshly ground black pepper

1. In a food processor (or blender), combine the mayonnaise, garlic, lemon juice, parsley, and chives, and season with salt and pepper. Blend until fully combined.

2. Pour into a sealed glass container and chill in the refrigerator for at least 30 minutes before serving. This sauce will keep in the refrigerator for up to 1 week.

INGREDIENT TIP Mince the garlic as finely as possible for best results. You can even grate it with a zester if you have one.

PER SERVING Calories: 204; Fat: 22g; Carbs: 3g; Net Carbs: 2g; Fiber: 1g; Protein: 1g

DIJON VINAIGRETTE

Serves 4 / Prep time: 5 minutes

This light, tangy dressing is especially good with salads containing tomatoes, berries, or other sweet elements—the Dijon mustard plays really well with such ingredients.

2 tablespoons Dijon mustard

Juice of ½ lemon

1 garlic clove, finely minced

1½ tablespoons red wine vinegar

Pink Himalayan salt

Freshly ground black pepper

3 tablespoons extra-virgin olive oil

1. In a small bowl, whisk the mustard, lemon juice, garlic, and red wine vinegar until well combined. Season with salt and pepper, and whisk again.

2. Slowly add the olive oil, a little bit at a time, whisking constantly.

3. Keep in a sealed glass container in the refrigerator for up to 1 week.

SUBSTITUTION TIP Feel free to replace the red wine vinegar with apple cider vinegar.

PER SERVING Calories: 99; Fat: 11g; Carbs: 1g; Net Carbs: 1g; Fiber: 1g; Protein: 1g

TRADITIONAL CAESAR DRESSING

Makes 1½ cups / Prep time: 10 minutes / Cook time: 5 minutes, plus 10 minutes to cool

Caesar dressing used to be a culinary production in high-caliber restaurants, with waiters in black ties mixing all the ingredients tableside in huge wooden bowls. This type of spectacle is no longer part of most dining experiences, but the dressing remains one of the most popular choices. If you want an even more authentic Caesar dressing, add a teaspoon of anchovy paste along with the mustard and vinegar.

2 teaspoons minced garlic

4 large egg yolks

¼ cup wine vinegar

½ teaspoon dry mustard

Dash Worcestershire sauce

1 cup extra-virgin olive oil

¼ cup freshly squeezed lemon juice

Pink Himalayan salt

Freshly ground black pepper

1. To a small saucepan, add the garlic, egg yolks, vinegar, mustard, and Worcestershire sauce and place over low heat.

2. Whisking constantly, cook the mixture until it thickens and is a little bubbly, about 5 minutes.

3. Remove the saucepan from the heat and let it stand for about 10 minutes to cool.

4. Transfer the egg mixture to a large stainless steel bowl. Whisking constantly, add the olive oil in a thin stream.

5. Whisk in the lemon juice and season the dressing with salt and pepper.

6. Transfer the dressing to an airtight container and keep in the refrigerator for up to 3 days.

INGREDIENT TIP If you have concerns about raw egg yolks, you can purchase pasteurized eggs in most large supermarket chains. They are found alongside regular and specialty eggs in the dairy section.

STORAGE TIP Mason jars are the perfect containers for keeping homemade salad dressings.

VARIATIONS There are many ways to make a Caesar dressing. Go ahead: Be creative!

- ¼ cup of sour cream adds a nice tang.
- Add Parmesan cheese to taste.

PER SERVING (2 TABLESPOONS) Calories: 180; Fat: 20g; Carbs: 1g; Net Carbs: 1g; Fiber: 0g; Protein: 1g

GREEN GODDESS DRESSING

Serves 4 / Prep time: 5 minutes

This simple dressing can be made in a flash and tastes absolutely divine when poured over salads and meaty main dishes. Try it over medallions of boneless beef top sirloin that have been grilled and cut into thick slices.

2 tablespoons buttermilk

¼ cup Greek yogurt

1 teaspoon apple cider vinegar

1 garlic clove, minced

1 tablespoon extra-virgin olive oil

1 tablespoon fresh parsley leaves

1. In a food processor (or blender), combine the buttermilk, yogurt, apple cider vinegar, garlic, olive oil, and parsley. Blend until fully combined.

2. Pour into a sealed glass container and chill in the refrigerator for at least 30 minutes before serving. This dressing will keep in the refrigerator for up to 1 week.

SUBSTITUTION TIP This dressing is also delicious if you use sour cream in place of the Greek yogurt, or if you mix some fresh chopped chives in with the parsley.

PER SERVING Calories: 62; Fat: 6g; Carbs: 1g; Net Carbs: 1g; Fiber: 0g; Protein: 1g

CHUNKY BLUE CHEESE DRESSING

Serves 4 / Prep time: 5 minutes

No doubt, a knock-out blue cheese dressing is a great addition to a wedge salad or a nice steak salad. But there may be nothing better than crispy hot wings dipped in this cold-and-creamy blue cheese dressing.

½ cup sour cream

½ cup Creamy Mayonnaise (page 33) or store-bought

Juice of ½ lemon

½ teaspoon Worcestershire sauce

Pink Himalayan salt

Freshly ground black pepper

2 ounces crumbled blue cheese

1. In a medium bowl, whisk the sour cream, mayonnaise, lemon juice, and Worcestershire sauce. Season with salt and pepper, and whisk again until fully combined.

2. Fold in the crumbled blue cheese until well combined.

3. Keep in a sealed glass container in the refrigerator for up to 1 week.

INGREDIENT TIP You can adjust the amount of blue cheese crumbles to use in the dressing. Add more if you like it chunky.

PER SERVING Calories: 306; Fat: 32g; Carbs: 3g; Net Carbs: 3g; Fiber: 0g; Protein: 7g

HERBED BALSAMIC DRESSING

Makes 1 cup / Prep time: 5 minutes

Having a foolproof salad dressing recipe you can whip up on a moment's notice is a cook's essential. Vinaigrettes are not complicated, but you do need the correct ratios to create emulsification between the acid and oil. Balsamic vinegar adds a pleasing sweetness to this dressing, and since a little goes a long way, you won't be getting too many carbs from the vinegar.

1 cup extra-virgin olive oil

¼ cup balsamic vinegar

2 tablespoons chopped fresh oregano

1 teaspoon chopped fresh basil

1 teaspoon minced garlic

Pink Himalayan salt

Freshly ground black pepper

1. In a small bowl, whisk the olive oil and vinegar until emulsified, about 3 minutes.

2. Whisk in the oregano, basil, and garlic until well combined, about 1 minute.

3. Season the dressing with salt and pepper.

4. Transfer the dressing to an airtight container, and store it in the refrigerator for up to 1 week. Give the dressing a vigorous shake before using.

PER SERVING (1 TABLESPOON) Calories: 83; Fat: 9g; Carbs: 0g; Net Carbs: 0g; Fiber: 0g; Protein: 0g

GREEN BASIL DRESSING

Makes 1 cup / Prep time: 10 minutes

Basil has a unique licorice-like taste and delicate deep green leaves that create a wonderful dressing for a summer salad. This herb is a very effective antibacterial, which means bacteria growth is almost impossible in this dressing. Basil is very high in vitamin K, copper, flavonoids, and manganese. Grow your own in terra cotta pots on your patio or windowsill so that you always have fresh basil handy for your cooking needs.

1 avocado, peeled and pitted
¼ cup sour cream
¼ cup extra-virgin olive oil
¼ cup chopped fresh basil

1 tablespoon freshly squeezed
 lime juice
1 teaspoon minced garlic
Pink Himalayan salt
Freshly ground black pepper

1. Place the avocado, sour cream, olive oil, basil, lime juice, and garlic in a food processor and pulse until smooth, scraping down the sides of the bowl once during processing.

2. Season the dressing with salt and pepper.

3. Keep the dressing in an airtight container in the refrigerator for 1 to 2 weeks.

PER SERVING (1 TABLESPOON) Calories: 173; Fat: 17g; Carbs: 1g; Net Carbs: 1g; Fiber: 0g; Protein: 5g

◀ Bulletproof Coffee, page 46

BULLETPROOF COFFEE

Serves 1 / Prep time: 5 minutes

Bulletproof Coffee is a staple beverage in a lot of keto diets. If you're doing intermittent fasting (see page 9), the fat-filled coffee can help you extend your fast, keeping you satiated until lunchtime. If you are not using Bulletproof Coffee for fasting and instead would like to add protein or collagen, you can do that as well (see Variations).

1½ cups hot coffee

2 tablespoons MCT oil powder or
  Bulletproof Brain Octane Oil

2 tablespoons butter or ghee

1. Pour the hot coffee into a blender.
2. Add the oil powder and butter, and blend until thoroughly mixed and frothy.
3. Pour into a large mug and enjoy.

INGREDIENT TIP If you're new to the keto diet, you will want to start slowly with the Brain Octane Oil. It is powerful, so you'll want to work your way up to 2 tablespoons over the course of a few weeks.

VARIATIONS If you are doing intermittent fasting, do not add protein to your Bulletproof Coffee—that will end your fast. But if you aren't fasting, the first two variations offer easy ways to add protein and create a more filling breakfast drink:

- Raw egg: To add protein, replace the MCT oil powder with 1 raw egg. The egg adds an appealing creamy texture, and although the hot coffee cooks the egg, there will be no hint of cooked proteins.
- Protein and collagen powder: You could also add a scoop or two of protein powder. Perfect Keto's Keto Collagen protein powder, which has a great chocolate flavor that is especially tasty in coffee, contains grass-fed collagen, MCT oil powder, and protein powder. The collagen is a good anti-inflammatory addition.
- Spiced: Add 1 teaspoon of ground cinnamon and a little sweetener to your Bulletproof mixture for a delicious spiced version. This adds no protein.

PER SERVING Calories: 463; Fat: 51g; Carbs: 0g; Net Carbs: 0g; Fiber: 0g; Protein: 1g

BERRY-AVOCADO SMOOTHIE

Serves 2 / Prep time: 5 minutes

This smoothie is delicious and filled with healthy fat, potassium, magnesium, and fiber. It makes a great breakfast or a satisfying, filling snack. Use the liquid stevia if you prefer sweeter smoothies.

1 cup unsweetened full-fat
  coconut milk
1 scoop Perfect Keto Exogenous
  Ketone Powder in peaches and cream
½ avocado

1 cup fresh spinach
½ cup berries, fresh or frozen
  (no sugar added if frozen)
½ cup ice cubes
¼ teaspoon liquid stevia (optional)

1. In a blender, combine the coconut milk, protein powder, avocado, spinach, berries, ice, and stevia (if using).

2. Blend until thoroughly mixed and frothy.

3. Pour into 2 glasses and serve immediately.

INGREDIENT TIP Adding avocado to a smoothie recipe may sound unusual, but it adds nutrition and healthy fat and contributes a creamy smoothness.

PER SERVING Calories: 355; Fat: 40g; Carbs: 16g; Net Carbs: 8g; Fiber: 6g; Protein: 4g

ALMOND BUTTER SMOOTHIE

Serves 2 / Prep time: 5 minutes

You may feel as though you're indulging in a milkshake when you drink this smoothie. But rest assured, it is very healthy and will power your body and mind for hours. Add the liquid stevia if you prefer sweeter smoothies.

1 cup unsweetened full-fat
  coconut milk
1 scoop Perfect Keto Exogenous
  Ketone Powder in chocolate sea salt
½ avocado

2 tablespoons almond butter
½ cup berries, fresh or frozen
  (no sugar added if frozen)
½ cup ice cubes
¼ teaspoon liquid stevia (optional)

1. In a blender, combine the coconut milk, protein powder, avocado, almond butter, berries, ice, and stevia (if using).

2. Blend until thoroughly mixed and frothy.

3. Pour into 2 glasses and serve immediately.

INGREDIENT TIP You can add 1 teaspoon of turmeric powder to boost this smoothie's anti-inflammatory power. Or you can add 1 tablespoon of chia seeds that have been soaked in coconut milk for at least 20 minutes. The seeds will add extra fiber, iron, calcium, and omega-3 fatty acids to the smoothie.

PER SERVING Calories: 446; Fat: 43g; Carbs: 16g; Net Carbs: 9g; Fiber: 7g; Protein: 7g

PEANUT BUTTER CUP SMOOTHIE

Serves 2 / Prep time: 5 minutes

Lovers of the popular candy featuring chocolate and peanut butter will enjoy the same flavor combination for breakfast or a filling snack.

1 cup water

¾ cup coconut cream

1 scoop chocolate protein powder

2 tablespoons natural peanut butter

3 ice cubes

1. In a blender, combine the water, coconut cream, protein powder, peanut butter, and ice.
2. Blend until smooth.
3. Pour into 2 glasses and serve immediately.

INGREDIENT TIP For a more chocolaty taste, add a teaspoon of good-quality cocoa powder and a couple drops of liquid stevia. These additions will not add any fat, protein, or carbs to the smoothie, just 3 calories per serving.

PER SERVING Calories: 486; Fat: 40g; Carbs: 11g; Net Carbs: 6g; Fiber: 5g; Protein: 30g

BERRY GREEN SMOOTHIE

Serves 2 / Prep time: 10 minutes

You might be taken aback by the unusual color of this smoothie—greenish brown—but the taste is similar to raspberry cheesecake. Kale is a perfect addition to smoothies because it has a less assertive taste than some other greens. It is also a spectacular source of vitamin K and very high in vitamins A and C.

1 cup water

½ cup raspberries

½ cup shredded kale

¾ cup cream cheese

1 tablespoon coconut oil

1 scoop vanilla protein powder

1. In a blender, combine the water, raspberries, kale, cream cheese, coconut oil, and protein powder.

2. Blend until smooth.

3. Pour into 2 glasses and serve immediately.

PER SERVING Calories: 436; Fat: 36g; Carbs: 11g; Net Carbs: 6g; Fiber: 5g; Protein: 28g

LEMON-CASHEW SMOOTHIE

Serves 1 / Prep time: 5 minutes

The cashew milk and heavy cream combine to create an absolutely luscious smoothie that is tart enough to be refreshing and still makes for a satisfying breakfast or snack. If you add a few ice cubes, it will be like enjoying a rich citrus sorbet instead of a healthy breakfast. A couple leaves of fresh mint will also enhance the fresh flavor.

1 cup unsweetened cashew milk

¼ cup heavy (whipping) cream

¼ cup freshly squeezed lemon juice

1 scoop plain protein powder

1 tablespoon coconut oil

1 teaspoon granulated sweetener, such as Swerve

1. In a blender, combine the cashew milk, heavy cream, lemon juice, protein powder, coconut oil, and sweetener.

2. Blend until smooth.

3. Pour into a glass and serve immediately.

SUBSTITUTION TIP Almond milk or coconut milk are also fine choices instead of cashew milk. Each type of milk adds a slightly different flavor to the smoothie, so try them all to find the right combination for your palate.

PER SERVING Calories: 503; Fat: 45g; Carbs: 15g; Net Carbs: 11g; Fiber: 4g; Protein: 29g

SPINACH-BLUEBERRY SMOOTHIE

Serves 2 / Prep time: 5 minutes

Blueberries are the second most popular berry in the United States and have one of the highest antioxidant contents of any food. Throwing a handful of this fruit in your morning smoothie adds vitamins K and C, magnesium, and copper to your diet. Look for organic berries because they have a higher antioxidant level than conventionally grown fruit.

1 cup unsweetened full-fat coconut milk

1 cup spinach

½ English cucumber, chopped

½ cup blueberries

1 scoop plain protein powder

2 tablespoons coconut oil

4 ice cubes

Mint sprigs, for garnish

1. In a blender, combine the coconut milk, spinach, cucumber, blueberries, protein powder, coconut oil, and ice.

2. Blend until smooth.

3. Pour into 2 glasses, garnish each with the mint, and serve immediately.

PER SERVING Calories: 353; Fat: 32g; Carbs: 9g; Net Carbs: 6g; Fiber: 3g; Protein: 15g

CREAMY CINNAMON SMOOTHIE

Serves 2 / Prep time: 5 minutes

Cinnamon is a lovely warm spice that often conjures up visions of holiday desserts or fragrant baked goods. Try to find Ceylon cinnamon instead of Cassia, because it does not contain courmarin, a toxin that affects the liver. Ceylon cinnamon is lighter in color and has a more delicate flavor than Cassia.

2 cups unsweetened full-fat
 coconut milk

1 scoop vanilla protein powder

5 drops liquid stevia

1 teaspoon ground cinnamon

½ teaspoon alcohol-free vanilla extract

1. In a blender, combine the coconut milk, protein powder, stevia, cinnamon, and vanilla.

2. Blend until smooth.

3. Pour into 2 glasses and serve immediately.

INGREDIENT TIP Most of the vanilla you will find in the grocery store probably has alcohol in it because vanilla extract in the United States cannot be called pure unless it is 35 percent alcohol. You can find vanilla extract without alcohol in specialty stores.

PER SERVING Calories: 492; Fat: 47g; Carbs: 8g; Net Carbs: 6g; Fiber: 2g; Protein: 18g

BLACKBERRY-CHIA PUDDING

Serves 2 / Prep time: 10 minutes, plus overnight to set

Loaded with fiber, iron, calcium, and omega-3 fatty acids, chia seeds are one of the most nutritious foods on the planet. The chia seeds soak in the coconut milk and soften overnight to help set the pudding mixture. Chia seeds help slow digestion, and the fat content of this dish helps keep you feeling satisfied for hours. Blackberries are a great low-carb option, and they add a lot of flavor and texture. This sweet treat makes a delicious breakfast or dessert.

1 cup unsweetened full-fat coconut milk

1 teaspoon liquid stevia

1 teaspoon alcohol-free vanilla extract

½ cup blackberries, fresh or frozen (no sugar added if frozen)

¼ cup chia seeds

1. In a food processor (or blender), process the coconut milk, stevia, and vanilla until the mixture starts to thicken.

2. Add the blackberries, and process until thoroughly mixed and purple. Fold in the chia seeds.

3. Divide the mixture between two small cups with lids, and refrigerate overnight or up to 3 days before serving.

COOKING TIP Using a food processor or blender is a must—if you just whisk the mixture by hand in a bowl, it will not thicken overnight.

PER SERVING Calories: 437; Fat: 38g; Carbs: 23g; Net Carbs: 8g; Fiber: 15g; Protein: 8g

NUT MEDLEY GRANOLA

Serves 8 / Prep time: 10 minutes / Cook time: 1 hour

Homemade granola is an incredibly versatile treat to have on hand for breakfast and snacks and as a healthy topping for a creamy cup of Greek yogurt. The combination and amount of nuts in this recipe create a wonderful keto macro, but you can add or omit different ingredients to suit your taste. Stay away from adding dried fruits, though, because they are very high in carbs.

2 cups shredded unsweetened coconut

1 cup sliced almonds

1 cup raw sunflower seeds

½ cup raw pumpkin seeds

½ cup walnuts

½ cup melted coconut oil

10 drops liquid stevia

1 teaspoon ground cinnamon

½ teaspoon ground nutmeg

1. Preheat the oven to 250°F. Line 2 baking sheets with parchment paper. Set aside.

2. In a large bowl, toss together the shredded coconut, almonds, sunflower seeds, pumpkin seeds, and walnuts until mixed.

3. In a small bowl, stir together the coconut oil, stevia, cinnamon, and nutmeg until blended.

4. Pour the coconut oil mixture into the nut mixture, and use your hands to blend until the nuts are very well coated.

5. Transfer the granola mixture to the baking sheets, and spread it out evenly.

6. Bake the granola, stirring every 10 to 15 minutes, until the mixture is golden brown and crunchy, about 1 hour.

7. Transfer the granola to a large bowl and let it cool, tossing frequently to break up the large pieces.

8. Store the granola in airtight containers in the refrigerator or freezer for up to 1 month.

PER SERVING Calories: 391; Fat: 38g; Carbs: 10g; Net Carbs: 4g; Fiber: 6g; Protein: 10g

BACON-ARTICHOKE OMELET

Serves 4 / Prep time: 10 minutes / Cook time: 10 minutes

Omelets are not just for breakfast, and this vegetable- and bacon-packed beauty is hearty enough for a light dinner. If you add a nice mixed green salad to the plate, you won't go over your carbs because the combination with the omelet should still be an excellent keto macro. If you have leftovers, try them cold the next day for a snack or lunch.

6 eggs, beaten

2 tablespoons heavy (whipping) cream

8 bacon slices, cooked and chopped

1 tablespoon extra-virgin olive oil

¼ cup chopped onion

½ cup chopped artichoke hearts (canned, packed in water)

Pink Himalayan salt

Freshly ground black pepper

1. In a small bowl, whisk together the eggs, heavy cream, and bacon until well blended, and set aside.

2. Place a large skillet over medium-high heat and add the olive oil.

3. Sauté the onion until tender, about 3 minutes.

4. Pour the egg mixture into the skillet, swirling it for 1 minute.

5. Cook the omelet, lifting the edges with a spatula to let the uncooked egg flow underneath, for 2 minutes.

6. Sprinkle the artichoke hearts on top, and flip the omelet. Cook for 4 minutes more, until the egg is firm. Flip the omelet over again so the artichoke hearts are on top.

7. Remove from the heat, cut the omelet into quarters, and season with salt and pepper. Transfer the omelet to plates and serve.

PER SERVING Calories: 435; Fat: 39g; Carbs: 5g; Net Carbs: 3g; Fiber: 2g; Protein: 17g

MUSHROOM FRITTATA

Serves 6 / Prep time: 10 minutes / Cook time: 25 minutes

Frittatas can be described as baked omelets or as crustless quiches, but no matter how you define them, they are delicious and simple. Any type of mushroom can be used for the recipe, depending on what you like or what you have in your refrigerator. If you want to use portobello mushrooms, scoop out the black gills so that your eggs don't turn an unsightly gray.

2 tablespoons extra-virgin olive oil

1 cup sliced fresh mushrooms

1 cup shredded spinach

6 bacon slices, cooked and chopped

10 large eggs, beaten

½ cup crumbled goat cheese

Pink Himalayan salt

Freshly ground black pepper

1. Preheat the oven to 350°F.
2. Place a large ovenproof skillet over medium-high heat and add the olive oil.
3. Sauté the mushrooms until lightly browned, about 3 minutes.
4. Add the spinach and bacon and sauté until the greens are wilted, about 1 minute.
5. Add the eggs and cook, lifting the edges of the frittata with a spatula so the uncooked egg flows underneath, for 3 to 4 minutes.
6. Sprinkle the top with the crumbled goat cheese, and season lightly with salt and pepper.
7. Bake until set and lightly browned, about 15 minutes.
8. Remove the frittata from the oven, and let it stand for 5 minutes.
9. Cut into 6 wedges and serve immediately.

SUBSTITUTION TIP If you're not keen on goat cheese, feta cheese tastes lovely with the other ingredients in this dish. Feta is higher in fat and lower in protein than goat cheese, so keep that in mind when considering your keto macros.

PER SERVING Calories: 316; Fat: 27g; Carbs: 1g; Net Carbs: 1g; Fiber: 0g; Protein: 16g

BREAKFAST BAKE

Serves 8 / Prep time: 10 minutes / Cook time: 50 minutes, plus 10 minutes to stand

Spaghetti squash adds a satisfying texture and bulk to this casserole as well as a plethora of nutritional benefits. It is high in vitamins A, B, and C, which are powerful antioxidants. Spaghetti squash is also an excellent source of beta-carotene, potassium, manganese, and calcium.

1 tablespoon extra-virgin olive oil, plus more for greasing the casserole dish

1 pound preservative-free or homemade sausage

8 large eggs

2 cups cooked spaghetti squash

1 tablespoon chopped fresh oregano

Pink Himalayan salt

Freshly ground black pepper

½ cup shredded Cheddar cheese

1. Preheat the oven to 375°F. Lightly grease a 9-by-13-inch casserole dish with olive oil and set aside.

2. Place a large ovenproof skillet over medium-high heat and add the olive oil.

3. Brown the sausage until cooked through, about 5 minutes. While the sausage is cooking, in a medium bowl, whisk together the eggs, squash, and oregano. Season lightly with salt and pepper.

4. Add the cooked sausage to the egg mixture, stir until just combined, and pour the mixture into the casserole dish.

5. Sprinkle the top of the casserole with the cheese, and cover the casserole loosely with aluminum foil.

6. Bake the casserole for 30 minutes, then remove the foil and bake for an additional 15 minutes.

7. Let the casserole stand for 10 minutes before serving.

PER SERVING Calories: 303; Fat: 24g; Carbs: 4g; Net Carbs: 3g; Fiber: 1g; Protein: 17g

AVOCADO AND EGGS

Serves 4 / Prep time: 10 minutes / Cook time: 20 minutes

These pale green egg-filled fruits provide a lovely light breakfast and the perfect keto macro to start the day. The avocados should be ripe but still firm so they hold together when baked. Avocados are very high in healthy fats, about 25 grams per cup, and are packed with antioxidants. The best way to peel an avocado is to nick the peel and remove it by hand. The greatest concentration of phytonutrients is in the darker flesh right next to the peel.

2 avocados, peeled, halved lengthwise, and pitted

4 large eggs

1 (4-ounce) chicken breast, cooked and shredded

¼ cup Cheddar cheese

Pink Himalayan salt

Freshly ground black pepper

1. Preheat the oven to 425°F.

2. Take a spoon and hollow out each of the avocado halves until the hole is about twice the original size.

3. Place the avocado halves in an 8-by-8-inch baking dish, hollow-side up.

4. Crack an egg into each hollow, and divide the shredded chicken among the avocado halves. Sprinkle the cheese on top of each and season lightly with salt and pepper.

5. Bake the avocados until the eggs are cooked through, 15 to 20 minutes.

6. Serve immediately.

PREP TIP Cooked chicken breast is very handy for many recipes, so bake 4 or 5 breasts at the beginning of the week and store them in a sealed plastic bag in the refrigerator after they are completely cooled. Cooked chicken will keep for up to 5 days in the refrigerator.

PER SERVING Calories: 324; Fat: 25g; Carbs: 8g; Net Carbs: 3g; Fiber: 5g; Protein: 19g

ONE PAN

DOUBLE-PORK FRITTATA

Serves 4 / Prep time: 5 minutes / Cook time: 25 minutes, plus 5 minutes to cool

Frittatas are frequently made with cheese, but this recipe calls for just heavy whipping cream. The result is so fluffy and delicious that you may never go back! For this recipe, you can use butter, all-natural pork lard, or the lard from bacon.

1 tablespoon butter or pork lard	Freshly ground black pepper
8 large eggs	4 ounces pancetta, chopped
1 cup heavy (whipping) cream	2 ounces prosciutto, thinly sliced
Pink Himalayan salt	1 tablespoon chopped fresh dill

1. Preheat the oven to 375°F. Coat a 9-by-13-inch baking pan with the butter.

2. In a large bowl, whisk the eggs and cream together. Season with salt and pepper, and whisk to blend.

3. Pour the egg mixture into the prepared pan. Sprinkle the pancetta in and distribute evenly throughout.

4. Tear off pieces of the prosciutto and place on top, then sprinkle with the dill.

5. Bake for about 25 minutes, or until the edges are golden and the eggs are just set.

6. Transfer to a rack to cool for 5 minutes.

7. Cut into 4 portions and serve hot.

INGREDIENT TIP All-natural pork lard is available from Fatworks as well as most butchers.

COOKING TIP You can use a greased muffin tin with this recipe to create individual egg bites. Just make sure to evenly distribute all the ingredients among the muffin cups.

VARIATIONS The great thing about a frittata is that you can add so many other ingredients to it. Here are a few variations you can try, but have fun coming up with your own combinations from whatever is in your refrigerator:

- Browned sausage and fresh spinach
- Chopped bacon, sliced fresh mushrooms, and fresh spinach
- Sliced black olives, sliced red peppers, and chopped fresh parsley
- Diced ham, sliced green peppers, and sliced scallions

PER SERVING Calories: 437; Fat: 39g; Carbs: 3g; Net Carbs: 3g; Fiber: 0g; Protein: 21g

SAUSAGE BREAKFAST STACKS

Serves 2 / Prep time: 10 minutes / Cook time: 15 minutes

The best part about making keto-friendly breakfasts is how many simple ingredients you can combine to make the perfect healthy fat–filled meal. Sausage patties topped with mashed avocado and a gooey, sunny-side-up egg are the perfect start to a morning.

8 ounces ground pork

½ teaspoon garlic powder

½ teaspoon onion powder

2 tablespoons ghee, divided

2 large eggs

1 avocado

Pink Himalayan salt

Freshly ground black pepper

1. Preheat the oven to 375°F.

2. In a medium bowl, mix well to combine the ground pork, garlic powder, and onion powder. Form the mixture into 2 patties.

3. In a medium skillet over medium-high heat, melt 1 tablespoon of ghee.

4. Add the sausage patties and cook for 2 minutes on each side, until browned.

5. Transfer the sausage to a baking sheet. Bake for 8 to 10 minutes, until cooked through.

6. Add the remaining 1 tablespoon of ghee to the skillet. When it is hot, crack the eggs into the skillet and cook without disturbing for about 3 minutes, until the whites are opaque and the yolks have set.

7. Meanwhile, in a small bowl, mash the avocado.

8. Season the eggs with salt and pepper.

9. Remove the cooked sausage patties from the oven.

10. Place a sausage patty on each of two warmed plates. Spread half of the mashed avocado on top of each sausage patty, and top each with a fried egg. Serve hot.

SUBSTITUTION TIP You can use precooked frozen sausage patties for an even quicker breakfast. Just make sure they are sugar-free.

PER SERVING Calories: 533; Fat: 44g; Carbs: 7g; Net Carbs: 3g; Fiber: 5g; Protein: 29g

SPICY BREAKFAST SCRAMBLE

Serves 2 / Prep time: 5 minutes / Cook time: 10 minutes

A breakfast scramble is one of those meals you can make with a variety of ingredients. This one is inspired by Mexican flavors, but you can just as easily make one with Italian- or Mediterranean-inspired flavors. The Mexican chorizo, a spicy sausage, provides the zesty meat base to this scramble, and with creamy eggs, cheese, and scallions, this easy breakfast will keep you satisfied for hours. Use pepper Jack cheese for extra spice.

2 tablespoons ghee

6 ounces Mexican chorizo or other spicy sausage

6 large eggs

2 tablespoons heavy (whipping) cream

Pink Himalayan salt

Freshly ground black pepper

½ cup shredded cheese, such as pepper Jack, divided

½ cup chopped scallions, white and green parts

1. In a large skillet over medium-high heat, melt the ghee. Add the sausage and sauté, browning for about 6 minutes, until cooked through.

2. In a medium bowl, whisk the eggs until frothy.

3. Add the cream, and season with salt and pepper. Whisk to blend thoroughly.

4. Leaving the fat in the skillet, push the sausage to one side. Add the egg mixture to the other side of the skillet and heat until almost cooked through, about 3 minutes.

5. When the eggs are almost done, mix in half of the shredded cheese.

6. Mix the eggs and sausage together in the skillet. Top with the remaining shredded cheese and the scallions.

7. Spoon onto two plates and serve hot.

SUBSTITUTION TIP If you can't find Mexican chorizo, you can use regular ground beef and spices such as garlic powder, cumin, and oregano.

VARIATIONS To take this scramble to the next level, you can add some toppings that will elevate the flavor profile and add healthy fat:

- Top the scramble with ½ sliced avocado, a diced jalapeño, and a dollop of sour cream.
- Top the scramble with 1 tablespoon of salsa, 1 tablespoon of sliced black olives, and 1 tablespoon of chopped fresh cilantro leaves.

PER SERVING Calories: 850; Fat: 70g; Carbs: 7g; Net Carbs: 6g; Fiber: 1g; Protein: 46g

BACON-JALAPEÑO EGG CUPS

Makes 6 egg cups / Prep time: 10 minutes / Cook time: 25 minutes, plus 10 minutes to cool

Bacon egg cups are the perfect keto breakfast, snack, or even side dish. The crispy bacon on the outside, mixed with the creamy egg middle and spicy jalapeño, will start your day with a kick. The cream cheese mixed with bits of jalapeño pepper provides just the right amount of heat.

FOR THE BACON

6 bacon slices

1 tablespoon butter

FOR THE EGGS

2 jalapeño peppers

4 large eggs

2 ounces cream cheese, at room temperature

Pink Himalayan salt

Freshly ground black pepper

¼ cup shredded Mexican blend cheese

TO MAKE THE BACON

1. Preheat the oven to 375°F.

2. While the oven is warming up, heat a large skillet over medium-high heat. Add the bacon slices and cook partially, about 4 minutes. Transfer the bacon to a paper towel–lined plate.

3. Coat six cups of a standard muffin tin with the butter. Place a partially cooked bacon strip in each cup to line the sides.

TO MAKE THE EGGS

1. Cut one jalapeño lengthwise, seed it, and mince it. Cut the remaining jalapeño into rings, discarding the seeds. Set aside.

2. In a medium bowl, beat the eggs with a hand mixer until well beaten. Add the cream cheese and diced jalapeño, season with salt and pepper, and beat again to combine.

3. Pour the egg mixture into the prepared muffin tin, filling each cup about two-thirds of the way up so they have room to rise.

4. Top each cup with some of the shredded cheese and a ring of jalapeño, and bake for 20 minutes.

5. Cool for 10 minutes, and serve hot.

SUBSTITUTION TIP If you don't have jalapeños available, or you don't like spicy food, you can use bell peppers or another vegetable with a little crunch, such as asparagus.

PER SERVING (1 EGG CUP) Calories: 159; Fat: 13g; Carbs: 1g; Net Carbs: 0g; Fiber: 0g; Protein: 9g

BACON, SPINACH, AND AVOCADO EGG WRAP

Serves 2 / Prep time: 10 minutes / Cook time: 10 minutes

To make an egg wrap, you cook the egg mixture like a flat omelet, which acts like a crêpe or a tortilla to enclose the other ingredients. This recipe calls for bacon, spinach, and avocado, but you can get creative with ingredients to wrap inside the egg mixture (see Variations).

6 bacon slices

2 large eggs

2 tablespoons heavy (whipping) cream

Pink Himalayan salt

Freshly ground black pepper

1 tablespoon butter, if needed

1 cup fresh spinach (or other greens of your choice)

½ avocado, sliced

1. In a medium skillet over medium-high heat, cook the bacon on both sides until crispy, about 8 minutes. Transfer the bacon to a paper towel–lined plate.

2. In a medium bowl, whisk the eggs and cream, and season with salt and pepper. Whisk again to combine.

3. Add half the egg mixture to the skillet with the bacon grease.

4. Cook the egg mixture for about 1 minute, or until set, then flip with a spatula and cook the other side for 1 minute.

5. Transfer the cooked egg mixture to a paper towel–lined plate to soak up extra grease.

6. Repeat steps 4 and 5 for the other half of the egg mixture. If the pan gets dry, add the butter.

7. Place half of the cooked egg mixture on each of two warmed plates. Top each with half of the spinach, bacon, and avocado slices.

8. Season with salt and pepper, and roll the wraps. Serve hot.

SUBSTITUTION TIP To make these wraps dairy-free, omit the heavy cream and just add an extra egg.

VARIATIONS Egg wraps provide an easy base for many different flavor combinations:
- Chopped romaine lettuce provides a nice crunch to go with the traditional bacon and tomato.
- For extra spice, add diced jalapeños or hot sauce to your egg mixture, along with sausage links and shredded cheese.

PER SERVING Calories: 336; Fat: 29g; Carbs: 5g; Net Carbs: 2g; Fiber: 3g; Protein: 17g

BACON AND EGG CAULIFLOWER HASH

Serves 2 / Prep time: 5 minutes / Cook time: 15 minutes, plus 5 minutes to cool

You don't need potatoes to make a delicious breakfast hash. Cauliflower, a low-carb vegetable, makes a great substitute. This hash recipe transforms the classic bacon-and-egg breakfast into an easy, complete, one-skillet meal.

6 bacon slices

½ head cauliflower, cut into small florets

2 garlic cloves, minced

1 medium onion, diced

1 tablespoon extra-virgin olive oil, if needed

4 large eggs

Pink Himalayan salt

Freshly ground black pepper

1. In a large skillet over medium-high heat, cook the bacon on both sides until crispy, about 8 minutes. Transfer the bacon to a paper towel–lined plate to drain and cool for 5 minutes. Transfer to a cutting board, and chop the bacon.

2. Turn the heat down to medium, and add the cauliflower, garlic, and onion to the bacon grease in the skillet. Sauté for 5 minutes. If the pan gets dry, add the olive oil. You want the cauliflower florets to just begin to brown before you add the eggs.

3. Using a spoon, make 4 wells in the mixture in the skillet, and crack an egg into each well. Season the eggs and hash with salt and pepper. Cook the eggs until they set, about 3 minutes.

4. Sprinkle the diced bacon onto the hash mixture, and serve hot.

INGREDIENT TIP Buy precut cauliflower florets, such as those from Trader Joe's, to save time and kitchen prep.

PER SERVING Calories: 395; Fat: 27g; Carbs: 15g; Nets Carbs: 11g; Fiber: 4g; Protein: 25g

SMOKED SALMON AND CREAM CHEESE ROLL-UPS

Serves 2 / Prep time: 25 minutes

Salmon roll-ups are usually considered appetizers, but they also make a delicious breakfast. These are inspired by bagels and lox, but without the carbohydrates.

4 ounces cream cheese, at room
  temperature
1 teaspoon grated lemon zest
1 teaspoon Dijon mustard
2 tablespoons chopped scallions, white
  and green parts

Pink Himalayan salt
Freshly ground black pepper
1 (4-ounce) package cold-smoked
  salmon (about 12 slices)

1. Put the cream cheese, lemon zest, mustard, and scallions in a food processor
   (or blender), and season with salt and pepper. Process until fully mixed and smooth.

2. Spread the cream cheese mixture on each slice of smoked salmon, and roll it up.
   Place the rolls on a plate seam-side down.

3. Serve immediately or refrigerate, covered in plastic wrap or in a lidded container,
   for up to 3 days.

SUBSTITUTION TIP You can substitute chopped fresh dill or capers for the scallions.

PER SERVING Calories: 268; Fat: 22g; Carbs: 4g; Net Carbs: 3g; Fiber: 1g; Protein: 14g

BRUSSELS SPROUTS, BACON, AND EGGS

Serves 2 / Prep time: 5 minutes / Cook time: 20 minutes

Chances are, Brussels sprouts haven't been on your breakfast menu before. But when mixed with eggs and bacon, they make a perfect breakfast that is healthy, beautiful, and super easy to make.

½ pound Brussels sprouts, cleaned, trimmed, and halved

1 tablespoon extra-virgin olive oil

Pink Himalayan salt

Freshly ground black pepper

Nonstick cooking spray

6 bacon slices, diced

4 large eggs

Pinch red pepper flakes

2 tablespoons grated Parmesan cheese

1. Preheat the oven to 400°F.
2. In a medium bowl, toss the halved Brussels sprouts in the olive oil, and season with salt and pepper.
3. Coat a 9-by-13-inch baking pan with cooking spray.
4. Put the Brussels sprouts and bacon in the pan, and roast for 12 minutes.
5. Take the pan out of the oven, and stir the Brussels sprouts and bacon. Using a spoon, create 4 wells in the mixture.
6. Carefully crack an egg into each well.
7. Season the eggs with salt, black pepper, and red pepper flakes.
8. Sprinkle the Parmesan cheese over the Brussels sprouts and eggs.
9. Bake in the oven for 8 more minutes, or until the eggs are cooked to your preference, and serve.

SUBSTITUTION TIP You can omit the Parmesan cheese and use your favorite chopped salted nuts instead.

PER SERVING Calories: 401; Fat: 29g; Carbs: 12g; Net Carbs: 7g; Fiber: 5g; Protein: 27g

BLT BREAKFAST SALAD

Serves 2 / Prep time: 10 minutes / Cook time: 5 minutes

Salads are not just for lunch or dinner. A hearty salad can be an amazing way to start any day, and salads are quick and easy to put together. An oozing, gooey egg mixed with the creamy avocado and crunchy bacon is the perfect way to start a day.

2 large eggs

5 ounces organic mixed greens

2 tablespoons extra-virgin olive oil

Pink Himalayan salt

Freshly ground black pepper

1 avocado, thinly sliced

5 grape tomatoes, halved

6 bacon slices, cooked and chopped

1. In a small saucepan filled with water over high heat, bring the water to a boil. Put the eggs on to softboil, turn the heat down to medium-high, and cook for about 6 minutes.

2. While the eggs are cooking, in a large bowl, toss the mixed greens with the olive oil and season with salt and pepper. Divide the dressed greens between two bowls.

3. Top the greens with the avocado slices, grape tomatoes, and bacon.

4. When the eggs are done, peel them, halve them, and place two halves on top of each salad. Season with more salt and pepper and serve.

SUBSTITUTION TIP Fresh spinach—or fresh kale, trimmed and stemmed and massaged with olive oil to tenderize it—would also be a delicious base for this salad.

PER SERVING Calories: 445; Fat: 39g; Carbs: 18g; Net Carbs: 4g; Fiber: 6g; Protein: 18g

CHEESY EGG AND SPINACH NEST

Serves 1 / Prep time: 5 minutes / Cook time: 10 minutes

Cheesy egg nests are one of the easiest but most visually impressive breakfasts you can make. In the skillet, surround a couple of sunny-side-up eggs with cheese to combine a crispy cheese edge with a gooey egg yolk. Top the nest with avocado, spinach, and Parmesan cheese for a delicious mixture of flavor and texture.

1 tablespoon extra-virgin olive oil
2 large eggs
Pink Himalayan salt
Freshly ground black pepper

½ cup shredded mozzarella cheese
½ avocado, diced
¼ cup chopped fresh spinach
1 tablespoon grated Parmesan cheese

1. In a medium skillet over medium-high heat, heat the olive oil.

2. Crack the eggs into the skillet right next to each other.

3. Season the eggs with salt and pepper.

4. When the egg whites start to set, after about 2 minutes, sprinkle the mozzarella cheese around the entire perimeter of the eggs.

5. Add the diced avocado and chopped spinach to the cheese "nest."

6. Sprinkle the Parmesan cheese over the eggs and the nest.

7. Cook until the edges of the mozzarella cheese just begin to brown and get crispy, 7 to 10 minutes.

8. Transfer to a warm plate and enjoy hot.

SUBSTITUTION TIP You can use fresh flat-leaf Italian parsley instead of spinach.

PER SERVING Calories: 563; Fat: 46g; Carbs: 9g; Net Carbs: 4g; Fiber: 5g; Protein: 31g

KALE-AVOCADO EGG SKILLET

Serves 2 / Prep time: 5 minutes / Cook time: 10 minutes

One-skillet egg dishes are a great way to combine flavors. This skillet meal uses mushrooms and kale to provide a hearty base to the healthy fats in eggs and avocado. Using low-carb vegetables instead of high-starch choices will give you a nourishing start to your day, without heaviness.

2 tablespoons extra-virgin olive oil, divided

2 cups sliced mushrooms

5 ounces fresh kale, stemmed and sliced into ribbons

1 avocado, sliced

4 large eggs

Pink Himalayan salt

Freshly ground black pepper

1. In a large skillet with a lid over medium heat, heat 1 tablespoon of olive oil.

2. Add the mushrooms to the pan, and sauté for about 3 minutes.

3. In a medium bowl, massage the kale with the remaining 1 tablespoon of olive oil for 1 to 2 minutes to help tenderize it. Add the kale to the skillet on top of the mushrooms, then place the slices of avocado on top of the kale.

4. Using a spoon, create 4 wells for the eggs. Crack one egg into each well. Season the eggs and kale with salt and pepper.

5. Cover the skillet and cook for about 5 minutes, or until the eggs reach your desired degree of doneness.

6. Serve hot.

SUBSTITUTION TIP You can add asparagus, tomatoes, or another keto-friendly vegetable to the kale if you wish.

PER SERVING Calories: 407; Fat: 34g; Carbs: 13g; Net Carbs: 6g; Fiber: 7g; Protein: 18g

EGG-IN-A-HOLE BREAKFAST BURGER

Serves 2 / Prep time: 5 minutes / Cook time: 15 minutes

A burger for breakfast is just plain fun and feels a little rebellious. And everyone knows a gooey egg makes any burger better! This burger is topped with crispy bacon, melted Cheddar cheese, and spicy Sriracha Mayo (page 34) for the perfect breakfast feast.

4 bacon slices

6 ounces ground beef

Pink Himalayan salt

Freshly ground black pepper

2 tablespoons butter

2 large eggs

2 slices Cheddar cheese

1 tablespoon Sriracha Mayo (page 34)

1. In a large skillet with a lid over medium-high heat, cook the bacon on both sides until crispy, about 8 minutes. Transfer the bacon to a paper towel–lined plate.

2. Form the ground beef into two burger patties. Use a small glass or cookie cutter to cut out the middle of each (like a donut). Take the cut-out meat and add it to the edges of the two burgers. Season the meat with salt and pepper.

3. In the skillet still set over medium-high heat, melt the butter. Add the burger patties, cook the first side for 2 minutes, and then flip.

4. Crack an egg into the middle of each burger, and cook until the whites are set, 1 to 2 minutes. Season the eggs with salt and pepper.

5. Top each egg with 1 slice of Cheddar cheese, turn the heat off, and cover the skillet to melt the cheese, about 2 minutes.

6. Transfer the burgers to two plates, top each with two bacon slices and some of the Sriracha mayo, and serve.

SUBSTITUTION TIP If you are not eating dairy, use avocado instead of Cheddar cheese and olive oil instead of butter.

PER SERVING Calories: 578; Fat: 48g; Carbs: 2g; Net Carbs: 2g; Fiber: 0g; Protein: 34g

PANCAKE "CAKE"

Serves 4 / Prep time: 5 minutes / Cook time: 20 minutes

Pancakes without any standing over the skillet or griddle while you're flipping? What's not to love! This recipe uses the Cream Cheese and Coconut Flour Pancake recipe (page 76), but in a larger batch cooked in the oven. The result is a light, puffy pancake "cake" that you can top with butter and low-carb syrup. If you want to add additional seasonings or ingredients, see the Variations on page 77.

4 tablespoons butter, plus more for the pan and the top of the cake

8 large eggs

8 ounces cream cheese, at room temperature

4 teaspoons liquid stevia

3 teaspoons baking powder

½ cup coconut flour

1. Preheat the oven to 425°F. Coat a 9-by-13-inch baking pan with butter.

2. In a food processor (or blender), process the eggs, cream cheese, stevia, baking powder, and coconut flour until thoroughly combined.

3. Mix in some add-ins (see Variations, page 77), if desired.

4. Spread out the 4 tablespoons of butter in the prepared pan.

5. Put the pan in the oven for 2 to 3 minutes to melt the butter. Let the butter bubble, but make sure it doesn't brown or burn. Remove from the oven.

6. Pour the batter into the pan.

7. Bake for about 15 minutes, or until a paring knife stuck into the center of the cake comes out clean.

8. Place the cake on a cooling rack, and melt a few more tablespoons of butter on top if you wish.

9. Cut the pancake "cake" into 4 pieces and serve warm.

INGREDIENT TIP For extra flavor, add 2 teaspoons of alcohol-free vanilla extract and 2 teaspoons of ground cinnamon to the cake mix.

PER SERVING Calories: 502; Fat: 43g; Carbs: 13g; Net Carbs: 8g; Fiber: 5g; Protein: 18g

CREAM CHEESE AND COCONUT FLOUR PANCAKES OR WAFFLES

Serves 2 (6 pancakes, 3 waffles) / Prep time: 5 minutes / Cook time: 10 minutes

Yes, you can have pancakes if you're following a keto lifestyle! These cream cheese–based pancakes have that authentic, puffy pancake feel. You can use the batter on a skillet or griddle for pancakes or in a waffle iron for waffles.

4 large eggs

4 ounces cream cheese,
   at room temperature

1 teaspoon liquid stevia

1½ teaspoons baking powder

4 tablespoons coconut flour

4 tablespoons butter, divided
   (for pancakes)

Nonstick cooking spray (for waffles)

TO MAKE PANCAKES

1. In a food processor (or blender), process the eggs, cream cheese, stevia, baking powder, and coconut flour until thoroughly combined.

2. Mix in some add-ins if desired (see Variations).

3. In a large skillet over medium-high heat, melt 2 tablespoons of butter, turning the skillet to spread it evenly in the bottom of the pan.

4. Pour the batter into the skillet in ¼-cup portions for 3 (4-inch) pancakes.

5. The pancakes will get puffy when it is time to flip them, after about 2 minutes. (They won't really get the air bubbles like a typical pancake, but they will set.) Cook for about 1 minute more, until lightly browned on the bottom.

6. Repeat with the remaining 2 tablespoons of butter for the remaining batter.

7. Serve hot.

TO MAKE WAFFLES

1. Preheat the closed waffle iron until it's nice and hot on medium-high heat.

2. In a food processor (or blender), process the eggs, cream cheese, stevia, baking powder, and coconut flour until thoroughly combined.

3. Mix in the add-ins (see Variations) if desired.

4. Open your waffle iron, and spray the top and bottom with nonstick cooking spray.

5. Pour in the batter in three portions, to not quite cover the waffle-iron surface; don't get it close to the edges, or it will spill out when it cooks.

6. Waffles are done when they quit steaming and are lightly browned and crisp. The time will vary depending on your waffle iron.

7. Serve hot.

VARIATIONS Use one or more of the following variations to customize your pancakes or waffles with seasonings or add-ins for a truly fabulous treat:

- Yes, you can use syrup: Just make sure it's a low-carb syrup, such as Walden Farms Calorie-Free Pancake Syrup. Walden Farms also makes a blueberry variety. To add some richness, heat up the syrup with 1 tablespoon of butter in a small saucepan over low heat.
- Add 2 teaspoons of alcohol-free vanilla extract and a sprinkle of cinnamon. If you love ground cinnamon, you can add up to 1 teaspoon, or as much (or as little) as you want.
- Make it chocolate: Add keto-friendly chocolate chips, such as Lily's Dark Chocolate Premium Baking Chips (sweetened with stevia).
- Make it "berry" delicious: Blackberries and raspberries are lowest in carbohydrates.
- Crush ½ cup of pork rinds and fold them into the mix. The pork rinds give the batter a bit more saltiness and a little crunch that's especially nice in waffles.
- Add 1 to 2 tablespoons of your favorite nut butter to the mix to give your pancakes a unique flavor. Brands such as Legendary Foods or Buff Bake have some particularly delicious flavors.

PER SERVING Calories: 604; Fat: 55g; Carbs: 13g; Net Carbs: 8g; Fiber: 5g; Protein: 18g

BREAKFAST QUESADILLA

Serves 2 / Prep time: 5 minutes / Cook time: 20 minutes

For a satisfying breakfast, try these quesadillas. Frying the eggs provides some gooey egg yolk in the middle, but you can, of course, scramble the eggs instead. The Mission brand of low-carb tortillas has just 4 net carbs per tortilla.

2 bacon slices

2 large eggs

Pink Himalayan salt

Freshly ground black pepper

1 tablespoon extra-virgin olive oil

2 low-carbohydrate tortillas

1 cup shredded Mexican blend
   cheese, divided

½ avocado, thinly sliced

1. In a medium skillet over medium-high heat, cook the bacon on both sides until crispy, about 8 minutes. Transfer the bacon to a paper towel–lined plate to drain and cool for 5 minutes. Transfer to a cutting board, and chop the bacon.

2. Turn the heat down to medium, and crack the eggs onto the hot skillet with the bacon grease. Season with salt and pepper.

3. Cook the eggs for 3 to 4 minutes, until the egg whites are set. If you want the yolks to set, you can cook them longer. Transfer the cooked eggs to a plate.

4. Pour the olive oil into the hot skillet. Place the first tortilla in the pan.

5. Add ½ cup of cheese, place slices of avocado on the cheese in a circle, top with both fried eggs, the chopped bacon, and the remaining ½ cup of cheese, and cover with the second tortilla.

6. Once the cheese starts melting and the bottom of the tortilla is golden, after about 3 minutes, flip the quesadilla. Cook for about 2 minutes on the second side, until the bottom is golden.

7. Cut the quesadilla into slices with a pizza cutter or a chef's knife and serve.

INGREDIENT TIP Be sure to use low-carb tortillas, such as Mission Whole Wheat Low-Carb Tortillas, which contain 4 net carbs each.

SUBSTITUTION TIP If you have Tajín, a seasoning mix, you can use that instead of salt and pepper for a nice kick of chiles, lime, and salt.

PER SERVING Calories: 569; Fat: 41g; Carbs: 27g; Net Carbs: 9g; Fiber: 18g; Protein: 27g

CREAM CHEESE MUFFINS

Makes 6 muffins / Prep time: 10 minutes / Cook time: 10 minutes

Just because you're going keto doesn't mean you can't have muffins! With almond flour providing the structure, these muffins rely on cream cheese mixed with heavy whipping cream for their delicious flavor and tender texture. The basic recipe also is an excellent base for savory or sweet additions (see Variations).

4 tablespoons melted butter, plus more for the muffin tin

1 cup almond flour

¾ tablespoon baking powder

2 large eggs, lightly beaten

2 ounces cream cheese mixed with 2 tablespoons heavy (whipping) cream

Handful shredded Mexican blend cheese

1. Preheat the oven to 400°F. Coat six cups of a muffin tin with butter.

2. In a small bowl, mix together the almond flour and baking powder.

3. In a medium bowl, mix together the eggs, cream cheese–heavy cream mixture, shredded cheese, and the melted butter.

4. Pour the flour mixture into the egg mixture, and beat with a hand mixer until thoroughly mixed.

5. Pour the batter into the prepared muffin cups.

6. Bake for 12 minutes, or until golden brown on top, and serve.

SUBSTITUTION TIP You can use almond meal instead of almond flour. The mix will have more texture because almond meal is less refined.

VARIATIONS

- Add savory Trader Joe's Everything But the Bagel Seasoning on top of the muffins prior to baking to give them a salty, sesame-seed flavor and texture.
- Add diced jalapeños to the mix for a spicy muffin.
- Add 1 tablespoon of grated lemon zest and a handful of blueberries to the mix for a sweeter muffin.

PER SERVING Calories: 247; Fat: 23g; Carbs: 6g; Net Carbs: 4g; Fiber: 2g; Protein: 8g

APPS & SNACKS

◄ Cheese Chips and Guacamole, page 86

BACON-PEPPER FAT BOMBS

Makes 12 fat bombs / Prep time: 10 minutes, plus 1 hour to chill

Fat bombs are designed to help you reach your daily macros with no fuss and little planning required. This cheesy bacon bomb is savory and delectable, with a satisfying kick from the black pepper. If you want a little more heat, add a pinch of cayenne. It will definitely add a little pep to your step.

2 ounces goat cheese, at room temperature

2 ounces cream cheese, at room temperature

¼ cup butter, at room temperature

8 bacon slices, cooked and chopped

Pinch freshly ground black pepper

1. Line a small baking sheet with parchment paper and set aside.
2. In a medium bowl, stir together the goat cheese, cream cheese, butter, bacon, and pepper until well combined.
3. Use a tablespoon to drop mounds of the bomb mixture onto the baking sheet until you have 12 even mounds, and place the sheet in the freezer until the fat bombs are very firm but not frozen, about 1 hour.
4. Store the fat bombs in a sealed container in the refrigerator for up to 2 weeks.

PER SERVING (1 FAT BOMB) Calories: 89; Fat: 8g; Carbs: 0g; Net Carbs: 0g; Fiber: 0g; Protein: 3g

SMOKED SALMON FAT BOMBS

Makes 12 fat bombs / Prep time: 10 minutes, plus 3 hours to chill

Many restaurants serve a popular appetizer that features smoked salmon and herb cream cheese spread on tortillas, rolled up, and cut into little bite-size rounds. This keto version omits the tortillas but still has all the rich, delicious flavor. Add a sprinkle of chopped fresh dill into the mixture if it suits your taste.

½ cup goat cheese, at room
temperature

½ cup butter, at room temperature

2 ounces smoked salmon

2 teaspoons freshly squeezed
lemon juice

Pinch freshly ground black pepper

1. Line a baking sheet with parchment paper and set aside.

2. In a medium bowl, stir together the goat cheese, butter, smoked salmon, lemon juice, and pepper until very well blended.

3. Use a tablespoon to scoop the salmon mixture onto the baking sheet until you have 12 even mounds.

4. Place the baking sheet in the refrigerator until the fat bombs are firm, 2 to 3 hours.

5. Store the fat bombs in a sealed container in the refrigerator for up to 1 week.

INGREDIENT TIP Smoked salmon has more stable omega-3 fatty acids than fresh fish, which means these healthy fats are less prone to oxidation. Look for better-quality smoked salmon because cheaper products are often smoked over sawdust.

PER SERVING (2 FAT BOMBS) Calories: 193; Fat: 18g; Carbs: 0g; Net Carbs: 0g; Fiber: 0g; Protein: 8g

WALNUT HERB-CRUSTED GOAT CHEESE

Serves 4 / Prep time: 10 minutes

Goat cheese is a marvelous tart creation that has about 12 grams of fat, 10 grams of protein, and zero carbs in a 2-ounce portion, which is the recommended serving size in this recipe. Try to find soft goat cheese because semihard and hard types actually do contain carbs. The soft product can be found in most grocery stores in prepackaged logs.

6 ounces chopped walnuts

1 tablespoon chopped fresh oregano

1 tablespoon chopped fresh parsley

1 teaspoon chopped fresh thyme

¼ teaspoon freshly ground
 black pepper

1 (8-ounce) log goat cheese

1. Place the walnuts, oregano, parsley, thyme, and pepper in a food processor and pulse until finely chopped.

2. Pour the walnut mixture onto a plate, and roll the goat cheese log in the nut mixture, pressing so the cheese is covered and the walnut mixture sticks to the log.

3. Wrap the cheese in plastic and store in the refrigerator for up to 1 week.

4. Slice and enjoy!

PER SERVING Calories: 304; Fat: 28g; Carbs: 4g; Net Carbs: 2g; Fiber: 2g; Protein: 12g

CRISPY PARMESAN CRACKERS

Makes 8 crackers / Prep time: 10 minutes / Cook time: 5 minutes

Parmesan cheese has a nice keto ratio, especially when combined with a little butter to create these lacy beauties. The cheese spreads out and melts into large, crispy, golden crackers that will satisfy any craving for a rich, savory treat. You can use grated Parmesan as well, as long as it is freshly grated. The pre-grated cheese you'll find on supermarket shelves won't cut it— it tends to be too dry and powdery to melt correctly.

1 teaspoon butter

8 ounces full-fat Parmesan cheese, shredded or freshly grated

1. Preheat the oven to 400°F.
2. Line a baking sheet with parchment paper, and lightly grease the paper with the butter.
3. Spoon the Parmesan cheese onto the baking sheet in 8 mounds, spread evenly apart.
4. Spread out the mounds with the back of a spoon until they are flat.
5. Bake the crackers until the edges are browned and the centers are still pale, about 5 minutes.
6. Remove the sheet from the oven, and remove the crackers with a spatula to paper towels. Lightly blot the tops with additional paper towels and let them completely cool.
7. Store in a sealed container in the refrigerator for up to 4 days.

PER SERVING (1 CRACKER) Calories: 133; Fat: 11g; Carbs: 1g; Net Carbs: 1g; Fiber: 0g; Protein: 11g

CHEESE CHIPS AND GUACAMOLE

Serves 2 / Prep time: 10 minutes / Cook time: 10 minutes

Chips and guacamole is one of those appetizers you miss when you are on a keto diet. But these cheese chips are so easy to make, there is no reason to miss corn chips. And you may even like these better!

FOR THE CHEESE CHIPS

1 cup shredded cheese
   (Mexican blend or other variety)

FOR THE GUACAMOLE

1 avocado, mashed

Juice of ½ lime

1 teaspoon diced jalapeño

2 tablespoons chopped fresh
   cilantro leaves

Pink Himalayan salt

Freshly ground black pepper

TO MAKE THE CHEESE CHIPS

1. Preheat the oven to 350°F. Line a baking sheet with parchment paper or a silicone baking mat.

2. Add ¼-cup mounds of shredded cheese to the pan, leaving plenty of space between them, and bake until the edges are brown and the middles have fully melted, about 7 minutes.

3. Set the pan on a cooling rack, and let the cheese chips cool for 5 minutes. The chips will be floppy when they first come out of the oven but will crisp as they cool.

TO MAKE THE GUACAMOLE

1. In a medium bowl, mix together the avocado, lime juice, jalapeño, and cilantro, and season with salt and pepper.

2. Top the cheese chips with the guacamole, and serve.

INGREDIENT TIP You can also add some of the diced jalapeños to the cheese mixture before baking the chips.

PER SERVING Calories: 323; Fat: 27g; Carbs: 8g; Net Carbs: 3g; Fiber: 5g; Protein: 15g

CRUNCHY PORK RIND ZUCCHINI STICKS

Serves 2 / Prep time: 5 minutes / Cook time: 25 minutes

Even if you aren't a fan of zucchini, you'll love these crunchy, salty zucchini sticks. They make a tempting appetizer or a satisfying snack. And they are a delicious side dish for just about any meal.

2 medium zucchini, halved lengthwise and seeded

¼ cup crushed pork rinds

¼ cup grated Parmesan cheese

2 garlic cloves, minced

2 tablespoons melted butter

Pink Himalayan salt

Freshly ground black pepper

Extra-virgin olive oil, for drizzling

1. Preheat the oven to 400°F. Line a baking sheet with aluminum foil or a silicone baking mat.

2. Place the zucchini halves cut-side up on the prepared baking sheet.

3. In a medium bowl, combine the pork rinds, Parmesan cheese, garlic, and melted butter, and season with salt and pepper. Mix until well combined.

4. Spoon the pork-rind mixture onto each zucchini stick, and drizzle each with a little olive oil.

5. Bake for about 20 minutes, or until the topping is golden brown.

6. Turn on the broiler to finish browning the zucchini sticks, 3 to 5 minutes, and serve.

INGREDIENT TIP You can use a spoon to hollow out the zucchini boats if you want to make a bit more room for toppings.

PER SERVING Calories: 231; Fat: 20g; Carbs: 8g; Net Carbs: 6g; Fiber: 2g; Protein: 9g

SALAMI, PEPPERONCINI, AND CREAM CHEESE PINWHEELS

Serves 2 / Prep time: 20 minutes, plus 6 hours to chill

These pinwheels are a great appetizer to bring to a gathering or just to keep in your refrigerator so that you have keto-friendly bites on hand. Fill the insides of these shapes with just about anything—sliced pepperoncini add zest to any dish. Another great thing about these pinwheels is that they require no cooking, just a little muscle to roll out the cream cheese.

8 ounces cream cheese, at room temperature

¼ pound salami, thinly sliced

2 tablespoons sliced pepperoncini

1. Lay out a sheet of plastic wrap on a large cutting board or counter.
2. Place the cream cheese in the center of the plastic wrap, and then add another layer of plastic wrap on top. Using a rolling pin, roll the cream cheese until it is even and about ¼ inch thick. Try to make the shape somewhat resemble a rectangle.
3. Pull off the top layer of plastic wrap.
4. Place the salami slices so they overlap to completely cover the cream cheese layer.
5. Place a new piece of plastic wrap on top of the salami layer so that you can flip over your cream cheese–salami rectangle. Flip the layer so the cream cheese side is up.
6. Remove the plastic wrap and add the sliced pepperoncini in a layer on top.
7. Roll the layered ingredients into a tight log, pressing the meat and cream cheese together. (You want it as tight as possible.) Then wrap the roll with plastic wrap and refrigerate for at least 6 hours so it will set.
8. Use a sharp knife to cut the log into slices and serve.

INGREDIENT TIP Pepperoncini are available at most grocery stores; Mezzetta is one popular brand. If you prefer, use chopped dill pickles, scallions, jalapeños, or sliced bell pepper instead.

PER SERVING Calories: 583; Fat: 54g; Carbs: 7g; Net Carbs: 7g; Fiber: 0g; Protein: 19g

BACON-WRAPPED JALAPEÑOS

Serves 4 / Prep time: 10 minutes / Cook time: 20 minutes

This might become your favorite fall and winter snack for tailgating or just watching your favorite team on TV. With only three ingredients, these jalapeño bites are easy to make, but they do take a good amount of prep time. (Put your family and friends to work prepping the ingredients so you don't miss the game!)

10 jalapeños

8 ounces cream cheese, at room temperature

1 pound bacon (you will use about half a slice per popper)

1. Preheat the oven to 450°F. Line a baking sheet with aluminum foil or a silicone baking mat.

2. Halve the jalapeños lengthwise, and remove the seeds and membranes (if you like the extra heat, leave them in). Place them on the prepared pan cut-side up.

3. Spread some cream cheese inside each jalapeño half.

4. Wrap a jalapeño half with a slice of bacon (depending on the size of the jalapeño, use a whole slice of bacon or half).

5. Secure the bacon around each jalapeño with 1 to 2 toothpicks so it stays put while baking.

6. Bake for 20 minutes, until the bacon is done and crispy.

7. Serve hot or at room temperature. Either way, they are delicious!

INGREDIENT TIP Wear thin rubber gloves when you are prepping a batch of fresh jalapeños. The capsaicin in the chile pepper soaks into your skin, and even after you wash your hands multiple times, it can still be irritating. It is so easy to forget and touch your eyes or face.

PER SERVING Calories: 164; Fat: 13g; Carbs: 1g; Net Carbs: 1g; Fiber: 0g; Protein: 9g

DEVILED EGGS

Makes 24 deviled eggs / Prep time: 30 minutes / Cook time: 15 minutes

Eggs can be a wonderful addition to the keto diet because they are an excellent source of fat and protein. Deviled eggs can be eaten as a quick snack or taken to a get-together on a pretty platter for everyone to enjoy. The basic recipe uses sour cream in the egg yolk mixture, which adds a satisfying creaminess and tang. Deviled eggs lend themselves to almost endless add-ins; start with the Variations following the recipe, and then let your imagination take hold!

12 large eggs

½ cup Creamy Mayonnaise (page 33) or store-bought

¼ cup sour cream

1 tablespoon ground mustard

Pink Himalayan salt

Freshly ground black pepper

1 teaspoon paprika

1. To hardboil the eggs, place them in a large saucepan and cover with 3 to 4 inches of water. Bring the water to a boil, turn off the heat, cover the pot, and let sit for 15 minutes. Drain the eggs and fill the pan with ice-cold water (you can add ice cubes, too). One by one, lightly tap the eggs on the countertop to crack and then peel them under cold running water. Put them on a paper towel–lined plate.

2. Halve the eggs lengthwise. With a small spoon, carefully remove the yolks, transfer the yolks to a small bowl, and mash them.

3. Add the mayonnaise, sour cream, and mustard, and season with salt and pepper. Mix with a fork until smooth.

4. Spoon the yolk mixture back into the indentations in the egg whites. Sprinkle with the paprika and serve.

INGREDIENT TIP For a more elegant presentation, pipe the filling into the egg white halves with a piping bag. If you don't have a piping bag, grab a zip-top sandwich bag and a drinking cup. Put the bag in the cup, folding the edges of the bag over the sides of the cup. Spoon the mix into the zip-top bag, lift the bag out of the cup, cut off a small corner, and there you have it—you've created a simple piping bag.

VARIATIONS A simple, classic deviled egg is great, but here are just a few ideas to take it to another level:

- BLT Deviled Eggs: Top the egg mixture with crumbled bacon, chopped tomato, and chopped basil, which acts as the "L." Everyone loves them, keto or not!
- Bacon-Jalapeño Deviled Eggs: This version uses the egg mixture with added crumbled bacon and diced jalapeños. Remove the seeds to decrease the heat level.
- Bacon-Avocado Deviled Eggs: Add ½ avocado to the egg mixture along with 1 tablespoon of freshly squeezed lime juice. Then crumble 2 slices of crisply cooked bacon on top. You can also replace the paprika with Tajín, a delicious Mexican seasoning salt made with chiles and lime.
- Bacon-Cheese Deviled Eggs: Omit the sour cream, ground mustard, and paprika. Mash the egg yolks with a fork and add ½ cup mayonnaise; 1 teaspoon Dijon mustard; ½ avocado, chopped; and ½ cup finely shredded Swiss cheese. Season with salt and black pepper to taste. Spoon or pipe the mixture into the egg whites, and top with 12 bacon slices that have been cooked and crumbled.

PER EGG HALF Calories: 74; Fat: 7g; Carbs: 1g; Net Carbs: 0g; Fiber: 0g; Protein: 3g

QUESO DIP

Serves 6 / Prep time: 5 minutes / Cook time: 10 minutes

Also known as chile con queso, this dip originated in Mexico and can be found in many places that serve Tex-Mex cuisine. Jalapeño peppers are hot because they contain capsaicin. They are considered about medium in heat on the Scoville scale, with about 2,500 to 8,000 heat units per pepper. If you want a hotter dip, choose a pepper with more heat units, such as a habanero or Scotch bonnet chile.

½ cup unsweetened full-fat
   coconut milk
½ jalapeño pepper, seeded and diced
1 teaspoon minced garlic
½ teaspoon onion powder
2 ounces goat cheese

6 ounces sharp Cheddar
   cheese, shredded
¼ teaspoon cayenne pepper
Keto crackers or low-carb vegetables,
   for serving

1. In a medium pot over medium heat, combine the coconut milk, jalapeño, garlic, and onion powder.

2. Bring the liquid to a simmer, then whisk in the goat cheese until smooth.

3. Add the Cheddar cheese and cayenne and whisk until the dip is thick, 30 seconds to 1 minute.

4. Pour into a serving dish and serve with keto crackers or low-carb vegetables.

PER SERVING Calories: 213; Fat: 19g; Carbs: 2g; Net Carbs: 2g; Fiber: 0g; Protein: 10g

BUFFALO CHICKEN DIP

Serves 2 / Prep time: 10 minutes / Cook time: 20 minutes

This dip is a great side dish for game day. It has all the taste of chicken wings, but in a dip.

Butter or extra-virgin olive oil, for
  greasing the pan
1 large, cooked boneless chicken
  breast, shredded
8 ounces cream cheese

½ cup shredded Cheddar cheese
½ cup Chunky Blue Cheese Dressing
  (page 41) or store-bought
¼ cup buffalo wing sauce (such as
  Frank's RedHot)

1. Preheat the oven to 375°F. Grease a small baking pan with the butter.
2. In a medium bowl, mix together the chicken, cream cheese, Cheddar cheese, blue cheese dressing, and wing sauce. Transfer the mixture to the prepared baking pan.
3. Bake for 20 minutes.
4. Pour into a dip dish and serve hot.

SERVING TIP Pair this dip with celery stalks or pork rinds.

PER SERVING Calories: 859; Fat: 73g; Carbs: 8g; Net Carbs: 8g; Fiber: 0g; Protein: 41g

CHICKEN-AVOCADO LETTUCE WRAPS

Serves 4 / Prep time: 10 minutes

Lettuce wraps are a spectacular method of enjoying sandwiches and toppings without adding undesirable carbs. The best lettuce to use is Boston, large red or green oak leaf, or romaine lettuce with the rib cut out. Cutting out the ribs allows you to roll the lettuce leaf without it cracking or ripping.

½ avocado, peeled and pitted

⅓ cup Creamy Mayonnaise (page 33) or store-bought

1 teaspoon freshly squeezed lemon juice

2 teaspoons chopped fresh thyme

1 (6-ounce) cooked chicken breast, chopped

Pink Himalayan salt

Freshly ground black pepper

8 large lettuce leaves

¼ cup chopped walnuts

1. In a medium bowl, mash the avocado with the mayonnaise, lemon juice, and thyme until well combined.

2. Stir in the chopped chicken, and season the filling with salt and pepper.

3. Spoon the chicken salad into the lettuce leaves, and top with the walnuts.

4. Serve 2 lettuce wraps per person.

PER SERVING Calories: 264; Fat: 20g; Carbs: 9g; Net Carbs: 6g; Fiber: 3g; Protein: 12g

CRAB SALAD-STUFFED AVOCADO

Serves 2 / Prep time: 20 minutes

Depending on the size of your avocados, this decadent dish could be a filling snack or a light lunch. It's perfectly acceptable to use frozen crab if fresh is not available, but take care to look for real crabmeat rather than cheaper imitation products. If using frozen crab, thaw it completely and squeeze out any extra liquid so your salad isn't soggy.

1 avocado, peeled, halved lengthwise, and pitted

½ teaspoon freshly squeezed lemon juice

4½ ounces Dungeness crabmeat

½ cup cream cheese

¼ cup chopped red bell pepper

¼ cup chopped, peeled English cucumber

½ scallion, chopped

1 teaspoon chopped fresh cilantro

Pink Himalayan salt

Freshly ground black pepper

1. Brush the cut edges of the avocado with the lemon juice, and set the halves aside on a plate.

2. In a medium bowl, stir together the crabmeat, cream cheese, red pepper, cucumber, scallion, cilantro, salt, and pepper until well mixed.

3. Divide the crab mixture between the avocado halves and store them, covered with plastic wrap, in the refrigerator until you want to serve them, up to 2 days.

INGREDIENT TIP Dungeness crab is in season from about December to April; this is the best time frame to purchase this sweet crustacean. Seafood Watch, an organization that rates the sustainability of seafood choices, rates Dungeness crab as sustainable seafood.

PER SERVING Calories: 389; Fat: 31g; Carbs: 10g; Net Carbs: 5g; Fiber: 5g; Protein: 19g

CHICKEN-PECAN SALAD CUCUMBER BITES

Serves 2 / Prep time: 15 minutes

The ingredients in many traditional recipes for chicken salad—chicken, celery, grapes, and pecans—make for a tasty and texturally satisfying combination. This recipe omits the grapes to make it keto- friendly, but cucumber slices step in to provide a fresh crunch. This dish is a super-easy, light dinner or a perfect appetizer. Wrapped and stored in the refrigerator, these bites can be kept for up to 2 days before serving, while still staying crunchy.

1 cup diced cooked chicken breast

2 tablespoons Creamy Mayonnaise (page 33) or store-bought

¼ cup chopped pecans

¼ cup diced celery

Pink Himalayan salt

Freshly ground black pepper

1 cucumber, peeled and cut into ¼-inch slices

1. In a medium bowl, mix together the chicken, mayonnaise, pecans, and celery. Season with salt and pepper.

2. Lay the cucumber slices out on a plate, and add a pinch of salt to each.

3. Top each cucumber slice with a spoonful of the chicken-salad mixture and serve.

PER SERVING Calories: 323; Fat: 24g; Carbs: 6g; Net Carbs: 4g; Fiber: 3g; Protein: 23g

KETO BREAD

Makes 1 loaf (12 slices) / Prep time: 5 minutes / Cook time: 25 minutes

Think that because you're going keto, you have to give up bread? Think again! This recipe is not only keto-friendly, but delicious and with a satisfying texture. It also works as a great basic recipe for creating sweet or savory versions (see Variations).

5 tablespoons butter, at room temperature, divided

6 large eggs, lightly beaten

1½ cups almond flour

3 teaspoons baking powder

1 scoop MCT oil powder, such as Perfect Keto's MCT Oil Powder (optional, but it is flavorless and adds high-quality fats)

Pinch pink Himalayan salt

1. Preheat the oven to 390°F. Coat a 9-by-5-inch loaf pan with 1 tablespoon of butter.

2. In a large bowl, use a hand mixer to mix the eggs, almond flour, remaining 4 tablespoons of butter, baking powder, MCT oil powder (if using), and salt until thoroughly blended. Pour into the prepared pan.

3. Bake for 25 minutes, or until a toothpick inserted in the center comes out clean.

4. Slice and serve.

VARIATIONS

- Keto Pumpkin Bread: Mix all the ingredients together along with ¼ can of pure pumpkin purée. (Make sure you aren't buying sugar-filled pumpkin pie mix; you just want plain pumpkin purée. Generally, canned pumpkin purée can be found year-round at most grocery stores, such as Target, Safeway, or Walmart; other stores, such as Trader Joe's, may carry it only seasonally.) Also mix in 2 to 3 teaspoons of liquid stevia, depending on how sweet you want the bread, and 1 tablespoon of pumpkin pie spice (a mixture of cinnamon, nutmeg, ginger, and allspice). Bake according to the recipe instructions.
- Keto Chocolate Chip Bread: Mix the ingredients as instructed, then fold in ½ cup of keto-friendly chocolate chips. One brand is Lily's Dark Chocolate Premium Baking Chips, which are sweetened with stevia.

PER SLICE Calories: 165; Fat: 15g; Carbs: 4g; Net Carbs: 2g; Fiber: 2g; Protein: 6g

VEGETABLES & SIDES

◀ Pesto Zucchini Noodles, page 118

PORTOBELLO MUSHROOM PIZZAS

Serves 4 / Prep time: 15 minutes / Cook time: 5 minutes

What would pizza be without gooey, melted mozzarella? Mozzarella is produced using a method that spins the cheese from milk and then cuts it, called pasta filata. Mozzarella is a good choice for the keto diet. It is high in fat (65 percent), contains about 32 percent protein, and has only 3 percent carbs.

4 large portobello
   mushrooms, stemmed
¼ cup extra-virgin olive oil
1 teaspoon minced garlic

1 medium tomato, cut into 4 slices
2 teaspoons chopped fresh basil
1 cup shredded mozzarella cheese

1. Preheat the oven to broil. Line a baking sheet with aluminum foil and set aside.

2. In a small bowl, toss the mushroom caps with the olive oil until well coated. Use your fingertips to rub the oil in without breaking the mushrooms.

3. Place the mushrooms on the baking sheet gill-side down and broil until they are tender on the tops, about 2 minutes.

4. Flip the mushrooms over and broil for 1 minute more.

5. Take the baking sheet out and spread the garlic over each mushroom, top each with a tomato slice, sprinkle with the basil, and top with the cheese.

6. Broil the mushrooms until the cheese is melted and bubbly, about 1 minute.

7. Serve.

SERVING TIP These pizzas pack a lot of flavor, so you'll need an assertive main course to share the plate with them. Some wonderful options could include Bacon-Wrapped Beef Tenderloin (page 209) or Sirloin with Blue Cheese Compound Butter (page 206). These juicy mushrooms make a tempting snack, as well.

PER SERVING Calories: 251; Fat: 20g; Carbs: 7g; Net Carbs: 4g; Fiber: 3g; Protein: 14g

BUTTERY SLOW-COOKER MUSHROOMS

Serves 2 / Prep time: 10 minutes / Cook time: 4 hours

Dry ranch dressing mix makes such a great seasoning for these mushrooms. Your house will smell incredible while they are cooking in the slow cooker. They make a wonderful snack as well as a delicious side dish for most meats. You can easily double or triple this recipe for a larger group.

6 tablespoons butter

1 tablespoon packaged dry ranch dressing mix

8 ounces fresh cremini mushrooms

2 tablespoons grated Parmesan cheese

1 tablespoon chopped fresh flat-leaf Italian parsley

1. With the crock insert in place, preheat the slow cooker to low.

2. Put the butter and the dry ranch dressing in the bottom of the slow cooker, and allow the butter to melt. Stir to blend the dressing mix and butter.

3. Add the mushrooms to the slow cooker, and stir to coat with the butter-dressing mixture. Sprinkle the top with the Parmesan cheese.

4. Cover and cook on low for 4 hours.

5. Use a slotted spoon to transfer the mushrooms to a serving dish. Top with the chopped parsley and serve.

SUBSTITUTION TIP If you don't have dry ranch dressing mix, you can obtain a similar result by combining equal amounts of onion powder, garlic powder, dried thyme, salt, pepper, dried parsley, and a dash of paprika.

PER SERVING Calories: 351; Fat: 36g; Carbs: 5g; Net Carbs: 4g; Fiber: 1g; Protein: 6g

MUSHROOMS WITH CAMEMBERT

Serves 4 / Prep time: 5 minutes / Cook time: 15 minutes

Mushrooms have an interesting, almost meaty texture, and they tend to soak up all the flavorings in a recipe. Mushrooms are very high in vitamin D, the only vegetable source of this nutrient, and are an excellent source of potassium and selenium. Mushrooms can help reduce your cravings for sweet foods and help prevent spikes in blood sugar that can cause overeating.

2 tablespoons butter

2 teaspoons minced garlic

1 pound button mushrooms, halved

4 ounces Camembert cheese, diced

Freshly ground black pepper

1. In a large skillet over medium-high heat, melt the butter.

2. Sauté the garlic until translucent, about 3 minutes.

3. Add the mushrooms and sauté until tender, about 10 minutes.

4. Stir in the cheese and sauté until melted, about 2 minutes.

5. Season with pepper and serve.

SERVING TIP A somewhat elegant dish like these cheesy mushrooms deserves to be matched with a gorgeous culinary partner. Very good choices include the Nut-Stuffed Pork Chops (page 217) or Lamb Chops with Kalamata Tapenade (page 222).

PER SERVING Calories: 161; Fat: 13g; Carbs: 4g; Net Carbs: 3g; Fiber: 1g; Protein: 9g

SAUTÉED ASPARAGUS WITH WALNUTS

Serves 4 / Prep time: 10 minutes / Cook time: 5 minutes

If you are a foodie, you probably wait with anticipation for spring and the slender, elegant asparagus spears that come into season at that time. Asparagus is a good choice for keto followers because although this veggie contains carbs, it is also very high in fiber, which results in a low net carb content. Asparagus is an antioxidant and anti-inflammatory, so it is excellent for eye health, helps fight cancers, and is wonderful for your heart.

1½ tablespoons extra-virgin olive oil

¾ pound asparagus, woody
  ends trimmed

Pink Himalayan salt

Freshly ground black pepper

¼ cup chopped walnuts

1. In a large skillet over medium-high heat, heat the olive oil.
2. Sauté the asparagus until the spears are tender and lightly browned, about 5 minutes.
3. Season with salt and pepper.
4. Remove the skillet from the heat, and toss the asparagus with the walnuts.
5. Serve.

SERVING TIP There are very few other ingredients that do not combine well with asparagus, so you have many delicious options for main dishes to serve with these tasty spears. Good choices to consider are Paprika Chicken (page 174) or Roasted Pork Loin with Grainy Mustard Sauce (page 218).

PER SERVING Calories: 124; Fat: 12g; Carbs: 4g; Net Carbs: 2g; Fiber: 2g; Protein: 3g

CREAMY BROCCOLI-BACON SALAD

Serves 2 / Prep time: 10 minutes, plus 1 hour to chill / Cook time: 10 minutes

This fresh, creamy cold salad is the perfect companion for grilled meats, fish, or any summer-friendly entrée. The crunchy raw broccoli is the star, but the honey mustard adds a nice sweet kick to the otherwise salty ingredients.

6 bacon slices
½ pound fresh broccoli, cut into
   small florets
¼ cup sliced almonds

⅓ cup Creamy Mayonnaise (page 33)
   or store-bought
1 tablespoon honey mustard dressing

1. In a large skillet over medium-high heat, cook the bacon on both sides until crispy, about 8 minutes. Transfer the bacon to a paper towel–lined plate to drain and cool for 5 minutes. When cool, break the bacon into crumbles.

2. In a large bowl, combine the broccoli with the almonds and bacon.

3. In a small bowl, mix together the mayonnaise and honey mustard.

4. Add the dressing to the broccoli salad, and toss to thoroughly combine.

5. Chill the salad for 1 hour or more before serving.

SUBSTITUTION TIP You can replace the sliced almonds with sunflower seeds.

VARIATIONS Consider adding these elements to the salad for a bit of crispness and sweetness:
- ½ red onion, chopped, or 2 scallions, chopped
- 2 carrots, shredded

PER SERVING Calories: 549; Fat: 49g; Carbs: 16g; Net Carbs: 11g: Fiber: 5g; Protein: 16g

BRUSSELS SPROUTS CASSEROLE

Serves 8 / Prep time: 15 minutes / Cook time: 30 minutes

Many people avoid Brussels sprouts because they look complicated to cook. And if you have ever overcooked them, you know that they produce an extremely unpleasant sulphur-like odor. But if you've shied away from them, you should rethink this nutritional powerhouse— they are delicious and have many health benefits. Brussels sprouts help fight cardiovascular disease and cancer, lower cholesterol levels, and can improve thyroid function. And they really are easy to cook well.

8 bacon slices

1 pound Brussels sprouts, blanched for 10 minutes and quartered

1 cup shredded Swiss cheese, divided

¾ cup heavy (whipping) cream

1. Preheat the oven to 400°F.
2. In a medium skillet over medium-high heat, cook the bacon on both sides until crispy, about 8 minutes.
3. Reserve 1 tablespoon of bacon fat to grease the casserole dish, and roughly chop the cooked bacon.
4. Lightly oil a casserole dish with the reserved bacon fat and set aside.
5. In a medium bowl, toss the Brussels sprouts with the chopped bacon and ½ cup of cheese, and transfer the mixture to the casserole dish.
6. Pour the heavy cream over the Brussels sprouts, and top the casserole with the remaining ½ cup of cheese.
7. Bake until the cheese is melted and lightly browned and the vegetables are heated through, about 20 minutes.
8. Serve.

SERVING TIP This rich dish needs a simple entrée on the plate so that you don't feel too full at the end of the meal. Consider Italian Beef Burgers (page 204) or Rosemary-Garlic Lamb Racks (page 224).

PER SERVING Calories: 299; Fat: 11g; Carbs: 7g; Net Carbs: 4g; Fiber: 3g; Protein: 12g

ROASTED BRUSSELS SPROUTS WITH BACON

Serves 2 / Prep time: 5 minutes / Cook time: 25 minutes

If you think you don't like Brussels sprouts, try roasting them—the crispy texture and almost nutty sweetness that roasting imparts may just change your mind. This dish is beyond easy because the bacon bits cook while the Brussels sprouts roast, all in just one pan, for a dish that's full of flavor.

½ pound Brussels sprouts, cleaned, trimmed, and halved

1 tablespoon extra-virgin olive oil

Pink Himalayan salt

Freshly ground black pepper

1 teaspoon red pepper flakes

6 bacon slices

1 tablespoon grated Parmesan cheese

1. Preheat the oven to 400°F.

2. In a medium bowl, toss the Brussels sprouts with the olive oil, season with salt and pepper, and add the red pepper flakes.

3. Cut the bacon strips into 1-inch pieces.

4. Place the Brussels sprouts and bacon on a baking sheet in a single layer. Roast for about 25 minutes. About halfway through the baking time, give the pan a little shake to move the sprouts around, or give them a stir. You want your Brussels sprouts crispy and browned on the outside.

5. Remove the Brussels sprouts from the oven. Divide them between two plates, top each serving with Parmesan cheese, and serve.

INGREDIENT TIP Just leave out the Parmesan cheese to make this dish dairy-free.

PER SERVING Calories: 248; Fat: 18g; Carbs: 11g; Net Carbs: 7g; Fiber: 5g; Protein: 14g

CHEESY MASHED CAULIFLOWER

Serves 4 / Prep time: 15 minutes / Cook time: 5 minutes

Mashed potatoes might be one of the foods you miss when starting your keto experience, but take heart—this lower-carb version is pretty close to its fluffy counterpart. The cheese, cream, and butter add lots of flavor and a certain creamy feel to the mashed cauliflower, and they create a wonderful base for other variations.

1 head cauliflower, chopped roughly
½ cup shredded Cheddar cheese
¼ cup heavy (whipping) cream

2 tablespoons butter, at room temperature
Pink Himalayan salt
Freshly ground black pepper

1. Place a large saucepan filled three-quarters full of water over high heat, and bring to a boil.

2. Blanch the cauliflower until tender, about 5 minutes, and drain.

3. Transfer the cauliflower to a food processor and add the cheese, heavy cream, and butter. Purée until very creamy and whipped.

4. Season with salt and pepper.

5. Serve.

SERVING TIP Creamy mashed vegetables seem to call out for delectable sauces to spoon over them. Two of the best come with the Garlic-Braised Short Ribs (page 208) and Coconut Chicken (page 175).

VARIATION Mash some roasted garlic in the cauliflower for a truly sublime side dish.

PER SERVING Calories: 183; Fat: 15g; Carbs: 6g; Net Carbs: 4g; Fiber: 2g; Protein: 8g;

ROASTED CAULIFLOWER WITH PROSCIUTTO, CAPERS, AND ALMONDS

Serves 2 / Prep time: 5 minutes / Cook time: 25 minutes

This dish can be a meal in itself, but it is also perfect as a side with any meat. The capers provide a nice pop of flavor, and the slivered almonds give it a surprising crunch.

12 ounces cauliflower florets

2 tablespoons leftover bacon grease or extra-virgin olive oil

Pink Himalayan salt

Freshly ground black pepper

2 ounces sliced prosciutto, torn into small pieces

¼ cup slivered almonds

2 tablespoons capers

2 tablespoons grated Parmesan cheese

1. Preheat the oven to 400°F. Line a baking pan with a silicone baking mat or parchment paper.

2. Put the cauliflower florets in the prepared baking pan with the bacon grease, and season with salt and pepper. Or if you are using olive oil instead, drizzle the cauliflower with olive oil and season with salt and pepper.

3. Roast the cauliflower for 15 minutes.

4. Stir the cauliflower so all sides are coated with the bacon grease.

5. Distribute the prosciutto pieces in the pan. Then add the slivered almonds and capers. Stir to combine. Sprinkle the Parmesan cheese on top, and roast for 10 minutes more.

6. Divide between two plates, using a slotted spoon so you don't get excess grease in the plates, and serve.

SUBSTITUTION TIP Sliced green olives work well if you don't have capers.

PREP TIP Whenever you cook bacon, think about making roasted cauliflower; you already have all that wonderful bacon grease left in the pan, and the cauliflower soaks it right up. You can also throw a couple of seasoned chicken breasts into the pan with the cauliflower for a complete meal in one pan.

PER SERVING Calories: 288; Fat: 24g; Carbs: 7g; Net Carbs: 4g; Fiber: 3g; Protein: 14g

CAULIFLOWER STEAKS WITH BACON AND BLUE CHEESE

Serves 2 / Prep time: 5 minutes / Cook time: 20 minutes

This recipe uses the familiar flavors of a wedge salad. But instead of lettuce, it has a warm, caramelized cauliflower steak as the base. Then it is topped with chunky blue cheese dressing and crispy bacon.

½ head cauliflower
1 tablespoon extra-virgin olive oil
Pink Himalayan salt
Freshly ground black pepper

4 bacon slices
2 tablespoons Chunky Blue Cheese Dressing (page 41) or store-bought (such as Trader Joe's)

1. Preheat the oven to 425°F. Line a baking sheet with aluminum foil or a silicone baking mat.

2. To prep the cauliflower steaks, remove and discard the leaves and cut the cauliflower into 1-inch-thick slices. You can also roast the extra floret crumbles that fall off with the steaks.

3. Place the cauliflower steaks on the prepared baking sheet, and brush with the olive oil. You want the surface just lightly coated with the oil so it gets caramelized. Season with salt and pepper. Place the bacon slices on the pan, along with the cauliflower floret crumbles.

4. Roast the cauliflower steaks for 20 minutes.

5. Place the cauliflower steaks on two plates. Drizzle with the blue cheese dressing, top with the crumbled bacon, and serve.

SUBSTITUTION TIP You could follow the same instructions to make this dish with cabbage steaks instead of cauliflower.

PER SERVING Calories: 254; Fat: 19g; Carbs: 11g; Net Carbs: 7g; Fiber: 4g; Protein: 11g

PESTO CAULIFLOWER STEAKS

Serves 2 / Prep time: 5 minutes / Cook time: 20 minutes

Making homemade pesto is easier than you may think. Whenever you buy a bunch of fresh basil for a recipe, you can use the leftovers to make pesto. And if you don't have almonds on hand, just opt for whatever nuts you do have around. The flavorful pesto paired with the melted cheese is a perfect topping for cauliflower steaks.

2 tablespoons extra-virgin olive oil,
    plus more for brushing
½ head cauliflower
Pink Himalayan salt
Freshly ground black pepper

2 cups fresh basil leaves
½ cup grated Parmesan cheese
¼ cup almonds
½ cup shredded mozzarella cheese

1. Preheat the oven to 425°F. Brush a baking sheet with olive oil or line with a silicone baking mat.

2. To prep the cauliflower steaks, remove and discard the leaves and cut the cauliflower into 1-inch-thick slices. You can roast the extra floret crumbles that fall off with the steaks.

3. Place the cauliflower steaks on the prepared baking sheet, and brush them with olive oil. You want the surface just lightly coated so it gets caramelized. Season with salt and pepper.

4. Roast the cauliflower steaks for 20 minutes.

5. Meanwhile, put the basil, Parmesan cheese, almonds, and 2 tablespoons of olive oil in a food processor (or blender), and season with salt and pepper. Mix until combined.

6. Spread some pesto on top of each cauliflower steak, and top with the mozzarella cheese. Return to the oven and bake until the cheese melts, about 2 minutes.

7. Place the cauliflower steaks on two plates, and serve hot.

SUBSTITUTION TIP If you have pine nuts on hand, which are more traditionally used in pesto, you can definitely use those in place of the almonds.

PER SERVING Calories: 448; Fat: 34g; Carbs: 17g; Net Carbs: 10g; Fiber: 7g; Protein: 24g

CAULIFLOWER "POTATO" SALAD

Serves 2 / Prep time: 10 minutes, plus 3 hours to chill / Cook time: 25 minutes

This recipe is another great example of how versatile cauliflower is. No one is going to be fooled into thinking this is an actual potato salad, but it is delicious in its own right. Feel free to add in some of the variations to really take it over the top!

½ head cauliflower
1 tablespoon extra-virgin olive oil
Pink Himalayan salt
Freshly ground black pepper

⅓ cup Creamy Mayonnaise (page 33) or store-bought
1 tablespoon mustard
¼ cup diced dill pickles
1 teaspoon paprika

1. Preheat the oven to 400°F. Line a baking sheet with aluminum foil or a silicone baking mat.

2. Cut the cauliflower into 1-inch pieces.

3. Put the cauliflower in a large bowl, add the olive oil, season with salt and pepper, and toss to combine.

4. Spread the cauliflower out on the prepared baking sheet and bake for 25 minutes, or just until the cauliflower begins to brown. Halfway through the cooking time, give the pan a couple of shakes or stir so all sides of the cauliflower cook.

5. In a large bowl, mix the cauliflower together with the mayonnaise, mustard, and pickles. Sprinkle the paprika on top, and chill in the refrigerator for 3 hours before serving.

INGREDIENT TIP Do not use precut cauliflower florets; the pieces can be too small or too large, and the salad won't have the same "potato salad" feel. Make sure you use bite-size pieces of cauliflower.

VARIATIONS These additions make this delicious salad even tastier:
- Chopped hardboiled eggs on top
- Diced celery and minced white onion added to the mix

PER SERVING Calories: 386; Fat: 37g; Carbs: 13g; Net Carbs: 8g; Fiber: 5g; Protein: 5g

LOADED CAULIFLOWER MASHED "POTATOES"

Serves 4 / Prep time: 10 minutes / Cook time: 10 minutes

Cauliflower is definitely a staple in a keto diet. It is very low in carbohydrates and is so versatile. In fact, many keto followers say it is just as good as a potato.

1 head fresh cauliflower, cut into cubes

2 garlic cloves, minced

6 tablespoons butter

2 tablespoons sour cream

Pink Himalayan salt

Freshly ground black pepper

1 cup shredded cheese (such as Colby Jack)

6 bacon slices, cooked and crumbled

1. Boil a large pot of water over high heat. Add the cauliflower. Reduce the heat to medium-low and simmer for 8 to 10 minutes, until fork-tender. (You can also steam the cauliflower if you have a steamer basket.)

2. Drain the cauliflower in a colander, and turn it out onto a paper towel–lined plate to soak up the water. Blot to remove any remaining water from the cauliflower pieces. This step is important; you want to get out as much water as possible so the mash won't be runny.

3. Add the cauliflower to the food processor (or blender) with the garlic, butter, and sour cream, and season with salt and pepper.

4. Mix for about 1 minute, stopping to scrape down the sides of the bowl every 30 seconds.

5. Divide the cauliflower mix evenly among four small serving dishes, and top each with the cheese and bacon crumbles. (The cheese should melt from the hot cauliflower. But if you want to reheat it, you can put the cauliflower in oven-safe serving dishes and pop them under the broiler for 1 minute to heat up the cauliflower and melt the cheese.)

6. Serve warm.

VARIATIONS Anything you would use to top mashed potatoes will work well on mashed cauliflower. Try the following additions:

- Instead of Colby cheese, you can sprinkle ¼ cup of grated Parmesan cheese over the top, with 2 slices of prosciutto, chopped, and 3 tablespoons of chopped chives. For crispy prosciutto, place it under the broiler briefly.

PER SERVING Calories: 757; Fat: 38g; Carbs: 17g; Net Carbs: 11g; Fiber: 6g; Protein: 29g

GARLICKY GREEN BEANS

Serves 4 / Prep time: 10 minutes / Cook time: 10 minutes

Sizzling, lightly caramelized green beans flavored generously with garlic are a perfect culinary storm of texture, color, and taste. You might find yourself whipping up a batch to eat as a snack instead of a side dish. Yellow wax beans or a combination of the two colors would also be a lovely choice if you want to vary the ingredients.

1 pound green beans, stemmed

2 tablespoons extra-virgin olive oil

1 teaspoon minced garlic

Pink Himalayan salt

Freshly ground black pepper

¼ cup freshly grated Parmesan cheese

1. Preheat the oven to 425°F. Line a baking sheet with aluminum foil and set aside.

2. In a large bowl, toss together the green beans, olive oil, and garlic until well mixed.

3. Season the beans lightly with salt and pepper.

4. Spread the beans on the baking sheet and roast until tender and lightly browned, stirring once, about 10 minutes.

5. Serve topped with the Parmesan cheese.

SERVING TIP Look for entrées with a quick cooking time so your entire meal can be on the table in less than 30 minutes. Try tender Herb Butter Scallops (page 153) or Pan-Seared Halibut with Citrus-Butter Sauce (page 156) for a lovely, speedy meal.

PER SERVING Calories: 104; Fat: 9g; Carbs: 2g; Net Carbs: 1g; Fiber: 1g; Protein: 4g

PARMESAN AND PORK RIND GREEN BEANS

Serves 2 / Prep time: 5 minutes / Cook time: 15 minutes

Roasting has become a popular way to prepare vegetables; this cooking method concentrates the flavors as well as imparting a satisfying texture. Drizzled in olive oil and seasoned with a bit of salt plus the Parmesan cheese and pork rinds, these roasted beans are bursting with flavor.

½ pound fresh green beans

2 tablespoons crushed pork rinds

2 tablespoons extra-virgin olive oil

1 tablespoon grated Parmesan cheese

Pink Himalayan salt

Freshly ground black pepper

1. Preheat the oven to 400°F.

2. In a medium bowl, combine the green beans, pork rinds, olive oil, and Parmesan cheese. Season with salt and pepper, and toss until the beans are thoroughly coated.

3. Spread the bean mixture on a baking sheet in a single layer, and roast for about 15 minutes. At the halfway point, give the pan a little shake to move the beans around, or just give them a stir.

4. Divide the beans between two plates and serve.

INGREDIENT TIP You can use any flavor of pork rinds to add additional zest to the green beans.

PER SERVING Calories: 175; Fat: 15g; Carbs: 8g; Net Carbs: 5g; Fiber: 3g; Protein: 6g

SAUTÉED CRISPY ZUCCHINI

Serves 4 / Prep time: 15 minutes / Cook time: 10 minutes

Anyone who has eaten a grilled cheese sandwich or picked the crispy edges off lasagna knows how incredible these cheesy bits taste. That rich, golden, crisp cheese is what you end up with on your sautéed zucchini when you prepare this recipe. The trick is to let the ingredients sit in the skillet after you add the cheese so it has the chance to melt and lightly caramelize.

2 tablespoons butter

4 zucchini, cut into ¼-inch-thick rounds

½ cup freshly grated Parmesan cheese

Freshly ground black pepper

1. In a large skillet over medium-high heat, melt the butter.

2. Add the zucchini and sauté until tender and lightly browned, about 5 minutes.

3. Spread the zucchini evenly in the skillet, sprinkle the Parmesan cheese over the vegetables, and season with pepper.

4. Cook without stirring until the Parmesan cheese is melted and crispy where it touches the skillet, about 5 minutes.

5. Serve.

SERVING TIP The crispy bits of cheese are perfect with the lightly caramelized vegetables and are an attractive pairing with most entrées. Paprika Chicken (page 174) or Lamb Leg with Sun-Dried Tomato Pesto (page 225) would be delicious with this recipe.

PER SERVING Calories: 94; Fat: 8g; Carbs: 1g; Net Carbs: 1g; Fiber: 0g; Protein: 4g

BAKED ZUCCHINI GRATIN

Serves 2 / Prep time: 10 minutes, plus 30 minutes to drain / Cook time: 25 minutes

This cheesy dish with a crispy pork-rind topping is a delicious low-carb alternative to potatoes gratin. The crushed pork rinds act like a bread-crumb topping, and you can use any flavor of pork rinds you prefer. Simply toss them in the food processor (or blender) for a few seconds to crush. The mixture of the Brie and Gruyère cheeses is what makes this dish so unique!

1 large zucchini, cut into
   ¼-inch-thick slices

Pink Himalayan salt

1 ounce Brie cheese, rind trimmed off

1 tablespoon butter

Freshly ground black pepper

⅓ cup shredded Gruyère cheese

¼ cup crushed pork rinds

1. Salt the zucchini slices, and put them in a colander in the sink for 45 minutes; the zucchini will shed much of their water.

2. Preheat the oven to 400°F.

3. When the zucchini have been "weeping" for about 30 minutes, in a small saucepan over medium-low heat, heat the Brie and butter, stirring occasionally, until the cheese has melted and the mixture is fully combined, about 2 minutes.

4. Arrange the zucchini in an 8-by-8-inch baking dish so the zucchini slices are overlapping a bit. Season with pepper.

5. Pour the Brie mixture over the zucchini, and top with the shredded Gruyère cheese.

6. Sprinkle the crushed pork rinds over the top.

7. Bake for about 25 minutes, until the dish is bubbling and the top is nicely browned, and serve.

SUBSTITUTION TIP You can use a crème de Brie soft cheese as well. Some have garlic or other herbs in them, which are tasty additions to this dish.

PER SERVING Calories: 355; Fat: 25g; Carbs: 5g; Net Carbs: 4g; Fiber: 2g; Protein: 28g

PESTO ZUCCHINI NOODLES

Serves 4 / Prep time: 15 minutes

The pesto recommended for this pretty side is the kale version found on page 30. Kale is touted as a super food for good reason, since this leafy green is very high in fiber, calcium, and vitamins A, C, and K. Kale helps lower cholesterol and reduces your risk for several cancers as well as boosting the immune system and detoxing the body.

4 small zucchini, ends trimmed

¾ cup Herb-Kale Pesto (page 30)

¼ cup grated or shredded Parmesan cheese

1. Use a spiralizer or peeler to cut the zucchini into "noodles," and put them in a large bowl.
2. Add the pesto and Parmesan cheese, and toss to coat.
3. Serve.

SERVING TIP This is a light side dish that is ready in an instant but packs a great deal of flavor. Try a simply flavored entrée to complement the freshness of the zucchini noodles, such as Pan-Seared Halibut with Citrus-Butter Sauce (page 156) or Rosemary-Garlic Lamb Racks (page 224).

PER SERVING Calories: 93; Fat: 8g; Carbs: 2g; Net Carbs: 2g; Fiber: 0g; Protein: 4g

GOLDEN ROSTI

ONE PAN

Serves 8 / Prep time: 15 minutes / Cook time: 20 minutes

Celeriac has a parsley-like flavor and fresh scent under its gnarled skin. This root vegetable is a good source of phosphorus, potassium, fiber, iron, and vitamin C. It is also very low in calories, with about 40 calories per cup.

8 bacon slices, chopped

1 cup shredded acorn squash

1 cup shredded raw celeriac

2 tablespoons grated or shredded
 Parmesan cheese

2 teaspoons minced garlic

1 teaspoon chopped fresh thyme

Pink Himalayan salt

Freshly ground black pepper

2 tablespoons butter

1. In a large skillet over medium-high heat, cook the bacon until crispy, about 8 minutes.

2. While the bacon is cooking, in a large bowl, mix together the squash, celeriac, Parmesan cheese, garlic, and thyme. Season the mixture generously with salt and pepper, and set aside.

3. Transfer the cooked bacon with a slotted spoon to the rosti mixture and stir to incorporate.

4. Remove all but 2 tablespoons of bacon fat from the skillet, and add the butter.

5. Reduce the heat to medium-low. Transfer the rosti mixture to the skillet, and spread it out evenly to form a large, round patty about 1 inch thick.

6. Cook until the bottom of the rosti is golden brown and crisp, about 5 minutes.

7. Flip the rosti over and cook until the other side is crispy and the middle is cooked through, about 5 minutes more.

8. Remove the skillet from the heat, cut the rosti into 8 pieces, and serve.

SERVING TIP Rosti is great with comfort food. Serve with Turkey Meatloaf (page 180) or Lamb Leg with Sun-Dried Tomato Pesto (page 225).

PER SERVING Calories: 171; Fat: 15g; Carbs: 3g; Net Carbs: 3g; Fiber: 0g; Protein: 5g

ROASTED RADISHES WITH BROWN BUTTER SAUCE

Serves 2 / Prep time: 10 minutes / Cook time: 15 minutes

These warm, buttery roasted radishes look and taste like you are eating a baby red potato. They are crispy on the outside, warm and smooth on the inside. The brown butter sauce makes this dish truly delicious.

2 cups halved radishes

1 tablespoon extra-virgin olive oil

Pink Himalayan salt

Freshly ground black pepper

2 tablespoons butter

1 tablespoon chopped fresh flat-leaf Italian parsley

1. Preheat the oven to 450°F.

2. In a medium bowl, toss the radishes in the olive oil and season with salt and pepper.

3. Spread the radishes on a baking sheet in a single layer. Roast for 15 minutes, stirring halfway through.

4. Meanwhile, when the radishes have been roasting for about 10 minutes, in a small, light-colored saucepan over medium heat, melt the butter completely, stirring frequently, and season with salt. When the butter begins to bubble and foam, continue stirring. When the bubbling diminishes a bit, the butter should be a nice nutty brown. The browning process should take about 3 minutes total. Transfer the browned butter to a heat-safe container.

5. Remove the radishes from the oven, and divide them between two plates. Spoon the brown butter over the radishes, top with the chopped parsley, and serve.

INGREDIENT TIP You can keep the stems on the radishes to roast them if you prefer them that way.

PER SERVING Calories: 181; Fat: 19g; Carbs: 4g; Net Carbs: 2g; Fiber: 2g; Protein: 1g

CREAMED SPINACH

ONE PAN

Serves 4 / Prep time: 10 minutes / Cook time: 30 minutes

Creamed vegetables, spinach in particular, have been around for several thousand years, although over the past several years, yogurt has often been used in the sauce instead of heavy cream. The finished dish is comforting and perfect for large potluck events when you need to bring something to contribute. If you want to cut some of the calories from the recipe, swap out the heavy cream for evaporated milk, but keep in mind that also changes the keto macro.

1 tablespoon butter
½ sweet onion, very thinly sliced
4 cups spinach, stemmed and
  thoroughly washed
¾ cup heavy (whipping) cream

¼ cup Herbed Chicken Stock (page 23)
  or store-bought chicken broth
Pinch pink Himalayan salt
Pinch freshly ground black pepper
Pinch ground nutmeg

1. In a large skillet over medium heat, melt the butter.
2. Sauté the onion until it is lightly caramelized, about 5 minutes.
3. Stir in the spinach, cream, and chicken stock, and season with salt, pepper, and nutmeg.
4. Sauté until the spinach is wilted, about 5 minutes.
5. Continue cooking the spinach until it is tender and the sauce is thickened, about 15 minutes.
6. Serve immediately.

SERVING TIP Adding some color to your meal highlights the simple presentation of this traditional side dish. Look to Roasted Salmon with Avocado Salsa (page XX) for some pizzazz or the subtler Stuffed Chicken Breasts (page XX).

PER SERVING Calories: 195; Fat: 20g; Carbs: 3g; Net Carbs: 1g; Fiber: 2g; Protein: 3g

CHAPTER SIX
SOUPS & SALADS

◄ Chopped Greek Salad, page 135

CREAMY TOMATO-BASIL SOUP

Serves 2 / Prep time: 5 minutes / Cook time: 15 minutes

With its fresh flavor and creamy texture, this recipe will make you forget about buying canned soup. But cans do have their place in this recipe: Using canned tomatoes means that you can make this soup year-round, even when fresh tomatoes aren't in season. And it's so easy, too!

1 (14.5-ounce) can diced tomatoes

2 ounces cream cheese

¼ cup heavy (whipping) cream

4 tablespoons butter

¼ cup chopped fresh basil leaves

Pink Himalayan salt

Freshly ground black pepper

1. Pour the tomatoes with their juices into a food processor (or blender) and purée until smooth.

2. In a medium saucepan over medium heat, cook the tomatoes, cream cheese, cream, and butter for 10 minutes, stirring occasionally, until all is melted and thoroughly combined.

3. Add the basil, and season with salt and pepper. Continue stirring for 5 minutes more, until completely smooth.

4. Pour the soup into two bowls and serve.

INGREDIENT TIPS

- You can use either plain, unseasoned diced tomatoes or, if you prefer, pack in more flavor by using diced tomatoes with Italian seasoning.
- If you wish, you can also use an immersion blender to make short work of smoothing the soup.

PER SERVING Calories: 239; Fat: 22g; Carbs: 9g; Net Carbs: 7g; Fiber: 2g; Protein: 3g

BROCCOLI-CHEESE SOUP

Serves 2 / Prep time: 5 minutes / Cook time: 20 minutes

When the temperature falls, a hearty soup is always welcome. Broccoli-Cheese Soup is one of those keto-perfect soups that make a complete entrée. Tasty and very filling.

2 tablespoons butter

1 cup broccoli florets, finely chopped

1 cup heavy (whipping) cream

1 cup Herbed Chicken Stock (page 23) or store-bought chicken or vegetable broth

Pink Himalayan salt

Freshly ground black pepper

1 cup shredded cheese, preferably sharp Cheddar, some reserved for topping

1. In a medium saucepan over medium heat, melt the butter.
2. Add the broccoli and sauté in the butter for about 5 minutes, until tender.
3. Add the cream and the chicken broth, stirring constantly. Season with salt and pepper. Cook, stirring occasionally, for 10 to 15 minutes, until the soup has thickened.
4. Turn down the heat to low, and begin adding the shredded cheese. Reserve a small handful of cheese for topping the bowls of soup. (Do not add all the cheese at once, or it may clump up.) Add small amounts, slowly, while stirring constantly.
5. Pour the soup into two bowls, top each with half of the reserved cheese, and serve.

INGREDIENT TIP If you prefer a smoother texture, you can use an immersion blender for the soup mixture before you add the cheese.

VARIATIONS This soup is a creamy, delicious canvas for additional flavors and textures:
- If you like your soup with a spicy kick, you can add ¼ teaspoon of red pepper flakes.
- For additional flavor, add 1 garlic clove, minced, and ¼ onion, diced, when you add the broccoli.
- Crumbled bacon (2 cooked slices) provides a tasty topping for the soup. Sprinkle it over the top.

PER SERVING Calories: 383; Fat: 37g; Carbs: 4g; Net Carbs: 4g; Fiber: 1g; Protein: 10g

CAULIFLOWER-CHEDDAR SOUP

Serves 8 / Prep time: 10 minutes / Cook time: 30 minutes

Cauliflower is a versatile vegetable that can be used in many keto recipes—such as this creamy soup. Cauliflower is an excellent source of vitamins C and K, omega-3 fatty acids, and manganese, which can help support digestion, improve brain function, and promote a healthy heart. Choose a snowy white head of cauliflower with crisp green leaves and absolutely no brown spots.

¼ cup butter

1 head cauliflower, chopped

½ sweet onion, chopped

4 cups Herbed Chicken Stock (page 23) or store-bought

½ teaspoon ground nutmeg

1 cup heavy (whipping) cream

Pink Himalayan salt

Freshly ground black pepper

1 cup shredded Cheddar cheese

1. In a large stockpot over medium heat, melt the butter.

2. Sauté the cauliflower and onion until tender and lightly browned, about 10 minutes.

3. Add the chicken stock and nutmeg to the pot, and bring the liquid to a boil.

4. Reduce the heat to low and simmer until the vegetables are very tender, about 15 minutes.

5. Remove the pot from the heat, stir in the cream, and purée the soup with an immersion blender or food processor until smooth.

6. Season the soup with salt and pepper and serve topped with the Cheddar cheese.

VARIATIONS As with any creamy soup, crunchy ingredients added on top can be a perfect contrast:
- Add crumbled bacon and chopped scallions atop the soup along with the cheese.
- Add hot sauce for an extra kick.

PER SERVING Calories: 227; Fat: 21g; Carbs: 4g; Net Carbs: 2g; Fiber: 2g; Protein: 8g

TACO SOUP

Serves 2 / Prep time: 5 minutes / Cook time: 4 hours 10 minutes

This soup has a nice kick of flavor from the taco seasoning mixed with the seasoned tomatoes. The base is creamy and rich. It's so rich, you could even make some low-carb tortilla chips and dip them into this delicious mixture. Browning the ground beef on the stovetop contributes extra flavor to the soup.

1 pound ground beef

Pink Himalayan salt

Freshly ground black pepper

2 cups Rich Beef Stock (page 22)
  or store-bought beef broth
  (such as Kettle & Fire Bone Broth)

1 (10-ounce) can diced tomatoes

1 tablespoon taco seasoning

8 ounces cream cheese

1. With the crock insert in place, preheat the slow cooker to low.

2. On the stovetop, in a medium skillet over medium-high heat, sauté the ground beef until browned, about 8 minutes, and season salt and pepper.

3. Add the ground beef, beef stock, tomatoes, taco seasoning, and cream cheese to the slow cooker.

4. Cover and cook on low for 4 hours, stirring occasionally.

5. Ladle into two bowls and serve.

SUBSTITUTION TIP Instead of ground beef, you can use spicy sausage.

INGREDIENT TIP For a really spicy kick, use Rotel diced tomatoes.

PER SERVING Calories: 422; Fat: 33g; Carbs: 6g; Net Carbs: 5g; Fiber: 1g; Protein: 25g

ONE POT

COCONUT AND CAULIFLOWER CURRY SHRIMP SOUP

Serves 2 / Prep time: 5 minutes / Cook time: 2 hours 15 minutes

The Asian flavors in this dish work on all levels: You have the spiciness of the red curry paste along with the creamy fat of coconut milk. Then the juicy shrimp and fresh cilantro finish off the dish.

8 ounces water

1 (13.5-ounce) can unsweetened full-fat coconut milk

2 cups riced/shredded cauliflower

2 tablespoons red curry paste

2 tablespoons chopped fresh cilantro leaves, divided

Pink Himalayan salt

Freshly ground black pepper

1 cup shrimp, peeled, deveined, and tails removed

1. With the crock insert in place, preheat the slow cooker to high.

2. Add the water, coconut milk, riced cauliflower, red curry paste, and 1 tablespoon of chopped cilantro, and season with salt and pepper. Stir to combine.

3. Cover and cook on high for 2 hours.

4. Season the shrimp with salt and pepper, add them to the slow cooker, and stir. Cook for an additional 15 minutes.

5. Ladle the soup into two bowls, top each with half of the remaining 1 tablespoon of chopped cilantro, and serve.

INGREDIENT TIPS

- You could also make this soup with cooked, shredded chicken breast.
- For convenience, buy packaged riced cauliflower, such as Trader Joe's.

PER SERVING Calories: 269; Fat: 21g; Carbs: 8g; Net Carbs: 5g; Fiber: 3g; Protein: 16g

ROASTED BRUSSELS SPROUTS SALAD WITH PARMESAN

Serves 2 / Prep time: 10 minutes / Cook time: 15 minutes

The difference between this dish and most roasted Brussels sprouts is that this one uses just the leaves of the sprouts, which makes the dish super light. Hazelnuts really play a starring role in this salad.

1 pound Brussels sprouts

1 tablespoon extra-virgin olive oil

Pink Himalayan salt

Freshly ground black pepper

¼ cup shaved or grated Parmesan cheese

¼ cup whole, skinless hazelnuts

1. Preheat the oven to 350°F. Line a baking sheet with a silicone baking mat or parchment paper.

2. Trim the bottom and core from each Brussels sprout with a small knife. This will release the leaves. (You can reserve the cores to roast later if you wish.)

3. Put the leaves in a medium bowl; you can use your hands to fully release all the leaves.

4. Toss the leaves with the olive oil, and season with salt and pepper.

5. Spread the leaves in a single layer on the baking sheet. Roast for 10 to 15 minutes, or until lightly browned and crisp.

6. Divide the roasted Brussels sprouts leaves between two bowls, top each with the shaved Parmesan cheese and hazelnuts, and serve.

SUBSTITUTION TIP If you don't have hazelnuts, use chopped almonds.

PER SERVING Calories: 287; Fat: 19g; Carbs: 23g; Net Carbs: 13g; Fiber: 10g; Protein: 14g

BLT SALAD

Serves 4 / Prep time: 15 minutes

The portions of this salad are quite small, but the combination of ingredients packs a hearty flavor burst. Using bacon fat in the dressing instead of olive oil adds to this already mouth-watering salad. Bacon fat will keep in a sealed container in the refrigerator for up to 1 week, so save it for other recipes whenever you cook bacon.

2 tablespoons melted bacon fat

2 tablespoons red wine vinegar

Freshly ground black pepper

4 cups shredded lettuce

1 tomato, chopped

6 bacon slices, cooked and chopped

2 hardboiled eggs, chopped

1 tablespoon roasted unsalted sunflower seeds

1 teaspoon toasted sesame seeds

1 cooked chicken breast, sliced (optional)

1. In a medium bowl, whisk together the bacon fat and vinegar until emulsified. Season with pepper.

2. Add the lettuce and tomato to the bowl, and toss the vegetables with the dressing.

3. Divide the salad among 4 plates, and top each with equal amounts of bacon, egg, sunflower seeds, sesame seeds, and chicken (if using). Serve.

SUBSTITUTION TIP If you want to try a warm bacon salad dressing, gently warm the bacon fat before whisking in the vinegar. Swap out regular lettuce for kale or spinach; the more robust greens will hold up better in the dressing.

PER SERVING Calories: 228; Fat: 18g; Carbs: 4g; Net Carbs: 2g; Fiber: 2g; Protein: 1g

WEDGE SALAD

Serves 2 / Prep time: 10 minutes / Cook time: 10 minutes

A crisp iceberg lettuce wedge topped with chunky blue cheese dressing is delicious on its own. But when you add juicy grape tomatoes and crunchy bacon? It's just perfect.

4 bacon slices

½ head iceberg lettuce, halved

2 tablespoons Chunky Blue Cheese Dressing (page 41) or store-bought, such as Trader Joe's

¼ cup blue cheese crumbles

½ cup halved grape tomatoes

1. In a large skillet over medium-high heat, cook the bacon on both sides until crispy, about 8 minutes. Transfer the bacon to a paper towel–lined plate to drain and cool for 5 minutes. Transfer to a cutting board, and chop the bacon.

2. Place the lettuce wedges on two plates. Top each with half of the blue cheese dressing, the blue cheese crumbles, the halved grape tomatoes, and the chopped bacon, and serve.

INGREDIENT TIP If you have a grill, you can drizzle each of your iceberg lettuce wedges with 1 tablespoon of extra-virgin olive oil, season with salt and pepper, and grill each side for about 1 minute to add some smoky flavor. Then dress the lettuce wedges as instructed.

PER SERVING Calories: 278; Fat: 20g; Carbs: 9g; Net Carbs: 7g; Fiber: 3g; Protein: 15g

MEXICAN EGG SALAD

Serves 2 / Prep time: 15 minutes / Cook time: 10 minutes

Who isn't a big fan of egg salad? You can eat it in bowl all by itself, but it also makes a great base for experimentation with different flavors and textures. This version of avocado egg salad brings fresh cilantro and diced jalapeños to the party for a little kick. Then for some crunch, put the egg salad on cheese chips! Cheese chips are so easy to make; you will love them.

FOR THE HARDBOILED EGGS

4 large eggs

FOR THE CHEESE CHIPS

½ cup shredded cheese (such as
  Mexican blend), divided

FOR THE MEXICAN EGG SALAD

1 jalapeño

1 avocado, halved

Pink Himalayan salt

Freshly ground black pepper

2 tablespoons chopped fresh cilantro

1. Preheat the oven to 350°F. Line a baking sheet with parchment paper or a silicone baking mat and set aside.

2. Hardboil the eggs for the salad by placing the eggs in a medium saucepan. Cover the eggs with water. Bring the water to a boil over high heat. Once it is boiling, turn off the heat, cover, and leave the saucepan on the burner for 10 to 12 minutes.

3. While the eggs are cooking, make the cheese chips. Put 2 (¼-cup) mounds of shredded cheese on the prepared pan and bake for about 7 minutes, or until the edges are brown and the middle has fully melted. Remove the cheese chips from the oven and allow to cool for 5 minutes; they will be floppy when they first come out but will crisp as they cool.

4. Using a slotted spoon, remove the eggs from the saucepan and run them under cold water for 1 minute or submerge in an ice bath. Gently tap the shells and peel.

5. To assemble the Mexican egg salad, place the hardboiled eggs in a medium bowl and chop them. Stem, rib, seed, and dice the jalapeño, and add it to the eggs. Mash the avocado with a fork. Season with salt and pepper. Add the avocado and cilantro to the eggs, and stir to combine.

6. Place the cheese chips on two plates, top with the egg salad, and serve.

INGREDIENT TIP For additional zest, add ½ teaspoon of Tajín (a Mexican seasoning salt that combines chiles, lime, and sea salt) and the juice of ½ lime to the egg salad.

PER SERVING Calories: 359; Fat: 29g; Carbs: 8g; Net Carbs: 3g; Fiber: 5g; Protein: 21g

BLUE CHEESE AND BACON KALE SALAD

Serves 2 / Prep time: 10 minutes / Cook time: 10 minutes

Kale salads have become very popular, and it's easy to see why. Massaging the kale leaves with olive oil breaks down the fibers and makes the greens more tender and easier to digest. Top the kale with bacon, blue cheese crumbles, and pecans, and you have a nutritious salad packed with unique flavors and textures.

4 bacon slices

2 cups stemmed and chopped fresh kale

1 tablespoon Herbed Balsamic Dressing (page 42) or store-bought vinaigrette

Pinch pink Himalayan salt

Pinch freshly ground black pepper

¼ cup pecans

¼ cup blue cheese crumbles

1. In a medium skillet over medium-high heat, cook the bacon on both sides until crispy, about 8 minutes. Transfer the bacon to a paper towel–lined plate.

2. Meanwhile, in a large bowl, massage the kale with the vinaigrette for 2 minutes. Add the and pepper. Let the kale sit while the bacon cooks, and it will get even softer.

3. Chop the bacon and pecans, and add them to the bowl. Sprinkle in the blue cheese.

4. Toss well to combine, portion onto two plates, and serve.

SUBSTITUTION TIP Use chopped almonds in place of the chopped pecans.

PER SERVING Calories: 353; Fat: 29g; Carbs: 10g; Net Carbs: 7g; Fiber: 3g; Protein: 16g

CHOPPED GREEK SALAD

Serves 2 / Prep time: 10 minutes

A Greek salad is a restaurant favorite, but it's definitely something you can enjoy at home. It is so fresh and easy to make. This one has just a few ingredients, but feel free to get creative with yours.

2 cups chopped romaine

½ cup halved grape tomatoes

¼ cup sliced black olives
    (such as Kalamata)

¼ cup feta cheese crumbles

2 tablespoons Herbed Balsamic
    Dressing (page 42) or store-bought
    vinaigrette

Pink Himalayan salt

Freshly ground black pepper

1 tablespoon extra-virgin olive oil

1. In a large bowl, combine the romaine, tomatoes, olives, feta cheese, and vinaigrette.

2. Season with salt and pepper, drizzle with the olive oil, and toss to combine.

3. Divide the salad between two bowls and serve.

SUBSTITUTION TIP You could replace the feta cheese with goat cheese.

VARIATIONS With Greek salad, there are so many great flavors you can add:

- Add red onion or finely chopped cucumbers for additional crunch and freshness, and chopped pepperoncini for a zesty kick.
- Finely chopped Genoa salami and pepperoni are good choices.

PER SERVING Calories: 202; Fat: 19g; Carbs: 4g; Net Carbs: 3g; Fiber: 2g; Protein: 4g

MEDITERRANEAN CUCUMBER SALAD

Serves 2 / Prep time: 10 minutes

This salad is simple, delicious, and packed with fresh flavors. The black olives and feta cheese add some healthy fats, while the cucumbers and tomatoes add that pop of freshness, making this a great side salad for any Mediterranean-inspired meat dish.

1 large cucumber, peeled and
  finely chopped

½ cup halved grape tomatoes

¼ cup halved black olives
  (such as Kalamata)

¼ cup crumbled feta cheese

Pink Himalayan salt

Freshly ground black pepper

2 tablespoons Herbed Balsamic
  Dressing (page 42) or store-bought
  vinaigrette

1. In a large bowl, combine the cucumber, tomatoes, olives, and feta cheese. Season with salt and pepper. Add the dressing and toss to combine.

2. Divide the salad between two bowls and serve.

INGREDIENT TIP This salad can be eaten immediately, but it is even better if you cover it and put it in the refrigerator to let the salad ingredients marinate in the dressing for a few hours.

PER SERVING Calories: 152; Fat: 13g; Carbs: 6g; Net Carbs: 4g; Fiber: 2g; Protein: 4g

AVOCADO CAPRESE SALAD

Serves 2 / Prep time: 10 minutes

Caprese salads are a classic. For a keto twist, this recipe adds avocado for additional healthy fats and arugula for a peppery flavor. These ingredients make the dish super filling, too.

2 cups arugula

1 tablespoon extra-virgin olive oil, divided

Pink Himalayan salt

Freshly ground black pepper

1 avocado, sliced

4 fresh mozzarella balls, sliced

1 Roma tomato, sliced

4 fresh basil leaves, cut into ribbons

1. In a large bowl, toss the arugula with ½ tablespoon of olive oil and season with salt and pepper.

2. Divide the arugula between two plates.

3. Top the arugula with the avocado, mozzarella, and tomatoes, and drizzle with the remaining ½ tablespoon of olive oil. Season with salt and pepper.

4. Sprinkle the basil on top and serve.

SUBSTITUTION TIP For an extra kick of flavor, replace the olive oil with a vinaigrette dressing, such as Herbed Balsamic Dressing (page 42) or Primal Kitchen Greek Vinaigrette.

PER SERVING Calories: 320; Fat: 27g; Carbs: 10g; Net Carbs: 5g; Fiber: 6g; Protein: 13g

AVOCADO EGG SALAD LETTUCE CUPS

Serves 2 / Prep time: 15 minutes / Cook time: 15 minutes

Have you ever thought of making egg salad with avocado instead of mayo? It adds a delicious flavor element. And for some enjoyable crunch, these cups feature sliced radishes.

FOR THE HARDBOILED EGGS

4 large eggs

FOR THE EGG SALAD

1 avocado, halved

Pink Himalayan salt

Freshly ground black pepper

½ teaspoon freshly squeezed
   lemon juice

4 butter lettuce cups, washed and
   patted dry with paper towels or a
   clean dish towel

2 radishes, thinly sliced

TO MAKE THE HARDBOILED EGGS

1. In a medium saucepan, cover the eggs with water. Place over high heat, and bring the water to a boil. Once it is boiling, turn off the heat, cover, and leave on the burner for 10 to 12 minutes.

2. Remove the eggs with a slotted spoon and run them under cold water for 1 minute or submerge them in an ice bath.

3. Then gently tap the shells and peel. Run cold water over your hands as you remove the shells.

TO MAKE THE EGG SALAD

1. In a medium bowl, chop the hardboiled eggs.

2. Add the avocado to the bowl, and mash the flesh with a fork. Season with salt and pepper, add the lemon juice, and stir to combine.

3. Place the 4 lettuce cups on two plates. Top the lettuce cups with the egg salad and the slices of radish and serve.

SUBSTITUTION TIP You could also use romaine hearts or baby cos lettuce.

PER SERVING Calories: 258; Fat: 20g; Carbs: 8g; Net Carbs: 3g; Fiber: 5g; Protein: 15g

TOMATO, AVOCADO, AND CUCUMBER SALAD

Serves 2 / Prep time: 10 minutes

You can assemble this flavorful salad in minutes. It's a perfect dish for a potluck because everyone will enjoy it. If they are available, use small Persian cucumbers for this salad—they are crisper and have very tiny seeds.

½ cup grape tomatoes, halved

4 small Persian cucumbers or 1 English cucumber, peeled and finely chopped

1 avocado, finely chopped

¼ cup crumbled feta cheese

2 tablespoons Herbed Balsamic Dressing (page 42) or store-bought vinaigrette

Pink Himalayan salt

Freshly ground black pepper

1. In a large bowl, combine the tomatoes, cucumbers, avocado, and feta cheese.

2. Add the vinaigrette, and season with salt and pepper. Toss to thoroughly combine.

3. Divide the salad between two plates and serve.

SUBSTITUTION TIP You could replace the feta cheese with goat cheese.

VARIATIONS The flavors and textures in this salad pair perfectly with the following additions:
- ½ red onion, finely chopped, for additional crunch and freshness
- Sliced black olives

PER SERVING Calories: 258; Fat: 23g; Carbs: 12g; Net Carbs: 6g; Fiber: 6g; Protein: 5g

SHRIMP AND AVOCADO SALAD

Serves 2 / Prep time: 5 minutes, plus 30 minutes to chill / Cook time: 2 minutes

This salad needs to chill for a bit before serving, but waiting that extra time is well worth it. To make the recipe super easy, you can buy cooked and peeled shrimp, or choose whichever kind of shrimp you like.

1 tablespoon extra-virgin olive oil

1 pound shrimp, peeled and deveined,
 tails removed

Pink Himalayan salt

Freshly ground black pepper

1 avocado, cubed

1 celery stalk, chopped

¼ cup Creamy Mayonnaise (page 33)
 or store-bought

1 teaspoon freshly squeezed lime juice

1. In a large skillet over medium heat, heat the olive oil. When the oil is hot, add the shrimp. Cook until they turn pink and opaque, about 3 minutes. Season with salt and pepper.

2. Transfer the shrimp to a medium bowl, cover, and refrigerate.

3. In a medium bowl, combine the avocado, celery, and mayonnaise. Add the lime juice, and season with salt. Stir to combine. Add the chilled shrimp, and toss to combine.

4. Cover the salad, and refrigerate to chill for 30 minutes before serving.

SUBSTITUTION TIP For an additional kick, use Tajín seasoning salt instead of pink Himalayan or sea salt. Tajín is a Mexican seasoning salt that combines chiles, lime, and sea salt.

VARIATIONS If you have fresh herbs or greens in the refrigerator, you might want to add them:

- Add chopped fresh dill to the salad mixture.
- Scoop the salad mixture onto butter lettuce cups or romaine leaves for added freshness and crunch.

PER SERVING Calories: 571; Fat: 41g; Carbs: 8g; Net Carbs: 3g; Fiber: 5g; Protein: 50g

SALMON CAESAR SALAD

Serves 2 / Prep time: 5 minutes / Cook time: 20 minutes

If you love salmon, this salad is for you. It's creamy and full of healthy fats, and it has the salty crunch of bacon. Who wouldn't prefer getting crunch from bacon instead of the standard carb-full croutons?

4 bacon slices

2 (6-ounce) salmon fillets

Pink Himalayan salt

Freshly ground black pepper

1 tablespoon ghee, if needed

½ avocado, sliced

2 romaine hearts or 2 cups
    chopped romaine

2 tablespoons Traditional Caesar
    Dressing (page 38) or store-bought

1. In a medium skillet over medium-high heat, cook the bacon on both sides until crispy, about 8 minutes. Transfer the bacon to a paper towel–lined plate.

2. Meanwhile, pat the salmon with a paper towel to remove excess water. Season both sides with salt and pepper.

3. With the bacon grease still in the skillet, add the salmon. If you need more grease in the pan, add the ghee to the bacon grease.

4. Cook the salmon for 5 minutes on each side, or until it reaches your preferred degree of doneness.

5. Tear the bacon into pieces. Season the avocado with salt and pepper.

6. Divide the romaine, bacon, and avocado between two plates.

7. Top the salads with the salmon fillets, drizzle Caesar dressing on top, and serve.

INGREDIENT TIP You could bake the bacon and salmon instead of using the skillet. Preheat the oven to 400°F, and line a baking sheet with aluminum foil. Place the bacon slices and salmon fillets on the baking sheet together. Bake for 15 minutes, then broil for 5 minutes, or until the top of the salmon browns.

PER SERVING Calories: 466; Fat: 32g; Carbs: 6g; Net Carbs: 3g; Fiber: 4g; Protein: 40g

SALMON AND SPINACH COBB SALAD

Serves 2 / Prep time: 5 minutes / Cook time: 25 minutes

The Cobb salad is a perfect keto food. It's fresh, full of healthy fats, and just plain delicious. Using salmon rather than the standard turkey or chicken is a great twist on an old favorite. And the warm, gooey egg yolk makes a super-flavorful dressing for the salad.

4 bacon slices

2 large eggs

2 (6-ounce) salmon fillets

Pink Himalayan salt

Freshly ground black pepper

1 tablespoon ghee, if needed

1 avocado, sliced

6 ounces organic baby spinach

¼ cup crumbled blue cheese

1 tablespoon extra-virgin olive oil

1. In a medium skillet over medium-high heat, cook the bacon on both sides until crispy, about 8 minutes. Transfer the bacon to a paper towel–lined plate.

2. Bring a small saucepan filled with water to a boil over high heat. Put the eggs on to softboil, turn the heat down to medium-high, and cook for about 6 minutes.

3. Meanwhile, pat the salmon fillets on both sides with a paper towel to remove excess moisture. Season both sides with salt and pepper.

4. With the bacon grease still in the skillet, add the salmon. If you need more grease in the pan, add some ghee to the bacon grease.

5. Cook the salmon on medium-high heat for 5 minutes on each side, or until it reaches your preferred degree of doneness.

6. Meanwhile, transfer the bacon to a cutting board and chop it. Peel the softboiled eggs. Season the avocado with salt and pepper.

7. Divide the spinach, bacon, and avocado between two plates.

8. Carefully halve the softboiled eggs and place them on the salads. Sprinkle the blue cheese crumbles over the salads.

9. Top with the salmon, drizzle the salads with the olive oil, and serve.

INGREDIENT TIP You could use arugula instead of spinach, or a crunchier green such as romaine, if you prefer.

VARIATIONS
- Add halved grape tomatoes for a pop of acidity and freshness.
- Add sliced black olives for an additional salty element.

PER SERVING Calories: 623; Fat: 43g; Carbs: 12g; Net Carbs: 5g; Fiber: 7g; Protein: 54g

TACO SALAD

Serves 2 / Prep time: 10 minutes / Cook time: 10 minutes

Taco salads are perfect for the keto diet if you don't use the taco shell. Making them at home is easy. Just brown some ground beef and combine it with a variety of fresh ingredients.

1 tablespoon ghee

1 pound ground beef

Pink Himalayan salt

Freshly ground black pepper

2 cups chopped romaine

1 avocado, cubed

½ cup halved grape tomatoes

½ cup shredded cheese
   (such as Mexican blend)

1. In a large skillet over medium-high heat, heat the ghee.

2. When the ghee is hot, add the ground beef, breaking it up into smaller pieces with a spoon. Stir, cooking until the beef is browned, about 10 minutes. Season with salt and pepper.

3. Divide the romaine between two bowls. Season with salt and pepper.

4. Add the avocado and tomatoes, top with the beef and shredded cheese, and serve.

SUBSTITUTION TIP You could replace salt and pepper with taco seasoning.

VARIATIONS

- Feel free to add a dollop of sour cream and some chopped scallions or jalapeños for crunch and healthy fat.
- Make your own tortilla strips: Cut a low-carb tortilla into strips, toss the strips in olive oil, season with salt and pepper, and bake in a single layer on a baking sheet for 10 minutes at 425°F.

PER SERVING Calories: 659; Fat: 52g; Carbs: 10g; Net Carbs: 4g; Fiber: 6g; Protein: 48g

CHEESEBURGER SALAD

Serves 2 / Prep time: 10 minutes / Cook time: 10 minutes

Have you ever ordered a lettuce-wrapped burger at a restaurant? This cheeseburger salad will give you the same taste, all mixed in one bowl. If you love the pickles in this recipe, go ahead and add more!

1 tablespoon ghee

1 pound ground beef

Pink Himalayan salt

Freshly ground black pepper

½ cup finely chopped dill pickles

2 cups chopped romaine

½ cup shredded Cheddar cheese

2 tablespoons ranch salad dressing
   (such as Primal Kitchen Ranch)

1. In a medium skillet over medium-high heat, heat the ghee.
2. When the ghee is hot, add the ground beef, breaking it up into smaller pieces with a spoon. Stir, cooking until the beef is browned, about 10 minutes. Season with salt and pepper.
3. Put the pickles in a large bowl, and add the romaine and cheese.
4. Using a slotted spoon, transfer the browned beef from the skillet to the bowl.
5. Top the salad with the dressing, and toss to thoroughly coat.
6. Divide the salad between two bowls and serve.

SUBSTITUTION TIP You could replace the ground beef with ground turkey.

VARIATIONS Your favorite burger toppings would also be tasty as toppings on this salad:
- For an extra tone of flavor, add a handful of diced onion to the salad, and 1 teaspoon of yellow mustard and ¼ teaspoon of paprika to the ranch dressing.
- Of course, you can also add chopped bacon.

PER SERVING Calories: 662; Fat: 50g; Carbs: 6g; Net Carbs: 4g; Fiber: 2g; Protein: 47g

CALIFORNIA STEAK SALAD

Serves 2 / Prep time: 15 minutes / Cook time: 10 minutes

Avocados and strawberries just scream California. In this recipe, they serve as the perfect companion to the skirt steak and the peppery flavor of arugula.

8 ounces skirt steak

Pink Himalayan salt

Freshly ground black pepper

2 tablespoons butter

2 cups arugula

1 tablespoon extra-virgin olive oil

1 avocado, sliced

2 fresh strawberries, sliced

¼ cup slivered, chopped almonds

1. Heat a large skillet over high heat.

2. Pat the steak dry with a paper towel, and season both sides with salt and pepper.

3. Add the butter to the skillet. When it melts, put the steak in the skillet.

4. Sear the steak for about 3 minutes on each side, for medium-rare.

5. Transfer the steak to a cutting board and let rest for at least 5 minutes.

6. In a large bowl, toss the arugula with the olive oil and a pinch each of salt and pepper.

7. Divide the arugula between two plates, and top with the sliced avocado, strawberries, and almonds.

8. Slice the skirt steak across the grain, top the salads with it, and serve.

SUBSTITUTION TIP Flank steak would work just as well as skirt steak. You can also use sliced cold leftover steak, which works beautifully.

PER SERVING Calories: 501; Fat: 41g; Carbs: 11g; Net Carbs: 4g; Fiber: 7g; Protein: 28g

SKIRT STEAK COBB SALAD

Serves 2 / Prep time: 15 minutes / Cook time: 10 minutes

Skirt steak is the perfect choice for topping a salad because it cooks quickly and is flavorful. Cook the skirt steak just to medium-rare to keep it tender, and cut it against the grain when serving. This salad doesn't call for marinating the steak ahead of time, but you can if you prefer. Rubbing the steak with salt and pepper and cooking it on a screaming hot pan with some oil is perfect.

8 ounces skirt steak

Pink Himalayan salt

Freshly ground black pepper

1 tablespoon butter

2 romaine hearts or 2 cups
   chopped romaine

½ cup halved grape tomatoes

¼ cup crumbled blue cheese

¼ cup pecans

1 tablespoon extra-virgin olive oil

1. Heat a large skillet over high heat.

2. Pat the steak dry with a paper towel, and season both sides with salt and pepper.

3. Add the butter to the skillet. When it melts, put the steak in the skillet.

4. Sear the steak for about 3 minutes on each side, for medium-rare.

5. Transfer the steak to a cutting board and let it rest for at least 5 minutes.

6. Meanwhile, divide the romaine between two plates, and top with the grape tomato halves, blue cheese, and pecans. Drizzle with the olive oil.

7. Slice the skirt steak across the grain, top the salads with it, and serve.

SUBSTITUTION TIP Flank steak works just as well as skirt steak.

VARIATIONS Salads are the perfect canvas for creativity when it comes to toppings. Look in your refrigerator and see what you have on hand. These options are just some of the great additions available:

- Balsamic dressing and a sliced hardboiled egg.
- Walnuts in place of the pecans, and 1 sliced avocado.

PER SERVING Calories: 451; Fat: 36g; Carbs: 7g; Net Carbs: 5g; Fiber: 3g; Protein: 30g

CHAPTER SEVEN
SEAFOOD & POULTRY ENTRÉES

◀ Baked Garlic and Paprika Chicken Legs, page 186

ONE PAN

SHRIMP AND SAUSAGE "BAKE"

Serves 4 / Prep time: 15 minutes / Cook time: 20 minutes

Chorizo, a fully cooked cured sausage common in Spanish, Portuguese, and Latin American cooking, can be either spicy or slightly sweet and has a distinctive red color from the copious amounts of paprika added during its creation. Chorizo is very high in protein, about 15 grams per 3-ounce portion, and is an excellent source of zinc, selenium, and vitamin B12.

2 tablespoons extra-virgin olive oil

6 ounces chorizo sausage, diced

½ pound shrimp, peeled and deveined

1 red bell pepper, chopped

½ small sweet onion, chopped

2 teaspoons minced garlic

¼ cup Herbed Chicken Stock (page 23) or store-bought chicken broth

Pinch red pepper flakes

1. In a large skillet over medium-high heat, heat the olive oil.

2. Sauté the sausage until it is warmed through, about 6 minutes.

3. Add the shrimp and sauté until it is opaque and just cooked through, about 3 minutes.

4. Transfer the sausage and shrimp to a bowl and set aside.

5. Add the red pepper, onion, and garlic to the skillet and sauté until tender, about 4 minutes.

6. Add the chicken stock to the skillet along with the cooked sausage and shrimp.

7. Bring the liquid to a simmer and simmer for 3 minutes.

8. Stir in the red pepper flakes and serve.

INGREDIENT TIP Shrimp is often not sustainably caught, and most farmed shrimp are not considered to be very good for you. When purchasing shrimp, look for US wild-caught shrimp from the Pacific or southern areas or West Coast farmed shrimp from fully recirculating farms.

PER SERVING Calories: 323; Fat: 24g; Carbs: 8g; Net Carbs: 6g; Fiber: 2g; Protein: 20g

SHRIMP AND AVOCADO LETTUCE CUPS

Serves 2 / Prep time: 10 minutes / Cook time: 5 minutes

Lettuce cups are such a great alternative to salad, and more fun to eat. You want to pick the largest butter lettuce leaves and fill them to the brim with yummy shrimp, creamy avocado, and juicy tomatoes. The recipe calls for a particularly zesty mayonnaise—spicy red pepper miso mayo—that adds a tasty kick to every food. It is available in most supermarkets, but if you can't find it, you can make your own Sriracha Mayo (page 34).

1 tablespoon ghee

½ pound shrimp, peeled, deveined, and tails removed

½ cup halved grape tomatoes

½ avocado, sliced

Pink Himalayan salt

Freshly ground black pepper

4 butter lettuce leaves, rinsed and patted dry

1 tablespoon store-bought spicy red pepper miso mayo or Sriracha Mayo (page 34)

1. In a medium skillet over medium-high heat, heat the ghee. Add the shrimp and cook until they turn pink and opaque, about 3 minutes. Season with salt and pepper.

2. Season the tomatoes and avocado with salt and pepper.

3. Divide the lettuce cups between two plates. Fill each cup with shrimp, tomatoes, and avocado. Drizzle the mayo sauce on top and serve.

PER SERVING Calories: 326; Fat: 11g; Carbs: 7g; Net Carbs: 4g; Fiber: 3g; Protein: 33g

GARLIC BUTTER SHRIMP

Serves 2 / Prep time: 10 minutes / Cook time: 15 minutes

You only have to wait 15 minutes to get this buttery goodness into your mouth! If you love a meal that can be made all in one pan and includes butter as one of the main ingredients, this is a perfect meal for you.

3 tablespoons butter

½ pound shrimp, peeled, deveined, and tails removed

Pink Himalayan salt

Freshly ground black pepper

1 lemon, halved

2 garlic cloves, crushed

¼ teaspoon red pepper flakes (optional)

1. Preheat the oven to 425°F.
2. Put the butter in an 8-by-8-inch baking dish, and pop it into the oven while it is preheating, just until the butter melts.
3. Sprinkle the shrimp with salt and pepper.
4. Slice one half of the lemon into thin slices, and cut the other half into 2 wedges.
5. In the baking dish, add the shrimp and garlic to the butter. The shrimp should be in a single layer. Add the lemon slices. Sprinkle the top of the fish with the red pepper flakes (if using).
6. Bake the shrimp for 15 minutes, stirring halfway through.
7. Remove the shrimp from the oven, and squeeze juice from the 2 lemon wedges over the dish. Serve hot.

INGREDIENT TIP Use the extra butter sauce to pour over zoodles or shirataki noodles (such as Miracle Noodles) to serve alongside the shrimp.

PER SERVING Calories: 329; Fat: 20g; Carbs: 5g; Net Carbs: 4g; Fiber: 1g; Protein: 32g

HERB BUTTER SCALLOPS

Serves 4 / Prep time: 10 minutes / Cook time: 10 minutes

Scallops are usually placed squarely in the category of foods best enjoyed in a restaurant because this sweet seafood is thought to be difficult to cook. Scallops are actually quite easy to prepare if you watch them carefully and don't leave them on the heat too long. They are very high in protein, selenium, and vitamin B12. These nutrients are crucial for cardiovascular health and can help lower your risk of arthritis and colon cancer.

1 pound sea scallops, small side muscles removed, rinsed and patted dry

Freshly ground black pepper

8 tablespoons butter, divided

2 teaspoons minced garlic

Juice of 1 lemon

2 teaspoons chopped fresh basil

1 teaspoon chopped fresh thyme

1. Pat the scallops dry with paper towels, and season them lightly with pepper.

2. In a large skillet over medium heat, melt 2 tablespoons of butter.

3. Arrange the scallops in the skillet, evenly spaced but not too close together, and sear each side until they are golden brown, about 2½ minutes per side.

4. Transfer the scallops to a plate and set aside.

5. Add the remaining 6 tablespoons of butter to the skillet and sauté the garlic until translucent, about 3 minutes.

6. Stir in the lemon juice, basil, and thyme and return the scallops to the skillet, turning to coat them in the sauce.

7. Serve immediately.

PER SERVING Calories: 306; Fat: 24g; Carbs: 4g; Net Carbs: 4g; Fiber: 0g; Protein: 19g

SCALLOPS WITH CREAMY BACON SAUCE

Serves 2 / Prep time: 5 minutes / Cook time: 20 minutes

This recipe features big, juicy scallops cooked just right and drenched in a creamy sauce. The bacon topping sends it, well, over the top!

4 bacon slices

1 cup heavy (whipping) cream

1 tablespoon butter

¼ cup grated Parmesan cheese

Pink Himalayan salt

Freshly ground black pepper

1 tablespoon ghee

8 large sea scallops, small side muscles removed, rinsed and patted dry

1. In a medium skillet over medium-high heat, cook the bacon on both sides until crispy, about 8 minutes. Transfer the bacon to a paper towel–lined plate.

2. Lower the heat to medium. Add the cream, butter, and Parmesan cheese to the bacon grease, and season with a pinch of salt and pepper. Reduce the heat to low and cook, stirring constantly, until the sauce thickens and is reduced by 50 percent, about 10 minutes.

3. In a separate large skillet over medium-high heat, heat the ghee until sizzling.

4. Season the scallops with salt and pepper, and add them to the skillet. Cook for just 1 minute per side. Do not crowd the scallops; if your pan isn't large enough, cook them in two batches. You want the scallops golden on each side.

5. Transfer the scallops to a paper towel–lined plate.

6. Divide the cream sauce between two plates, crumble the bacon on top of the cream sauce, and top with 4 scallops each. Serve immediately.

INGREDIENT TIP When shopping for scallops, choose sea scallops, which are much larger than bay scallops. Also, avoid frozen scallops—they are harder to work with.

VARIATIONS This recipe is very rich, so fresh flavors make perfect additions:

- Toss 6 ounces of fresh spinach in a small skillet with 1 tablespoon of butter over medium-high heat. Cook just until wilted, about 1 minute. Fold into the cream sauce just before serving the scallop dish.
- Squeeze the juice from ½ lemon, and stir it into the cream sauce before serving. Garnish the scallops with 1 tablespoon of chopped fresh Italian parsley.

PER SERVING Calories: 782; Fat: 73g; Carbs: 11g; Net Carbs: 10g; Fiber: 0g; Protein: 24g

PAN-SEARED HALIBUT WITH CITRUS-BUTTER SAUCE

Serves 4 / Prep time: 10 minutes / Cook time: 15 minutes

Citrus fruits are absolutely delicious and are bursting with nutrients. Both lemons and oranges are excellent sources of vitamin C, which boosts the immune system and can help detoxify your body. The acid from citrus is a wonderful addition to most fish and seafood recipes.

4 (5-ounce) halibut fillets, each about 1 inch thick

Pink Himalayan salt

Freshly ground black pepper

¼ cup butter

2 teaspoons minced garlic

1 shallot, minced

3 tablespoons dry white wine

1 tablespoon freshly squeezed lemon juice

1 tablespoon freshly squeezed orange juice

2 teaspoons chopped fresh parsley

2 tablespoons extra-virgin olive oil

1. Pat the fish dry with paper towels, then lightly season the fillets with salt and pepper. Set aside on a paper towel–lined plate.

2. In a small saucepan over medium heat, melt the butter.

3. Sauté the garlic and shallot until tender, about 3 minutes.

4. Whisk in the white wine, lemon juice, and orange juice and bring the sauce to a simmer, cooking until it thickens slightly, about 2 minutes.

5. Remove the sauce from the heat and stir in the parsley; set aside.

6. In a large skillet over medium-high heat, heat the olive oil.

7. Panfry the fish until lightly browned and just cooked through, turning them over once, about 10 minutes in total.

8. Serve the fish immediately with a spoonful of sauce for each fillet.

SUBSTITUTION TIP Any firm white-fleshed fish will be delicious with this creamy sauce. Try haddock, tilapia, or sea bass.

PER SERVING Calories: 319; Fat: 26g; Carbs: 2g; Net Carbs: 2g; Fiber: 0g; Protein: 22g

SIMPLE FISH CURRY

ONE PAN

Serves 4 / Prep time: 10 minutes / Cook time: 25 minutes

Curry is a sauce-based recipe originating in India and adapted by many cultures. The ubiquitous spice mixture often contains a multitude of ingredients, such as cumin, coriander, turmeric, ginger, cloves, paprika, and cinnamon. It's adapted so well to many cuisines because no matter the ingredients used—vegetables, meats, fish, eggs, butter, coconut—the spices bring the dish together beautifully.

2 tablespoons coconut oil

1½ tablespoons grated fresh ginger

2 teaspoons minced garlic

1 tablespoon curry powder

½ teaspoon ground cumin

2 cups unsweetened full-fat coconut milk

16 ounces firm white fish, cut into 1-inch chunks

1 cup shredded kale

2 tablespoons chopped fresh cilantro

1. In a large saucepan over medium heat, melt the coconut oil.

2. Sauté the ginger and garlic until lightly browned, about 2 minutes.

3. Stir in the curry powder and cumin and sauté until very fragrant, about 2 minutes.

4. Stir in the coconut milk, and bring the liquid to a boil.

5. Reduce the heat to low and simmer for about 5 minutes to infuse the milk with the spices.

6. Add the fish and cook until the fish is cooked through, about 10 minutes.

7. Stir in the kale and cilantro and simmer until wilted, about 2 minutes.

8. Serve.

PER SERVING Calories: 416; Fat: 31g; Carbs: 5g; Net Carbs: 4g; Fiber: 1g; Protein: 26g

ROASTED SALMON WITH AVOCADO SALSA

Serves 4 / Prep time: 15 minutes / Cook time: 15 minutes

A simple, fresh salsa is often the best topping for a juicy piece of fish, and creamy avocados are a perfect choice for the base. Take the salsa ingredients out of the refrigerator an hour or so before serving the fish so they come to room temperature. The taste of the avocado will be much stronger than when this fruit is completely chilled. You can also grill the salmon for this recipe—this fish holds up well under higher heat and does not dry out.

FOR THE SALSA

1 avocado, peeled, pitted, and diced

1 scallion, white and green
   parts, chopped

½ cup halved cherry tomatoes

Juice and zest of 1 lemon

FOR THE FISH

1 teaspoon ground cumin

½ teaspoon ground coriander

½ teaspoon onion powder

¼ teaspoon pink Himalayan salt

Pinch freshly ground black pepper

Pinch cayenne pepper

4 (4-ounce) skinless salmon fillets

2 tablespoons extra-virgin olive oil

TO MAKE THE SALSA

1. In a small bowl, smash the avocado with a fork and stir it together with the scallion, tomatoes, lemon juice, and lemon zest until mixed.

2. Set aside.

TO MAKE THE FISH

1. Preheat the oven to 400°F. Line a baking sheet with aluminum foil and set aside.

2. In a small bowl, stir together the cumin, coriander, onion powder, salt, black pepper, and cayenne until well mixed.

3. Rub the salmon fillets with the spice mix, and place them on the baking sheet.

4. Drizzle the fillets with the olive oil, and roast the fish until it is just cooked through, about 15 minutes.

5. Serve the salmon topped with the avocado salsa.

PER SERVING Calories: 320; Fat: 26g; Carbs: 4g; Net Carbs: 1g; Fiber: 3g; Protein: 22g

CHEESY GARLIC SALMON

Serves 4 / Prep time: 15 minutes / Cook time: 10 minutes

Salmon has such a satisfying firm texture and strong flavor that it can handle the garlic and cheese in this dish. Salmon is one of the healthiest fish choices, with loads of nutrients such as vitamin D and omega-3 fatty acids. Wild salmon caught in the Pacific off the US and Canadian coasts have a very high level of these disease-busting anti-inflammatory nutrients and antioxidants.

½ cup Asiago cheese

2 tablespoons freshly squeezed lemon juice

2 tablespoons butter, at room temperature

2 teaspoons minced garlic

1 teaspoon chopped fresh basil

1 teaspoon chopped fresh oregano

4 (5-ounce) salmon fillets

1 tablespoon extra-virgin olive oil

1. Preheat the oven to 350°F. Line a baking sheet with parchment paper and set aside.

2. In a small bowl, stir together the Asiago cheese, lemon juice, butter, garlic, basil, and oregano.

3. Pat the salmon dry with paper towels, and place the fillets on the baking sheet skin-side down. Divide the topping evenly among the fillets and spread it across the fish using a knife or the back of a spoon.

4. Drizzle the fish with the olive oil, and bake until the topping is golden and the fish is just cooked through, about 12 minutes.

5. Serve.

PER SERVING Calories: 357; Fat: 28g; Carbs: 2g; Net Carbs: 2g; Fiber: 0g; Protein: 24g

PARMESAN-GARLIC SALMON WITH ASPARAGUS

Serves 2 / Prep time: 10 minutes / Cook time: 15 minutes

For this recipe, you can use either individual fillets of salmon or one large fillet. The delicious garlic-butter sauce covers the salmon and asparagus, creating wonderful flavor.

2 (6-ounce) salmon fillets, skin on

Pink Himalayan salt

Freshly ground black pepper

1 pound fresh asparagus, ends
   snapped off

3 tablespoons butter

2 garlic cloves, minced

¼ cup grated Parmesan cheese

1. Preheat the oven to 400°F. Line a baking sheet with aluminum foil or a silicone baking mat.

2. Pat the salmon dry with a paper towel, and season both sides with salt and pepper.

3. Place the salmon in the middle of the prepared pan, and arrange the asparagus around the salmon.

4. In a small saucepan over medium heat, melt the butter. Add the garlic and stir until the garlic just begins to brown, about 3 minutes.

5. Drizzle the garlic-butter sauce over the salmon and asparagus, and top both with the Parmesan cheese.

6. Bake until the salmon is cooked and the asparagus is crisp-tender, about 12 minutes. You can switch the oven to broil at the end of cooking time for about 3 minutes to get a nice char on the asparagus.

7. Serve hot.

SUBSTITUTION TIP If you don't have asparagus, you could use fresh green beans.

PER SERVING Calories: 434; Fat: 26g; Carbs: 10g; Net Carbs: 6g; Fiber: 5g; Protein: 42g

SEARED-SALMON SHIRATAKI RICE BOWLS

Serves 2 / Prep time: 10 minutes, plus 30 minutes to marinate / Cook time: 10 minutes

This dish, although not a true "poke," was inspired by the same flavors.

2 (6-ounce) salmon fillets, skin on

4 tablespoons soy sauce (or coconut aminos), divided

2 small Persian cucumbers or ½ large English cucumber

1 tablespoon ghee

1 (8-ounce) pack Miracle Shirataki Rice

1 avocado, diced

Pink Himalayan salt

Freshly ground black pepper

1. Place the salmon in an 8-by-8-inch baking dish, and add 3 tablespoons of soy sauce. Cover and marinate in the refrigerator for 30 minutes.

2. Meanwhile, slice the cucumbers thinly, put them in a small bowl, and add the remaining 1 tablespoon of soy sauce. Set aside to marinate.

3. In a medium skillet over medium heat, melt the ghee. Add the salmon fillets skin-side down. Pour some of the soy sauce marinade over the salmon, and sear the fish for 3 to 4 minutes on each side.

4. Meanwhile, in a large saucepan, cook the shirataki rice per package instructions:

5. Rinse the shirataki rice in cold water in a colander.

6. In a saucepan filled with boiling water, cook the rice for 2 minutes.

7. Pour the rice into the colander. Dry out the pan.

8. Transfer the rice to the dry pan and dry roast over medium heat until dry and opaque.

9. Season the avocado with salt and pepper.

10. Place the salmon fillets on a plate, and remove the skin. Cut the salmon into bite-size pieces.

11. Assemble the rice bowls: In two bowls, make a layer of the cooked Miracle Rice. Top each with the cucumbers, avocado, and salmon, and serve.

VARIATIONS The fun part of poke bowls is customizing the toppings! Here are a few to try:

- Store-bought spicy red pepper miso mayo or Sriracha Mayo (page 34)
- Furikake (sesame seed and seaweed mixture)
- Fresh cooked crab
- Sliced scallions
- Fresh sliced, peeled ginger
- Wasabi

PER SERVING Calories: 328; Fat: 18g; Carbs: 8g; Net Carbs: 5g; Fiber: 3g; Protein: 36g

PORK RIND SALMON CAKES

Serves 2 / Prep time: 10 minutes / Cook time: 10 minutes

This fish-cake recipe is easy to make because it uses canned salmon. The taste is amazing, and you can enjoy knowing that you're eating a high-quality product. The crushed pork rinds help hold the cakes together, like a bread-crumb crust but with more flavor.

6 ounces canned Alaska wild salmon, drained (such as Wild Planet)

2 tablespoons crushed pork rinds

1 large egg, lightly beaten

3 tablespoons Creamy Mayonnaise (page 33) or store-bought, divided

Pink Himalayan salt

Freshly ground black pepper

1 tablespoon ghee

½ tablespoon Dijon mustard

1. In a medium bowl, mix to combine the salmon, pork rinds, egg, and 1½ tablespoons of mayonnaise. Season with salt and pepper.

2. With the salmon mixture, form patties the size of hockey pucks or smaller. Keep patting the patties until they keep together.

3. In a medium skillet over medium-high heat, melt the ghee. When the ghee sizzles, place the salmon patties in the pan. Cook for about 3 minutes per side, until browned. Transfer the patties to a paper towel–lined plate.

4. In a small bowl, mix together the remaining 1½ tablespoons of mayonnaise and the mustard.

5. Serve the salmon cakes with the mayo-mustard dipping sauce.

INGREDIENT TIP When possible, purchase wild-caught salmon from the Pacific coast instead of farm-raised. Some stores will carry both, so make sure you read the labels. (Atlantic salmon is generally farm-raised.)

PER SERVING Calories: 362; Fat: 31g; Carbs: 1g; Net Carbs: 1g; Fiber: 0g; Protein: 24g

CREAMY DILL SALMON

Serves 2 / Prep time: 10 minutes / Cook time: 10 minutes

This salmon recipe is so easy and so creamy that it's an excellent choice for serving guests. Mayonnaise, besides being delicious, helps keep fish or poultry juicy and is a great way to get some healthy fats. And the fresh dill is the perfect herbal accent for salmon.

2 tablespoons ghee, melted

2 (6-ounce) salmon fillets, skin on

Pink Himalayan salt

Freshly ground black pepper

¼ cup Creamy Mayonnaise (page 33) or store-bought

1 tablespoon Dijon mustard

2 tablespoons minced fresh dill

Pinch garlic powder

1. Preheat the oven to 450°F. Coat a 9-by-13-inch baking dish with the ghee.

2. Pat dry the salmon with paper towels, season on both sides with salt and pepper, and place in the prepared baking dish.

3. In a small bowl, mix to combine the mayonnaise, mustard, dill, and garlic powder.

4. Slather the mayonnaise sauce on top of both salmon fillets so that it fully covers the tops.

5. Bake for 7 to 9 minutes, depending on how you like your salmon—7 minutes for medium-rare and 9 minutes for well-done—and serve.

INGREDIENT TIP A lot of people might be unsure about eating the skin of the salmon, but a large amount of the healthy fats in salmon is found in the skin. Also, cooking the fish with the skin on helps retain moisture while cooking.

PER SERVING Calories: 510; Fat: 41g; Carbs: 2g; Net Carbs: 2g; Fiber: 1g; Protein: 33g

SOLE ASIAGO

Serves 4 / Prep time: 10 minutes / Cook time: 10 minutes

Sole is a flat fish, which means both of its eyes are on one side of its head. It looks rather strange, but when filleted, it is delicious. Sole is not a threatened species, but it is overfished in some areas, so it is not as plentiful as it was in the past. This tender, delicate fish freezes very well; if you cannot find fresh fillets, frozen fillets will work, too.

4 (4-ounce) sole fillets

¾ cup ground almonds

¼ cup Asiago cheese

2 large eggs, beaten

2½ tablespoons melted coconut oil

1. Preheat the oven to 350°F. Line a baking sheet with parchment paper and set aside.
2. Pat the fish dry with paper towels.
3. Stir together the ground almonds and cheese in a small bowl.
4. Place the bowl with the beaten eggs in it next to the almond mixture.
5. Dredge a sole fillet in the beaten egg, then press the fish into the almond mixture so it is completely coated. Place on the baking sheet and repeat until all the fillets are breaded.
6. Brush both sides of each piece of fish with the coconut oil.
7. Bake the sole until it is cooked through, about 8 minutes in total.
8. Serve immediately.

PER SERVING Calories: 406; Fat: 31g; Carbs: 6g; Net Carbs: 3g; Fiber: 3g; Protein: 29g

BAKED COCONUT HADDOCK

Serves 4 / Prep time: 10 minutes / Cook time: 10 minutes

A lovely golden nut crust not only adds fabulous flavor to fish, it also helps prevent overcooking of the fillets so they stay moist. This protective coating can be almost any type of nut, from delicate almonds to more robust pecans. Just substitute the other nuts in the same amount as the hazelnuts in the recipe.

4 (5-ounce) haddock fillets

Pink Himalayan salt

Freshly ground black pepper

1 cup shredded unsweetened coconut

¼ cup ground hazelnuts

2 tablespoons coconut oil, melted

1. Preheat the oven to 400°F. Line a baking sheet with parchment paper and set aside.

2. Pat the fillets very dry with paper towels, and lightly season with salt and pepper.

3. Stir together the shredded coconut and hazelnuts in a small bowl.

4. Dredge the fish fillets in the coconut mixture so that both sides of each piece are thickly coated.

5. Place the fish on the baking sheet, and lightly brush both sides of each piece with the coconut oil.

6. Bake the haddock until the topping is golden and the fish flakes easily with a fork, about 12 minutes total.

7. Serve.

PREP TIP The breading of the fish can be done ahead, up to 1 day, if you just want to pop the fish in the oven when you get home. Place the breaded fish on the baking sheet, and cover it with plastic wrap in the refrigerator until you wish to bake it.

PER SERVING Calories: 299; Fat: 24g; Carbs: 4g; Net Carbs: 1g; Fiber: 3g; Protein: 20g

BAKED LEMON-BUTTER FISH

Serves 2 / Prep time: 10 minutes / Cook time: 20 minutes

The lemon provides the bright counterpoint to the mild, buttery, flaky fish, and the capers give the dish a zesty pop.

4 tablespoons butter, plus more
  for coating

2 (5-ounce) tilapia fillets

Pink Himalayan salt

Freshly ground black pepper

2 garlic cloves, minced

Zest and juice of 1 lemon

2 tablespoons capers, rinsed
  and chopped

1. Preheat the oven to 400°F. Coat an 8-by-8-inch baking dish with butter.

2. Pat dry the tilapia with paper towels, and season on both sides with salt and pepper. Place in the prepared baking dish.

3. In a medium skillet over medium heat, melt the butter. Add the garlic and cook for 3 to 5 minutes, until slightly browned but not burned.

4. Remove the garlic butter from the heat, and mix in the lemon zest and 2 tablespoons of lemon juice.

5. Pour the lemon-butter sauce over the fish, and sprinkle the capers around the baking pan.

6. Bake for 12 to 15 minutes, until the fish is just cooked through, and serve.

SUBSTITUTION TIP You could use any mild white fish with this recipe. Even salmon is delicious with the lemon-butter sauce.

PER SERVING Calories: 299; Fat: 26g; Carbs: 5g; Net Carbs: 3g; Fiber: 1g; Protein: 16g

FISH TACO BOWL

Serves 2 / Prep time: 10 minutes / Cook time: 15 minutes

This Fish Taco Bowl makes the most of just a few ingredients, with exciting punches of chile, lime, and red pepper from the Tajín seasoning salt. The coleslaw mix is a time-saver, and the crunch of the cabbage provides a nice counterpoint to the smooth avocado.

2 (5-ounce) tilapia fillets

1 tablespoon extra-virgin olive oil

4 teaspoons Tajín seasoning salt, divided

2 cups presliced coleslaw cabbage mix

1 tablespoon store-bought spicy red pepper miso mayo or Sriracha Mayo (page 34), plus more for serving

1 avocado, mashed

Pink Himalayan salt

Freshly ground black pepper

1. Preheat the oven to 425°F. Line a baking sheet with aluminum foil or a silicone baking mat.

2. Rub the tilapia with the olive oil, then coat it with 2 teaspoons of Tajín seasoning salt. Place the fish in the prepared pan.

3. Bake for 15 minutes, or until the fish is opaque when you pierce it with a fork. Put the fish on a cooling rack and let it sit for 5 minutes.

4. Meanwhile, in a medium bowl, gently mix to combine the coleslaw and the mayo. You don't want the cabbage super wet, so add just enough sauce to dress it. Add the mashed avocado and the remaining 2 teaspoons of Tajín seasoning salt to the coleslaw, and season with salt and pepper. Divide the salad between two bowls.

5. Use two forks to shred the fish into small pieces, and add it to the bowls.

6. Top the fish with a drizzle of mayo and serve.

SUBSTITUTION TIP If you don't have spicy red pepper miso mayo or Sriracha Mayo, the Avocado-Lime Crema (page 32) will also work nicely.

PER SERVING Calories: 315; Fat: 24g; Carbs: 12g; Net Carbs: 5g; Fiber: 7g; Protein: 16g

STUFFED CHICKEN BREASTS

Serves 4 / Prep time: 30 minutes, plus 30 minutes to chill / Cook time: 30 minutes

This dish might perfectly complement a complicated risotto in a fancy fine-dining restaurant. The trick to perfect stuffed chicken breasts is to cut a perfect pocket—not too deep, but with enough space to completely enclose the filling. If it isn't enclosed, the filling will simply melt in the oven, leaving an empty pocket.

1 tablespoon butter

¼ cup chopped sweet onion

½ cup goat cheese, at room temperature

¼ cup Kalamata olives, chopped

¼ cup chopped roasted red pepper

2 tablespoons chopped fresh basil

4 (5-ounce) chicken breasts, skin-on

2 tablespoons extra-virgin olive oil

1. Preheat the oven to 400°F.

2. In a small skillet over medium heat, melt the butter. Sauté the onion until tender, about 3 minutes.

3. Transfer the onion to a medium bowl, and add the cheese, olives, red pepper, and basil. Stir until well blended, then refrigerate for about 30 minutes.

4. Cut horizontal pockets into each chicken breast, and stuff them evenly with the filling. Secure the two sides of each breast with toothpicks.

5. In a large ovenproof skillet over medium-high heat, heat the olive oil.

6. Brown the chicken on both sides, about 10 minutes in total.

7. Place the skillet in the oven and roast until the chicken is just cooked through, about 15 minutes. Remove the toothpicks and serve.

SUBSTITUTION TIP If fresh basil is not available in the grocery store or your garden, try using a premade paste or frozen basil in the filling. You can also use a spoon of pesto for added flavor.

PER SERVING Calories: 389; Fat: 30g; Carbs: 3g; Net Carbs: 3g; Fiber: 0g; Protein: 25g

ONE PAN

LEMON-BUTTER CHICKEN

Serves 4 / Prep time: 10 minutes / Cook time: 40 minutes

Chicken is a staple food in many households—it combines so well with many other ingredients, and its mild flavor is a favorite even among picky eaters. If your budget allows, look for organic grass-fed chicken at your local grocery store because it tastes better than the meat from factory-farmed birds. Organic grass-fed chicken also contains more vitamin A and omega-3 fatty acids.

4 bone-in, skin-on chicken thighs

Pink Himalayan salt

Freshly ground black pepper

2 tablespoons butter, divided

2 teaspoons minced garlic

½ cup Herbed Chicken Stock (page 23)

½ cup heavy (whipping) cream

Juice of ½ lemon

1. Preheat the oven to 400°F.

2. Lightly season the chicken thighs with salt and pepper.

3. In a large ovenproof skillet over medium-high heat, melt 1 tablespoon of butter.

4. Brown the chicken thighs until golden on both sides, about 6 minutes in total. Transfer the thighs to a plate and set aside.

5. Add the remaining 1 tablespoon of butter and sauté the garlic until translucent, about 2 minutes.

6. Whisk in the chicken stock, cream, and lemon juice.

7. Bring the sauce to a boil, then return the chicken to the skillet.

8. Place the skillet in the oven, covered. Braise until the chicken is cooked through, about 30 minutes, and serve.

INGREDIENT TIP Chicken thighs often get overlooked in favor of the more popular breasts, but they have more flavor and are juicier. Thighs are also less expensive than chicken breasts and are a smart choice at least once per week for people on a budget.

PER SERVING Calories: 294; Fat: 26g; Carbs: 4g; Net Carbs: 3g; Fiber: 1g; Protein: 12g

CHICKEN BACON BURGERS

Serves 6 / Prep time: 10 minutes / Cook time: 25 minutes

The absolute best method of cooking these juicy herbed burgers is over a medium-heat grill, but this oven-baked recipe works very well too.

1 pound ground chicken

8 bacon slices, chopped

¼ cup ground almonds

1 teaspoon chopped fresh basil

¼ teaspoon pink Himalayan salt

Pinch freshly ground black pepper

2 tablespoons coconut oil

4 large lettuce leaves

1 avocado, peeled, pitted, and sliced

1. Preheat the oven to 350°F. Line a baking sheet with parchment paper and set aside.

2. In a medium bowl, combine the chicken, bacon, ground almonds, basil, salt, and pepper until well mixed.

3. Form the mixture into 6 equal patties.

4. In a large skillet over medium-high heat, heat the coconut oil.

5. Pan sear the chicken patties until brown on both sides, about 6 minutes in total.

6. Place the browned patties on the baking sheet and bake until completely cooked through, about 15 minutes.

7. Serve on the lettuce leaves, topped with the avocado slices.

PREP TIP For a make-ahead meal, double the batch. Place the formed burgers between layers of parchment paper, and wrap them tightly in plastic or place them in a sealed freezer bag. Store in the freezer, and simply thaw and cook for an easy dinner at a later time.

PER SERVING Calories: 374; Fat: 33g; Carbs: 3g; Net Carbs: 1g; Fiber: 2g; Protein: 18g

PAPRIKA CHICKEN

Serves 4 / Prep time: 10 minutes / Cook time: 25 minutes

Paprika is a glorious red spice created by grinding dried sweet red bell peppers and chile peppers into a fine powder. It's available in sweet, hot, and smoked varieties, to name just a few. The rich color and piquant flavor of paprika infuses the other ingredients in this recipe. Paprika also adds some health benefits to the recipe, such as protecting eyes from macular degeneration.

4 (4-ounce) chicken breasts, skin on
Pink Himalayan salt
Freshly ground black pepper
1 tablespoon extra-virgin olive oil
½ cup chopped sweet onion

½ cup heavy (whipping) cream
2 teaspoons smoked paprika
½ cup sour cream
2 tablespoons chopped fresh parsley

1. Lightly season the chicken with salt and pepper.

2. In a large skillet over medium-high heat, heat the olive oil.

3. Sear the chicken on both sides until almost cooked through, about 15 minutes in total. Transfer the chicken to a plate.

4. Add the onion to the skillet and sauté until tender, about 4 minutes.

5. Stir in the cream and paprika, and bring the liquid to a simmer.

6. Return the chicken and any accumulated juices to the skillet, and simmer the chicken for about 5 minutes, until completely cooked.

7. Stir in the sour cream, and remove the skillet from the heat.

8. Serve topped with the parsley.

PER SERVING Calories: 389; Fat: 30g; Carbs: 4g; Net Carbs: 4g; Fiber: 0g; Protein: 25g

COCONUT CHICKEN

Serves 4 / Prep time: 15 minutes / Cook time: 25 minutes

One of the main components of this recipe is rich, creamy coconut milk, which is a popular keto ingredient. The various types of coconut milk available might be confusing, but the best is the canned variety with a thick layer of coconut cream on top. Either stir the cream into the milk or skim it off for other recipes after opening the can.

2 tablespoons extra-virgin olive oil

4 (4-ounce) chicken breasts, cut into 2-inch chunks

½ cup chopped sweet onion

1 cup unsweetened full-fat coconut milk

1 tablespoon curry powder

1 teaspoon ground cumin

1 teaspoon ground coriander

¼ cup chopped fresh cilantro

1. In a large saucepan over medium-high heat, heat the olive oil.

2. Sauté the chicken until almost cooked through, about 10 minutes.

3. Add the onion and sauté for an additional 3 minutes.

4. In a medium bowl, whisk together the coconut milk, curry powder, cumin, and coriander.

5. Pour the sauce into the saucepan with the chicken, and bring the liquid to a boil.

6. Reduce the heat and simmer until the chicken is tender and the sauce has thickened, about 10 minutes.

7. Serve the chicken with the sauce, topped with the cilantro.

PER SERVING Calories: 382; Fat: 31g; Carbs: 5g; Net Carbs: 4g; Fiber: 1g; Protein: 23g

CHICKEN-BASIL ALFREDO WITH SHIRATAKI NOODLES

Serves 2 / Prep time: 10 minutes / Cook time: 15 minutes

At first you might find shirataki noodles puzzling, because the cooking process for these noodles is different from what you are used to. But they can totally satisfy your pasta craving. This decadent "pasta" dish uses shirataki noodles, creamy Alfredo sauce, chicken, and fresh herbs. It is so filling and delicious!

1 (7-ounce) package Miracle Noodle Fettuccini Shirataki Noodles

1 tablespoon extra-virgin olive oil

4 ounces cooked shredded chicken

Pink Himalayan salt

Freshly ground black pepper

1 cup Alfredo Sauce (page 31), or any keto-friendly brand you like

¼ cup grated Parmesan cheese

2 tablespoons chopped fresh basil leaves

1. In a colander, rinse the noodles with cold water (shirataki noodles naturally have a smell, and rinsing with cold water will help remove this).

2. Fill a large saucepan with water and bring to a boil over high heat. Cook according to package directions, then drain.

3. Transfer the noodles to a large, dry skillet over medium-low heat to evaporate any moisture. Do not grease the skillet; it must be dry. Transfer the noodles to a plate and set aside.

4. In the saucepan over medium heat, heat the olive oil. Add the cooked chicken. Season with salt and pepper.

5. Pour the Alfredo sauce over the chicken, and cook until warm, about 5 minutes. Season with more salt and pepper.

6. Add the dried noodles to the sauce mixture, and toss until combined.

7. Divide the pasta between two plates, top each with the Parmesan cheese and chopped basil, and serve.

INGREDIENT TIP For convenience, you can use a store-bought rotisserie chicken.

SUBSTITUTION TIP To make this meal vegetarian, you need only replace the shredded chicken with sautéed mushrooms.

PER SERVING Calories: 673; Fat: 61g; Carbs: 4g; Net Carbs: 4g; Fiber: 0g; Protein: 29g

CHICKEN QUESADILLA

Serves 2 / Prep time: 5 minutes / Cook time: 5 minutes

There is something so simple and satisfying about a chicken quesadilla. It is one of those universally loved dishes. There are a lot of low-carb tortilla options on the market now, which makes it easier than ever to enjoy a quesadilla without taking in lots of carbs.

1 tablespoon extra-virgin olive oil
2 low-carbohydrate tortillas,
   such as Mission Whole Wheat
   Low-Carb Tortillas

½ cup shredded Mexican blend
   cheese, divided
2 ounces shredded chicken
1 teaspoon Tajín seasoning salt
2 tablespoons sour cream

1. In a large skillet over medium-high heat, heat the olive oil. Add a tortilla, then layer on top ¼ cup of cheese, the chicken, the Tajín seasoning, and the remaining ¼ cup of cheese. Top with the second tortilla.

2. Using a spatula, peek under the edge of the bottom tortilla to monitor how it is browning. Once the bottom tortilla gets golden and the cheese begins to melt, after about 2 minutes, flip the quesadilla over. The second side will cook faster, about 1 minute.

3. Once the second tortilla is crispy and golden, transfer the quesadilla to a cutting board and let sit for 2 minutes. Cut the quesadilla into 4 wedges using a pizza cutter or chef's knife.

4. Transfer half of the quesadilla to each of two plates. Add 1 tablespoon of sour cream to each plate, and serve hot.

INGREDIENT TIPS

- A store-bought rotisserie chicken works well for this dish.
- The olive oil in the skillet is what makes the tortilla beautifully golden and crispy.

VARIATIONS You can add nearly endless numbers of tasty elements to a quesadilla. Try traditional Mexican inclusions or unexpected combinations:

- Leftover sliced steak and avocado slices are delicious fillings.
- For an Italian take on a quesadilla, try shredded mozzarella, pepperoni, sliced pepperoncini, and grated Parmesan.

PER SERVING Calories: 414; Fat: 28g; Carbs: 24g; Net Carbs: 7g; Fiber: 17g; Protein: 26g

GARLIC-PARMESAN CHICKEN WINGS

Serves 2 / Prep time: 10 minutes / Cook time: 3 hours

These slow-cooker chicken wings will fill your house with amazing butter and garlic fragrances all day. At the very end of the cooking time, just pop them under the broiler to get them to crispy perfection.

8 tablespoons (1 stick) butter

2 garlic cloves, minced

1 tablespoon dried Italian seasoning

¼ cup grated Parmesan cheese plus ½ cup, divided

Pink Himalayan salt

Freshly ground black pepper

1 pound chicken wings

1. With the crock insert in place, preheat the slow cooker to high. Line a baking sheet with aluminum foil or a silicone baking mat.

2. Put the butter, garlic, Italian seasoning, and ¼ cup of Parmesan cheese in the slow cooker, and season with salt and pepper. Allow the butter to melt, and stir the ingredients until well mixed.

3. Add the chicken wings, and stir until coated with the butter mixture.

4. Cover the slow cooker and cook for 2 hours and 45 minutes.

5. Preheat the broiler.

6. Transfer the wings to the prepared baking sheet, sprinkle the remaining ½ cup of Parmesan cheese over the wings, and cook under the broiler until crispy, about 5 minutes.

7. Serve hot.

INGREDIENT TIP Try a combination of fresh (not frozen) chicken wingettes and drummettes.

PER SERVING Calories: 738; Fat: 66g; Carbs: 4g; Net Carbs: 4g; Fiber: 0g; Protein: 39g

CHICKEN SKEWERS WITH PEANUT SAUCE

ONE PAN

Serves 2 / Prep time: 10 minutes, plus 1 hour to marinate / Cook time: 15 minutes

A traditional chicken satay would generally have a lot more ingredients than this recipe, but this recipe was inspired by those flavors. The spicy peanut sauce is irresistible! Add as much or as little Sriracha sauce as you want to control the spice level.

1 pound boneless skinless chicken breast, cut into chunks

3 tablespoons soy sauce (or coconut aminos), divided

½ teaspoon Sriracha sauce plus ¼ teaspoon, divided

3 teaspoons toasted sesame oil, divided

Ghee, for oiling

2 tablespoons natural peanut butter

Pink Himalayan salt

Freshly ground black pepper

1. In a large zip-top bag, combine the chicken chunks with 2 tablespoons of soy sauce, ½ teaspoon of Sriracha sauce, and 2 teaspoons of sesame oil. Seal the bag, and let the chicken marinate for an hour or so in the refrigerator or up to overnight.

2. If you are using wood 8-inch skewers, soak them in water for 30 minutes before using.

3. Preheat your grill pan or grill to low. Oil the grill pan with ghee.

4. Thread the chicken chunks onto the skewers.

5. Cook the skewers over low heat for 10 to 15 minutes, flipping halfway through.

6. Meanwhile, mix the peanut dipping sauce. Stir together the remaining 1 tablespoon of soy sauce, ¼ teaspoon of Sriracha sauce, 1 teaspoon of sesame oil, and the peanut butter. Season with salt and pepper.

7. Serve the chicken skewers with a small dish of the peanut sauce.

INGREDIENT TIP Coconut aminos tastes just like soy sauce but is gluten-free and Paleo-friendly.

COOKING TIP If you don't have a grill pan, you can use a large skillet.

PER SERVING Calories: 586; Fat: 29g; Carbs: 6g; Net Carbs: 5g; Fiber: 1g; Protein: 75g

BRAISED CHICKEN THIGHS WITH KALAMATA OLIVES

Serves 2 / Prep time: 10 minutes / Cook time: 40 minutes

Chicken thighs are so tender and tasty, with crispy skin—but it takes a little practice to get them right. The key is starting them on the stovetop, leaving them alone so the skin can get nice and crispy, and then transferring them to the oven to finish cooking and get tender. Use a cast iron skillet or other oven-safe pan.

4 chicken thighs, skin on
Pink Himalayan salt
Freshly ground black pepper
2 tablespoons ghee

½ cup Herbed Chicken Stock (page 23) or store-bought chicken broth
1 lemon, ½ sliced and ½ juiced
½ cup pitted Kalamata olives
2 tablespoons butter

1. Preheat the oven to 375°F.
2. Pat the chicken thighs dry with paper towels, and season with salt and pepper.
3. In a medium oven-safe skillet or high-sided baking dish over medium-high heat, melt the ghee. When the ghee has melted and is hot, add the chicken thighs, skin-side down, and leave them for about 8 minutes, or until the skin is brown and crispy.
4. Flip the chicken and cook for 2 minutes on the second side. Around the chicken thighs, pour in the chicken broth, and add the lemon slices, lemon juice, and olives.
5. Transfer to the oven and bake for about 30 minutes, until the chicken is cooked through.
6. Add the butter to the broth mixture.
7. Divide the chicken and olives between two plates and serve.

INGREDIENT TIP You can use any of your favorite olives in this dish instead of Kalamata if you like.

PER SERVING Calories: 567; Fat: 47g; Carbs: 4g; Net Carbs: 2g; Fiber: 2g; Protein: 33g

BUTTERY GARLIC CHICKEN

Serves 2 / Prep time: 5 minutes / Cook time: 40 minutes, plus 5 minutes to rest

Chicken drenched in butter? What's not to love! This chicken is so moist and delicious, and you will definitely want to spoon all of the excess butter over the top at the end.

2 tablespoons ghee, melted

2 boneless skinless chicken breasts

Pink Himalayan salt

Freshly ground black pepper

1 tablespoon dried Italian seasoning

4 tablespoons butter

2 garlic cloves, minced

¼ cup grated Parmesan cheese

1. Preheat the oven to 375°F. Choose a baking dish large enough to hold both chicken breasts, and coat it with the ghee.

2. Pat dry the chicken breasts and season with salt, pepper, and Italian seasoning. Place the chicken in the baking dish.

3. In a medium skillet over medium heat, melt the butter. Add the minced garlic, and cook for about 5 minutes. You want the garlic very lightly browned but not burned.

4. Remove the butter-garlic mixture from the heat, and pour it over the chicken breasts.

5. Roast the chicken in the oven for 30 to 35 minutes, until cooked through. Sprinkle the Parmesan cheese on top of each chicken breast. Let the chicken rest in the baking dish for 5 minutes.

6. Divide the chicken between two plates, spoon the butter sauce over the chicken, and serve.

SUBSTITUTION TIP If you don't have dried Italian seasoning, you can make your own mix from dried herbs and spices you may have in your cupboard. Mix together as many of these ingredients as you have: 1 teaspoon each of dried basil, oregano, thyme, rosemary, sage, garlic powder, and cilantro.

PER SERVING Calories: 642; Fat: 45g; Carbs: 2g; Net Carbs: 2g; Fiber: 0g; Protein: 57g

CHEESY BACON AND BROCCOLI CHICKEN

Serves 2 / Prep time: 10 minutes / Cook time: 1 hour

Smothered in cream cheese and topped with bacon, plain chicken breasts are transformed into a rich and elegant meal. This recipe gives you instructions for baking the chicken breast and bacon, but when you happen to have leftovers of both items, you can put this together super fast.

2 tablespoons ghee

2 boneless skinless chicken breasts

Pink Himalayan salt

Freshly ground black pepper

4 bacon slices

6 ounces cream cheese, at room
  temperature

2 cups frozen broccoli florets, thawed

½ cup shredded Cheddar cheese

1. Preheat the oven to 375°F.
2. Choose a baking dish large enough to hold both chicken breasts, and coat it with the ghee.
3. Pat dry the chicken breasts with a paper towel, and season with salt and pepper.
4. Place the chicken breasts and bacon slices in the baking dish, and bake for 25 minutes.
5. Transfer the chicken to a cutting board, and use two forks to shred it. Season it again with salt and pepper.
6. Place the bacon on a paper towel–lined plate to crisp up, then crumble it.
7. In a medium bowl, mix to combine the cream cheese, shredded chicken, broccoli, and half of the bacon crumbles. Transfer the chicken mixture to the baking dish, and top with the Cheddar and the remaining half of the bacon crumbles.
8. Bake until the cheese is bubbling and browned, about 35 minutes, and serve.

INGREDIENT TIP You could replace the broccoli with cauliflower if you prefer.

PER SERVING Calories: 935; Fat: 66g; Carbs: 10g; Net Carbs: 8g; Fiber: 3g; Protein: 75g

PARMESAN BAKED CHICKEN

Serves 2 / Prep time: 5 minutes / Cook time: 20 minutes

This chicken dish may be the easiest recipe of all time: You basically smother the chicken in mayonnaise, and the mayonnaise makes it tender and juicy. Topped with crushed pork rinds and kissed with Italian seasoning, this dish is perfect for a keto diet.

2 tablespoons ghee

2 boneless skinless chicken breasts

Pink Himalayan salt

Freshly ground black pepper

½ cup Creamy Mayonnaise (page 33) or store-bought

¼ cup grated Parmesan cheese

1 tablespoon dried Italian seasoning

¼ cup crushed pork rinds

1. Preheat the oven to 425°F. Choose a baking dish large enough to hold both chicken breasts, and coat it with the ghee.

2. Pat dry the chicken breasts with a paper towel, season with salt and pepper, and place in the prepared baking dish.

3. In a small bowl, mix to combine the mayonnaise, Parmesan cheese, and Italian seasoning.

4. Slather the mayonnaise mixture evenly over the chicken breasts, and sprinkle the crushed pork rinds on top of the mayonnaise mixture.

5. Bake until the topping is browned, about 20 minutes, and serve.

INGREDIENT TIP You can leave out the pork rinds if you don't have them in your pantry, but they add a nice texture.

PER SERVING Calories: 850; Fat: 67g; Carbs: 2g; Net Carbs: 2g; Fiber: 0g; Protein: 60g

CRUNCHY CHICKEN MILANESE

Serves 2 / Prep time: 10 minutes / Cook time: 10 minutes

When in doubt, make this chicken dish. It's hard to imagine anyone not liking it. The key to the dish is pounding the chicken thin so that it cooks quickly.

2 boneless skinless chicken breasts

½ cup coconut flour

1 teaspoon ground cayenne pepper

Pink Himalayan salt

Freshly ground black pepper

1 large egg

½ cup crushed pork rinds

2 tablespoons extra-virgin olive oil

1. Pound the chicken breasts with a heavy mallet until they are about ½ inch thick. (If you don't have a kitchen mallet, you can use the thick rim of a heavy plate.)

2. Prepare two separate prep plates and one small, shallow bowl:

3. On plate 1, mix the coconut flour and cayenne pepper, and season with salt and pepper.

4. Crack the egg into the small bowl, and lightly beat it with a fork or whisk.

5. On plate 2, put the crushed pork rinds.

6. In a large skillet over medium-high heat, heat the olive oil.

7. Dredge 1 chicken breast on both sides in the coconut-flour mixture. Dip the chicken into the egg, and coat both sides. Dredge the chicken in the pork-rind mixture, pressing the pork rinds into the chicken so they stick. Place the coated chicken in the hot skillet, and repeat with the other chicken breast.

8. Cook the chicken for 3 to 5 minutes on each side, until brown, crispy, and cooked through. Serve.

SUBSTITUTION TIP You can replace the cayenne pepper with grated Parmesan cheese if you prefer less spice.

PER SERVING Calories: 604; Fat: 29g; Carbs: 17g; Net Carbs: 7g; Fiber: 10g; Protein: 65g

BAKED GARLIC AND PAPRIKA CHICKEN LEGS

Serves 2 / Prep time: 10 minutes / Cook time: 55 minutes

Drumsticks are always worth the wait. The combination of flavors of the garlic, paprika, and herbs will excite your palate.

1 pound chicken drumsticks, skin on

Pink Himalayan salt

Freshly ground black pepper

2 tablespoons ghee

2 garlic cloves, minced

1 teaspoon paprika

1 teaspoon dried Italian seasoning

½ pound fresh green beans

1 tablespoon extra-virgin olive oil

1. Preheat the oven to 425°F. Line a 9-by-13-inch baking pan with aluminum foil or a silicone baking mat.

2. Pat the chicken legs dry with paper towels, put them in a large bowl, and apply salt and pepper all over the skin on both sides.

3. In a small saucepan over medium-low heat, combine the ghee, garlic, paprika, and Italian seasoning. Stir to combine for 30 seconds, and let sit for 5 minutes while the flavors combine.

4. Pour the sauce over the chicken legs, and toss to coat evenly. Season with more salt and pepper.

5. Arrange the chicken legs on one side of the prepared pan, leaving room for the vegetables later.

6. Bake the chicken for 30 minutes, then remove the pan from the oven. Spread the green beans over the empty half of the pan, and turn the chicken legs. Drizzle the beans with the olive oil, and season with salt and pepper.

7. Roast for 15 to 20 minutes more, until the chicken is cooked through and the skin is crispy, and serve.

SUBSTITUTION TIP You can replace the Italian herbs with any herbs or spices you prefer, such as an Indian spice mix (like garam masala) or Chinese five-spice powder.

PER SERVING Calories: 700; Fat: 45g; Carbs: 10g; Net Carbs: 6g; Fiber: 4g; Protein: 63g

CREAMY SLOW-COOKER CHICKEN

Serves 2 / Prep time: 10 minutes / Cook time: 4 hours 15 minutes

A creamy slow cooker meal is perfect for those chilly days. You can make this dish very quickly and then enjoy the aromas for the next 4 hours while it cooks. The fresh spinach added toward the end of the cooking time adds beautiful color and freshness.

1 tablespoon ghee

2 boneless skinless chicken breasts

1 cup Alfredo Sauce (page 31), or any keto-friendly brand you like

¼ cup chopped sun-dried tomatoes

¼ cup grated Parmesan cheese

Pink Himalayan salt

Freshly ground black pepper

2 cups fresh spinach

1. In a medium skillet over medium-high heat, melt the ghee. Add the chicken and cook, about 4 minutes on each side, until brown.

2. With the crock insert in place, transfer the chicken to the slow cooker. Set the slow cooker to low.

3. In a small bowl, mix to combine the Alfredo sauce, sun-dried tomatoes, and Parmesan cheese, and season with salt and pepper. Pour the sauce over the chicken.

4. Cover and cook on low for 4 hours, or until the chicken is cooked through.

5. Add the fresh spinach. Cover and cook for 5 minutes more, until the spinach is slightly wilted, and serve.

SUBSTITUTION TIP You can replace the chicken with pork chops and follow the same instructions.

PER SERVING Calories: 900; Fat: 66g; Carbs: 9g; Net Carbs: 7g; Fiber: 2g; Protein: 70g

RKEY MEATLOAF

s 6 / Prep time: 10 minutes / Cook time: 35 minutes, plus 10 minutes to rest

Good meatloaf is an art and a successful staple dish for many home cooks. It is one of the ultimate comfort foods. Meatloaf needs the perfect ratio of meat, fats, vegetables, and spices to be tender and flavorful. The best part about meatloaf is that it freezes beautifully, so you can make a double batch and keep one for a quick meal at another time.

1 tablespoon extra-virgin olive oil

½ sweet onion, chopped

1½ pounds ground turkey

⅓ cup heavy (whipping) cream

¼ cup freshly grated Parmesan cheese

1 tablespoon chopped fresh parsley

Pinch pink Himalayan salt

Pinch freshly ground black pepper

1. Heat the oven to 450°F.
2. In a small skillet over medium heat, heat the olive oil.
3. Sauté the onion until it is tender, about 4 minutes.
4. Transfer the onion to a large bowl and add the turkey, cream, Parmesan cheese, parsley, salt, and pepper.
5. Stir until the ingredients are combined and hold together. Press the mixture into a 9-by-5-inch loaf pan.
6. Bake until cooked through, about 30 minutes.
7. Let the meatloaf rest for 10 minutes and serve.

PER SERVING Calories: 216; Fat: 19g; Carbs: 1g; Net Carbs: 1g; Fiber: 0g; Protein: 15g

TURKEY RISSOLES

Serves 4 / Prep time: 10 minutes / Cook time: 25 minutes

Chicken is often the first choice for poultry in most home kitchens, but turkey tastes fabulous, is inexpensive, and is very healthy. It is low in fat and high in protein. When cooking with it, make sure some of your other recipe ingredients are high in fat so that you hit your keto macro. Turkey can help boost your immunity because it contains an amino acid called tryptophan, which supports the immune system.

1 pound ground turkey

1 scallion, white and green parts, finely chopped

1 teaspoon minced garlic

Pinch pink Himalayan salt

Pinch freshly ground black pepper

1 cup ground almonds

2 tablespoons extra-virgin olive oil

1. Preheat the oven to 350°F. Line a baking sheet with aluminum foil and set aside.

2. In a medium bowl, mix together the turkey, scallion, garlic, salt, and pepper until well combined.

3. Shape the turkey mixture into 8 patties and flatten them out.

4. Place the ground almonds in a shallow bowl, and dredge the turkey patties in the ground almonds to coat.

5. In a large skillet over medium heat, heat the olive oil.

6. Brown the turkey patties on both sides, about 10 minutes in total.

7. Transfer the patties to the baking sheet. Bake until cooked through, flipping them once, about 15 minutes in total, and serve.

PREP TIP Make the entire recipe from start to finish. Place the cooled turkey patties in sealed plastic bags and store them in the refrigerator for up to 3 days or in the freezer for up to 1 month. Take them out of the freezer and thaw for a quick dinner or snack, or reheat them right from the refrigerator.

PER SERVING Calories: 440; Fat: 34g; Carbs: 7g; Net Carbs: 3g; Fiber: 4g; Protein: 27g

CHAPTER EIGHT
BEEF, PORK & LAMB ENTRÉES

◄ Steak and Egg Bibimbap, page 198

BEEF AND BELL PEPPER "POTATO SKINS"

Serves 2 / Prep time: 10 minutes / Cook time: 20 minutes

Here's a creative low-carb take on potato skins. The big slices of bell pepper provide the "skin" to hold all the yummy ingredients while also offering a fresh, crisp taste. For additional flavor variations, add Mexican-inspired ingredients such as diced onion, diced jalapeño or green chiles, chopped fresh cilantro, freshly squeezed lime juice (for the crema), or hot sauce.

1 tablespoon ghee
½ pound ground beef
Pink Himalayan salt
Freshly ground black pepper
3 large bell peppers, in different colors

½ cup shredded cheese (such as Mexican blend)
1 avocado
¼ cup sour cream

1. Preheat the oven to 400°F. Line a baking sheet with aluminum foil or a silicone baking mat.

2. In a large skillet over medium-high heat, melt the ghee. When the ghee is hot, add the ground beef and season with salt and pepper. Stir occasionally with a wooden spoon, breaking up the beef chunks. Continue cooking until the beef is done, 7 to 10 minutes.

3. Meanwhile, cut the bell peppers to get your "potato skins" ready: Cut off the top of each pepper, slice it in half, and pull out the seeds and ribs. If the pepper is large, you can cut it into quarters; use your best judgment to come up with a potato skin–size "boat."

4. Place the bell peppers on the prepared baking sheet.

5. Spoon the ground beef into the peppers, sprinkle the cheese on top of each, and bake for 10 minutes.

6. Meanwhile, in a medium bowl, combine the avocado and sour cream to create an avocado crema. Mix until smooth.

7. When the peppers and beef are done baking, divide them between two plates, top each with the avocado crema, and serve.

SUBSTITUTION TIP You could also use ground turkey instead of ground beef.

PER SERVING Calories: 707; Fat: 52g; Carbs: 22g; Net Carbs: 13g; Fiber: 10g; Protein: 40g

BEEF AND BROCCOLI ROAST

Serves 2 / Prep time: 10 minutes / Cook time: 4 hours 30 minutes

Eating in Asian restaurants can pose a problem when you're following a keto diet because many of the sauces contain sugar or brown sugar. By making a copycat meal like this roast at home, you will know exactly what's inside. The recipe is not authentic, but it is yummy, and you need only five ingredients, plus a little salt and pepper, and a few hours for the slow cooker to create tender beef, crisp broccoli, and a salty sauce.

1 pound beef chuck roast

Pink Himalayan salt

Freshly ground black pepper

½ cup Rich Beef Stock (page 22) or store-bought beef broth, plus more if needed

¼ cup soy sauce (or coconut aminos)

1 teaspoon toasted sesame oil

1 (16-ounce) bag frozen broccoli

1. With the crock insert in place, preheat the slow cooker to low.

2. On a cutting board, season the chuck roast with salt and pepper, and slice the roast thin. Put the sliced beef in the slow cooker.

3. In a small bowl, mix together the beef broth, soy sauce, and sesame oil. Pour over the beef.

4. Cover and cook on low for 4 hours.

5. Add the frozen broccoli, and cook for 30 minutes more. If you need more liquid, add additional beef broth.

6. Serve hot.

SERVING TIP Spoon this recipe over shirataki rice or cauliflower rice (see Serving Tip, page 214).

PER SERVING Calories: 806; Fat: 49g; Carbs: 18g; Net Carbs: 12g; Fiber: 6g; Protein: 74g

SKIRT STEAK WITH CHIMICHURRI SAUCE

Serves 2 / Prep time: 10 minutes, plus all day to marinate / Cook time: 10 minutes

This dish has such a bold and savory combination of flavors. The key is marinating the skirt steak as long as you can to get it tender, and then it will melt in your mouth. The sliced steak is then topped with zesty garlic chimichurri sauce before serving, jolting your taste buds into a happy dance.

¼ cup soy sauce

½ cup extra-virgin olive oil

Juice of 1 lime

2 tablespoons apple cider vinegar

1 pound skirt steak

Pink Himalayan salt

Freshly ground black pepper

2 tablespoons ghee

¼ cup chimichurri sauce
  (such as Elvio's)

1. In a small bowl, mix together the soy sauce, olive oil, lime juice, and apple cider vinegar. Pour into a large zip-top bag, and add the skirt steak. Marinate for as long as possible: at least all day or, ideally, overnight.

2. Dry the steak with a paper towel. Season both sides of the steak with salt and pepper.

3. In a large skillet over high heat, melt the ghee. Add the steak and sear for about 4 minutes on each side, until well browned. Transfer the steak to a chopping board to rest for at least 5 minutes.

4. Slice the skirt steak against the grain. Divide the slices between two plates, top with the chimichurri sauce, and serve.

INGREDIENT TIP You can also make your own chimichurri sauce with a combination of ⅛ cup of cilantro, ⅛ cup of minced red onion, ⅛ cup of chopped parsley, 1 minced garlic clove, 1 tablespoon of olive oil, and 1 tablespoon of apple cider vinegar. Season with salt and freshly ground black pepper.

PER SERVING Calories: 718; Fat: 46g; Carbs: 6g; Net Carbs: 4g; Fiber: 2g; Protein: 70g

BARBACOA BEEF ROAST

Serves 2 / Prep time: 10 minutes / Cook time: 8 hours

Restaurant versions of barbacoa can have eleven or twelve ingredients, but this one has only five. It is still packed full of flavor, and after 8 hours it will fall apart when you shred it.

1 pound beef chuck roast

Pink Himalayan salt

Freshly ground black pepper

4 chipotle peppers in adobo sauce (such as La Costeña)

1 (6-ounce) can green jalapeño chiles

2 tablespoons apple cider vinegar

½ cup Rich Beef Stock (page 22) or store-bought beef broth

1. With the crock insert in place, preheat the slow cooker to low.

2. Season the beef chuck roast on both sides with salt and pepper. Put the roast in the slow cooker.

3. In a food processor (or blender), combine the chipotle peppers and their adobo sauce, jalapeños, and apple cider vinegar, and pulse until smooth. Add the beef broth, and pulse a few more times. Pour the chile mixture over the top of the roast.

4. Cover and cook on low for 8 hours.

5. Transfer the beef to a cutting board, and use two forks to shred the meat.

6. Serve hot.

INGREDIENT TIP You can also use beef brisket for this roast.

PER SERVING Calories: 723; Fat: 46g; Carbs: 7g; Net Carbs: 2g; Fiber: 5g; Protein: 66g

MISSISSIPPI POT ROAST

Serves 4 / Prep time: 5 minutes / Cook time: 8 hours

Mississippi Pot Roast is likely to become a favorite, because it is so simple and packed with flavor. The pepperoncini, ranch dressing, and gravy packets contribute some excellent flavors.

1 pound beef chuck roast

Pink Himalayan salt

Freshly ground black pepper

1 (1-ounce) packet dry Au Jus Gravy Mix

1 (1-ounce) packet dry ranch dressing

8 tablespoons butter (1 stick)

1 cup whole pepperoncini (such as Mezzetta)

1. With the crock insert in place, preheat the slow cooker to low.
2. Season both sides of the beef chuck roast with salt and pepper. Put in the slow cooker.
3. Sprinkle the gravy mix and ranch dressing packets on top of the roast.
4. Place the butter on top of the roast, and sprinkle the pepperoncini around it.
5. Cover and cook on low for 8 hours.
6. Shred the beef using two forks, and serve hot.

INGREDIENT TIP This recipe is also delicious with boneless chicken breasts instead of the beef.

PER SERVING Calories: 504; Fat: 34g; Carbs: 6g; Net Carbs: 6g; Fiber: 0g; Protein: 36g

STEAK AND EGG BIBIMBAP

Serves 2 / Prep time: 10 minutes / Cook time: 20 minutes

Bibimbap, which means "mixed rice" in Korean, is an increasingly popular Asian dish. While this recipe is unlike a traditional version, it has the key ingredients: beef, a runny egg, and vegetables. Make this when you have leftovers—most vegetables will work well.

FOR THE GROUND BEEF

1 tablespoon ghee

½ pound ground beef or steak, minced

Pink Himalayan salt

Freshly ground black pepper

1 tablespoon soy sauce
  (or coconut aminos)

FOR THE EGG AND CAULIFLOWER RICE

2 tablespoons ghee, divided

2 large eggs

1 large cucumber, peeled and cut
  into matchsticks

1 tablespoon soy sauce

1 cup cauliflower rice (see Serving tip,
  page 214)

Pink Himalayan salt

Freshly ground black pepper

TO MAKE THE GROUND BEEF

1. In a large skillet over medium-high heat, heat the ghee. Add the ground beef, and season with salt and pepper. Using a wooden spoon, stir occasionally, breaking the beef apart. Continue cooking until the beef is done, 7 to 10 minutes.

2. Add the soy sauce and stir. Turn the heat to medium-low and simmer while you make the egg and cauliflower rice.

TO MAKE THE EGG AND CAULIFLOWER RICE

1. In a second large skillet over medium-high heat, heat 1 tablespoon of ghee. When the ghee is very hot, crack the eggs into it. When the whites have cooked through, after 2 to 3 minutes, carefully transfer the eggs to a plate.

2. In a small bowl, marinate the cucumber matchsticks in the soy sauce.

3. Clean out the skillet from the eggs, and add the remaining 1 tablespoon of ghee to the pan over medium-high heat. Add the cauliflower rice, season with salt and pepper, and stir, cooking for 5 minutes. Turn the heat up to high at the end of the cooking to get a nice crisp on the "rice."

4. Divide the rice between two bowls.

5. Top the rice in each bowl with an egg, the ground beef, and the marinated cucumber matchsticks and serve.

INGREDIENT TIP You could also make this recipe with ground turkey instead of ground beef.

VARIATIONS You can add so many vegetables and other ingredients to a bibimbap, so take a look in your refrigerator and get creative. Here are just a few suggestions:

- Kimchi
- Sriracha, drizzled on top
- Bean sprouts
- Carrot matchsticks
- Chopped mushrooms
- Chopped scallions

PER SERVING Calories: 590; Fat: 45g; Carbs: 8g; Net Carbs: 5g; Fiber: 4g; Protein: 39g

TACO CHEESE CUPS

Serves 2 / Prep time: 10 minutes / Cook time: 20 minutes

Cheese cups are versatile and very easy to make. Once you master the cheese chips, you will no doubt start making cheese taco shells, cheese bowls, cheese everything! These Mexican-themed taco cups include flavorful beef, fresh avocado, cool sour cream, and of course the crunch of the cheese cup. Delicious and fun to eat!

FOR THE CHEESE CUPS

2 cups shredded cheese
  (such as Mexican blend)

FOR THE GROUND BEEF

1 tablespoon ghee
½ pound ground beef
½ (1.25-ounce) package
  taco seasoning
¼ cup water

FOR THE TACO CUPS

½ avocado, diced
Pink Himalayan salt
Freshly ground black pepper
2 tablespoons sour cream

TO MAKE THE CHEESE CUPS

1. Preheat the oven to 350°F. Line a baking sheet with parchment paper or a silicone baking mat.

2. Place 4 (½-cup) mounds of the cheese on the prepared pan. Bake for about 7 minutes, or until the edges are brown and the middle has melted. You want these slightly larger than a typical tortilla chip.

3. Put the pan on a cooling rack for 2 minutes while the cheese chips cool. The chips will be floppy when they first come out of the oven, but they will begin to crisp as they cool.

4. Before they are fully crisp, move the cheese chips to a muffin tin. Form the cheese chips around the shape of the muffin cups to create small bowls. (The chips will fully harden in the muffin tin, which will make them really easy to fill.)

TO MAKE THE GROUND BEEF

1. In a medium skillet over medium-high heat, heat the ghee.

2. When the ghee is hot, add the ground beef and sauté for about 8 minutes, until browned.

3. Drain the excess grease. Stir in the taco seasoning and water, and bring to a boil. Turn the heat to medium-low and simmer for 5 minutes.

TO MAKE THE TACO CUPS

1. Place two taco cups on each of two plates. Using a slotted spoon, spoon the ground beef into the taco cups.

2. Season the diced avocado with salt and pepper, and divide it among the taco cups.

3. Add a dollop of sour cream to each taco cup and serve.

STORAGE TIP The taco cups will keep well for 2 to 3 days in a sealed container in the refrigerator.

VARIATIONS Just like a taco shell, these taco cheese cups can be used to hold any number of flavor combinations:

- Diced tomatoes, onions, and jalapeños can be added to the ground beef.
- Use pepper Jack cheese for an extra kick.

PER SERVING Calories: 894; Fat: 68g; Carbs: 12g; Net Carbs: 9g; Fiber: 3g; Protein: 57g

BLTA CUPS

ONE
PAN

Serves 2 (2 jumbo-size muffin cups each) / Prep time: 5 minutes /
Cook time: 20 minutes, plus 10 minutes to rest

What's better than a cup made of bacon? Almost anything goes well with bacon, but bacon paired with lettuce, tomato, and avocado is a classic. You'll love these bacon cups, which are full of flavor.

12 bacon slices

¼ head romaine lettuce, chopped

½ avocado, diced

½ cup halved grape tomatoes

2 tablespoons sour cream

1. Preheat the oven to 400°F. You will need a muffin tin, either jumbo size or standard.

2. Turn the muffin tin upside down, and lay it on a baking sheet. Make a cross with 2 bacon strip halves over the upside-down muffin tin. Take 2 more bacon strip halves and put them around the perimeter of the crossed halves. Take 1 full bacon strip and circle it around the base of the upside down tin and then use a toothpick to hold that piece together tightly. Repeat to make 4 cups total.

3. Bake for 20 minutes, or until the bacon is crispy. Transfer to a cooling rack and let rest for at least 10 minutes.

4. Once the bacon cups have become firm, carefully remove them from the muffin cups and place two cups on each of two plates. Fill the cups evenly with the romaine, add the avocado, tomatoes, and a dollop of sour cream, and serve.

INGREDIENT TIP The bacon cups will store well covered in the refrigerator for up to 3 days, so you might want to make extra!

PER SERVING (2 CUPS) Calories: 354; Fat: 28g; Carbs: 6.5g; Net Carbs: 3g; Fiber: 3.5g; Protein: 19.5g

CHEESEBURGER CASSEROLE

Serves 6 / Prep time: 10 minutes / Cook time: 40 minutes

Casseroles are the epitome of comfort food, and the no-fuss preparation is attractive for anyone who has a busy schedule to maintain. The flavor of this dish will remind you of sizzling cheese-topped beef burgers right off the barbecue on a balmy summer evening. If you have leftovers, either enjoy them for lunch the next day or freeze them for up to 2 weeks.

1 pound ground beef

½ cup chopped sweet onion

2 teaspoons minced garlic

1½ cups shredded aged
  Cheddar, divided

½ cup heavy (whipping) cream

1 large tomato, chopped

1 teaspoon minced fresh basil

¼ teaspoon pink Himalayan salt

⅛ teaspoon freshly ground
  black pepper

1. Preheat the oven to 350°F.

2. In a large skillet over medium-high heat, heat the ground beef.

3. Brown the beef until cooked through, about 8 minutes, and spoon off any excess fat.

4. Stir in the onion and garlic and cook until the vegetables are tender, about 4 minutes.

5. Transfer the beef and vegetables to an 8-by-8-inch casserole dish.

6. In medium bowl, stir together 1 cup of shredded cheese and the cream, tomato, basil, salt, and pepper until well combined.

7. Pour the cream mixture over the beef mixture, and top the casserole with the remaining ½ cup of shredded cheese.

8. Bake until the casserole is bubbly and the cheese is melted and lightly browned, about 30 minutes.

9. Serve.

VARIATIONS To add some acidity, try any of the following:

- Add ½ cup diced pickles into the beef mixture.
- Sliced pepperoncini works well, too, if you aren't a fan of pickles.
- Add ¼ cup of a low-sugar tomato sauce, such as Rao's brand, to the cream mixture.

PER SERVING Calories: 410; Fat: 33g; Carbs: 3g; Net Carbs: 3g; Fiber: 0g; Protein: 20g

ITALIAN BEEF BURGERS

Serves 4 / Prep time: 10 minutes / Cook time: 10 minutes

Sometimes it is more fun to plan the toppings on a burger than is to make the burger itself. You can top these juicy patties with whatever catches your imagination, such as bacon, avocado, Creamy Mayonnaise (page 33), or simple tomato slices—or all of the above and more. Tomatoes are a wonderful choice because they are very high in vitamins A, C, and K and a phytonutrient called lycopene, which can help prevent certain cancers and support a healthy cardiovascular system.

1 pound ground beef

¼ cup ground almonds

2 tablespoons chopped fresh basil

1 teaspoon minced garlic

¼ teaspoon pink Himalayan salt

1 tablespoon extra-virgin olive oil

1 tomato, cut into 4 thick slices

¼ sweet onion, sliced thinly

1. In a medium bowl, mix together the ground beef, ground almonds, basil, garlic, and salt until well combined.

2. Form the beef mixture into four equal patties, and flatten each to about ½ inch thick.

3. In a large skillet over medium-high heat, heat the olive oil.

4. Panfry the burgers until cooked through, flipping them once, about 12 minutes in total.

5. Pat away any excess grease with paper towels, and serve the burgers with a slice of tomato and onion.

SUBSTITUTION TIP Ground lamb is a perfect choice if you do not want to use ground beef; just make sure the ground meat is not too lean. Try to get 70% lean or less so that your fat macros are not too low.

PER SERVING Calories: 441; Fat: 37g; Carbs: 4g; Net Carbs: 3g; Fiber: 1g; Protein: 22g

FETA-STUFFED BURGERS

Serves 2 / Prep time: 10 minutes / Cook time: 10 minutes

Who doesn't love a burger? Especially a burger stuffed with cheese! The combo of the beef and lamb with classic Mediterranean flavors is a winner.

2 tablespoons fresh mint leaves, finely chopped

1 scallion, white and green parts, thinly sliced

1 tablespoon Dijon mustard

Pink Himalayan salt

Freshly ground black pepper

12 ounces (6 ounces each) ground beef and ground lamb mixture

2 ounces crumbled feta cheese

1 tablespoon ghee

1. In a large bowl, mix to combine the mint leaves with the scallion and mustard. Season with salt and pepper.

2. Add the ground beef and lamb to the bowl. Mix together thoroughly, and form into 4 patties.

3. Press the feta crumbles into 2 of the patties, and put the other 2 patties on top so the cheese is in the middle. Pinch all the way around the edges of the burgers to seal in the feta cheese.

4. In a medium skillet over medium heat, heat the ghee. Add the burger patties to the hot oil. Cook each side for 4 to 5 minutes, until done to your preference, and serve.

SUBSTITUTION TIP You could use just ground beef or just ground lamb for this recipe if you prefer.

PER SERVING Calories: 607; Fat: 48g; Carbs: 2g; Net Carbs: 2g; Fiber: 1g; Protein: 41g

SIRLOIN WITH BLUE CHEESE COMPOUND BUTTER

Serves 4 / Prep time: 10 minutes, plus 1 hour to chill /
Cook time: 15 minutes, plus 10 minutes to rest

Compound butters—butter mixed with another ingredient such as an herb or a cheese—are an easy, quick way to get intense flavor in your recipes. The heat of the prepared meats, poultry, or vegetables melts the butter into a scrumptious pool with no work beyond cutting a disk of butter off the prepared log. Compound butters will keep in the freezer, tightly wrapped, for up to a month.

6 tablespoons butter, at room
  temperature

4 ounces blue cheese, such as Stilton
  or Roquefort

4 (5-ounce) beef sirloin steaks

1 tablespoon extra-virgin olive oil

Pink Himalayan salt

Freshly ground black pepper

1. Place the butter in a blender and pulse until the butter is whipped, about 2 minutes.

2. Add the cheese, and pulse until just incorporated.

3. Spoon the butter mixture onto a sheet of plastic wrap and roll it into a log about 1½ inches in diameter by twisting both ends of the plastic wrap in opposite directions.

4. Refrigerate the butter until completely set, about 1 hour.

5. Slice the butter into ½-inch disks and set them on a plate in the refrigerator until you are ready to serve the steaks. Store leftover butter in the refrigerator for up to 1 week.

6. Preheat a barbecue to medium-high heat.

7. Let the steaks come to room temperature.

8. Rub the steaks all over with the olive oil, and season them with salt and pepper.

9. Grill the steaks until they reach your desired doneness, about 6 minutes per side for medium.

10. If you do not have a barbecue, put the steaks in a baking pan and broil in a preheated oven for 7 minutes per side for medium.

11. Let the steaks rest for 10 minutes. Serve each topped with a disk of the compound butter.

PER SERVING Calories: 544; Fat: 44g; Carbs: 0g; Net Carbs: 0g; Fiber: 0g; Protein: 35g

GARLIC-BRAISED SHORT RIBS

Serves 4 / Prep time: 10 minutes / Cook time: 2 hours, 10 minutes

Garlic infuses these ribs with a complex flavor and adds a plethora of important nutrients, because this allium is the source of about 70 phytochemicals, calcium, selenium, and manganese. Garlic has been used for centuries as a medicinal ingredient for its detoxing qualities and to lower blood pressure. Including garlic as a regular part of your diet is even thought to cut your risk of getting the common cold.

4 (4-ounce) beef short ribs
Pink Himalayan salt
Freshly ground black pepper
1 tablespoon extra-virgin olive oil

2 teaspoons minced garlic
½ cup dry red wine
3 cups Rich Beef Stock (page 22)
  or store-bought beef broth

1. Preheat the oven to 325°F.
2. Season the beef ribs on all sides with salt and pepper.
3. In a deep ovenproof skillet with a lid over medium-high heat, heat the olive oil.
4. Sear the ribs on all sides until browned, about 6 minutes in total. Transfer the ribs to a plate.
5. Add the garlic to the skillet and sauté until translucent, about 3 minutes.
6. Whisk in the red wine to deglaze the pan. Be sure to scrape all the browned bits from the meat from the bottom of the pan. Simmer the wine until it is slightly reduced, about 2 minutes.
7. Add the beef stock, ribs, and any accumulated juices on the plate back to the skillet, and bring the liquid to a boil.
8. Cover the skillet and place it in the oven to braise the ribs until the meat is fall-off-the-bone tender, about 2 hours.
9. Serve the ribs with a spoonful of the cooking liquid drizzled over each serving.

PER SERVING Calories: 481; Fat: 38g; Carbs: 5g; Net Carbs: 2g; Fiber: 3g; Protein: 29g

BACON-WRAPPED BEEF TENDERLOIN

Serves 4 / Prep time: 10 minutes / Cook time: 15 minutes, plus 10 minutes to rest

This is a throwback to a popular dish from the '80s, when many things were wrapped in bacon despite the moratorium on fats. Bacon-wrapped steaks were found on every restaurant menu because the salty richness of the bacon combined beautifully with the lean tenderloin. If you are looking for higher omega-3 fatty acids and vitamin E in your beef, source out organic grass-fed animals.

4 (4-ounce) beef tenderloin steaks
Pink Himalayan salt
Freshly ground black pepper

8 bacon slices
1 tablespoon extra-virgin olive oil

1. Preheat the oven to 450°F.
2. Season the steaks with salt and pepper.
3. Wrap each steak snugly around the edges with 2 slices of bacon, and secure the bacon with toothpicks.
4. In a large skillet over medium-high heat, heat the olive oil.
5. Pan sear the steaks for 4 minutes per side, and transfer them to a baking sheet.
6. Roast the steaks until they reach your desired doneness, about 6 minutes for medium.
7. Remove the steaks from the oven and let them rest for 10 minutes.
8. Remove the toothpicks and serve.

INGREDIENT TIP Bacon has a bad reputation in many nutritionist circles because it can be very high in preservatives and sodium, depending on the brand and processing. Look for organic bacon with no additives, preferably from a reputable butcher.

PER SERVING Calories: 565; Fat: 49g; Carbs: 0g; Net Carbs: 0g; Fiber: 0g; Protein: 28g

BUTTER AND HERB PORK CHOPS

Serves 2 / Prep time: 5 minutes / Cook time: 25 minutes

Sometimes the simplest flavors are the most delicious. It is hard to go wrong with herbs, butter, and olive oil. The flavors complement the pork beautifully, and the dish bakes quickly so it can go from the kitchen to the dinner table in no more than 30 minutes.

1 tablespoon butter, plus more for coating the dish

2 boneless pork chops

Pink Himalayan salt

Freshly ground black pepper

1 tablespoon dried Italian seasoning

1 tablespoon chopped fresh flat-leaf Italian parsley

1 tablespoon extra-virgin olive oil

1. Preheat the oven to 350°F. Choose a baking dish that will hold both pork chops, and coat it with the butter.

2. Pat the pork chops dry with a paper towel, place them in the prepared baking dish, and season with salt, pepper, and Italian seasoning.

3. Top with the fresh parsley, drizzle the olive oil over both pork chops, and top each chop with ½ tablespoon of butter.

4. Bake for 20 to 25 minutes, until the meat is pale and mostly white with mostly clear juices. (Thinner pork chops will cook faster than thicker ones.)

5. Place the pork chops on two plates, spoon the buttery juices over the meat, and serve hot.

SERVING TIP This dish is particularly delicious with mashed cauliflower (try Cheesy Mashed Cauliflower on page 107).

PER SERVING Calories: 333; Fat: 23g; Carbs: 0g; Net Carbs: 0g; Fiber: 0g; Protein: 31g

PARMESAN PORK CHOPS AND ROASTED ASPARAGUS

Serves 2 / Prep time: 10 minutes / Cook time: 25 minutes

This recipe is perfect for a weeknight meal since everything cooks on one pan. You'll love these, especially their crispy pork rind and Parmesan "breading." The roasted asparagus also contributes some crunchy goodness.

¼ cup grated Parmesan cheese

¼ cup crushed pork rinds

1 teaspoon garlic powder

2 boneless pork chops

Pink Himalayan salt

Freshly ground black pepper

Extra-virgin olive oil, for drizzling

½ pound asparagus spears, tough ends snapped off

1. Preheat the oven to 350°F. Line a baking sheet with aluminum foil or a silicone baking mat.

2. In a medium bowl, mix to combine the Parmesan cheese, pork rinds, and garlic powder.

3. Pat the pork chops dry with a paper towel, and season with salt and pepper.

4. Place a pork chop in the bowl with the Parmesan–pork rind mixture, and press the "breading" to the pork chop so it sticks. Place the coated pork chop on the prepared baking sheet. Repeat for the second pork chop.

5. Drizzle a small amount of olive oil over each pork chop.

6. Place the asparagus on the baking sheet around the pork chops. Drizzle with olive oil, and season with salt and pepper. Sprinkle any leftover Parmesan cheese–pork rind mixture over the asparagus.

7. Bake for 20 to 25 minutes, until the meat is pale and mostly white with mostly clear juices. (Thinner pork chops will cook faster than thicker ones.)

8. Serve hot.

INGREDIENT TIP There are a lot of different flavors of pork rinds available now. Feel free to use any of them to add a unique flavor profile to this dish.

PER SERVING Calories: 370; Fat: 21g; Carbs: 6g; Net Carbs: 4g; Fiber: 3g; Protein: 40g

SAME PORK AND GREEN BEANS

Serves 2 / Prep time: 5 minutes / Cook time: 10 minutes

This dinner is quick and flavorful. It celebrates Asian flavors in a healthy and hearty dish that you can create in just minutes on a busy night.

2 boneless pork chops

Pink Himalayan salt

Freshly ground black pepper

2 tablespoons toasted sesame
  oil, divided

2 tablespoons soy sauce

1 teaspoon Sriracha sauce

1 cup fresh green beans

1. On a cutting board, pat the pork chops dry with a paper towel. Slice the chops into strips, and season with salt and pepper.

2. In a large skillet over medium heat, heat 1 tablespoon of sesame oil.

3. Add the pork strips and cook for 7 minutes, stirring occasionally.

4. In a small bowl, mix to combine the remaining 1 tablespoon of sesame oil, the soy sauce, and the Sriracha sauce. Pour into the skillet with the pork.

5. Add the green beans to the skillet, reduce the heat to medium-low, and simmer for 3 to 5 minutes.

6. Divide the pork, green beans, and sauce between two wide, shallow bowls and serve.

SUBSTITUTION TIP If Sriracha sauce is too spicy for you, you can add peeled, minced fresh ginger instead, which will add flavor and kick but not heat.

PER SERVING Calories: 366; Fat: 24g; Carbs: 5g; Net Carbs: 3g; Fiber: 2g; Protein: 33g

SLOW-COOKER BARBECUE RIBS

Serves 2 / Prep time: 10 minutes / Cook time: 4 hours

Ribs are such a treat. The slow cooker works really well for making ribs. There are many tasty sugar-free barbecue sauces available at the supermarket, making this recipe ever so simple.

1 pound pork ribs

Pink Himalayan salt

Freshly ground black pepper

1 (1.25-ounce) package dry rib-seasoning rub

½ cup sugar-free barbecue sauce

1. With the crock insert in place, preheat the slow cooker to high.

2. Generously season the pork ribs with salt, pepper, and dry rib-seasoning rub.

3. Stand the ribs up along the walls of the slow-cooker insert, with the bonier side facing inward.

4. Pour the barbecue sauce on both sides of the ribs, using just enough to coat.

5. Cover, cook for 4 hours, and serve.

INGREDIENT TIP The ribs will be very tender, so be careful removing them from the slow cooker.

PER SERVING Calories: 956; Fat: 72g; Carbs: 5g; Net Carbs: 5g; Fiber: 0g; Protein: 68g

KALUA PORK WITH CABBAGE

Serves 2 / Prep time: 10 minutes / Cook time: 8 hours

The "plate lunch" is a popular item in Honolulu, and kalua pork is a favorite among the locals. Plate lunch always has a scoop of white rice and macaroni salad, which obviously don't go with the keto lifestyle, but you can pair the kalua pork with keto-friendly alternatives (see Serving tip).

1 pound boneless pork butt roast
Pink Himalayan salt
Freshly ground black pepper

1 tablespoon smoked paprika or
   liquid smoke
½ cup water
½ head cabbage, chopped

1. With the crock insert in place, preheat the slow cooker to low.
2. Generously season the pork roast with salt, pepper, and smoked paprika.
3. Place the pork roast in the slow-cooker insert, and add the water.
4. Cover and cook on low for 7 hours.
5. Transfer the cooked pork roast to a plate. Put the chopped cabbage in the bottom of the slow cooker, and put the pork roast back in on top of the cabbage.
6. Cover and cook the cabbage and pork roast on low for 1 hour.
7. Remove the pork roast from the slow cooker, and place it on a baking sheet. Use two forks to shred the pork.
8. Serve the shredded pork hot with the cooked cabbage.
9. Reserve the liquid from the slow cooker to remoisten the pork and cabbage when reheating leftovers.

SERVING TIP You can serve the kalua pork alone or over cauliflower rice, or you can enjoy it on a low-carb roll. To make cauliflower rice, simply process cauliflower florets in your food processor or blender to achieve a rice-like consistency. Then sauté the cauliflower rice in olive oil or ghee in a skillet over medium heat for about 5 minutes.

PER SERVING Calories: 550; Fat: 41g; Carbs: 10g; Net Carbs: 5g; Fiber: 5g; Protein: 39g

SPICY PORK BURGERS

Serves 2 / Prep time: 10 minutes / Cook time: 10 minutes, plus 5 minutes to rest

People don't think about ground pork enough when it comes to burgers! Ground pork works beautifully for burgers, and I love adding fresh ingredients to the meat and then topping the dish with the burst of heat that you get from mixing mayonnaise with Sriracha. Whether you eat your burger with a knife and fork or add lettuce leaves to wrap it up, this is the perfect keto burger.

12 ounces ground pork

2 scallions, white and green parts,
  thinly sliced

1 tablespoon toasted sesame oil

Pink Himalayan salt

Freshly ground black pepper

1 tablespoon ghee

2 tablespoons Sriracha Mayo (page 34)

1. In a large bowl, mix to combine the ground pork with the scallions and sesame oil, and season with salt and pepper. Form the pork mixture into 2 patties. Create an imprint with your thumb in the middle of each burger so the pork will heat evenly.

2. In a large skillet over medium-high heat, heat the ghee. When the ghee has melted and is very hot, add the burger patties and cook for 4 minutes on each side.

3. Transfer the burgers to a plate and let rest for at least 5 minutes.

4. Top the burgers with the Sriracha Mayo and serve.

INGREDIENT TIP Sriracha is spicy, so use as little or as much as you want based on your heat tolerance.

PER SERVING Calories: 575; Fat: 49g; Carbs: 2g; Net Carbs: 1g; Fiber: 1g; Protein: 31g

BLUE CHEESE PORK CHOPS

Serves 2 / Prep time: 5 minutes / Cook time: 10 minutes

You could put this blue cheese sauce on top of just about anything and it would be amazing, but it's especially delicious with pork chops. The ingredients of this recipe are perfect for the keto diet, and it's very quick to make.

2 boneless pork chops

Pink Himalayan salt

Freshly ground black pepper

2 tablespoons butter

⅓ cup blue cheese crumbles

⅓ cup heavy (whipping) cream

⅓ cup sour cream

1. Pat the pork chops dry, and season with salt and pepper.

2. In a medium skillet over medium heat, melt the butter. When the butter melts and is very hot, add the pork chops and sear on each side for 3 minutes, until golden brown on each side.

3. Transfer the pork chops to a plate and let rest for 3 to 5 minutes.

4. In a medium saucepan over medium heat, melt the blue cheese crumbles, stirring frequently so they don't burn.

5. Add the cream and the sour cream to the pan with the blue cheese. Let simmer for a few minutes, stirring occasionally.

6. For an extra kick of flavor in the sauce, pour the pork-chop pan juice into the cheese mixture and stir. Let simmer while the pork chops are resting.

7. Put the pork chops on two plates, pour the blue cheese sauce over the top of each, and serve.

INGREDIENT TIP The blue cheese sauce is also delicious poured over vegetables.

PER SERVING Calories: 669; Fat: 34g; Carbs: 4g; Net Carbs: 4g; Fiber: 0g; Protein: 41g

NUT-STUFFED PORK CHOPS

Serves 4 / Prep time: 20 minutes / Cook time: 30 minutes

Pork is a healthy choice that falls somewhere between poultry and red meat on the nutrition spectrum, which is why pork is often called the "other white meat." Pork is very high in protein and vitamin D and low in saturated fat. You will have to combine pork with ingredients higher in fat, such as the nuts and goat cheese in this recipe, to meet your keto macros.

3 ounces goat cheese

½ cup chopped walnuts

¼ cup toasted chopped almonds

1 teaspoon chopped fresh thyme

4 center-cut pork chops, butterflied

Pink Himalayan salt

Freshly ground black pepper

2 tablespoons extra-virgin olive oil

1. Preheat the oven to 400°F.
2. In a small bowl, make the filling by stirring together the goat cheese, walnuts, almonds, and thyme until well mixed.
3. Season the pork chops inside and outside with salt and pepper. Stuff each chop, pushing the filling to the bottom of the cut section. Secure the stuffing with toothpicks through the meat.
4. In a large skillet over medium-high heat, heat the olive oil. Pan sear the pork chops until they're browned on each side, about 10 minutes in total.
5. Transfer the pork chops to a baking dish and roast in the oven until cooked through, about 20 minutes.
6. Serve after removing the toothpicks.

PER SERVING Calories: 481; Fat: 38g; Carbs: 5g; Net Carbs: 2g; Fiber: 3g; Protein: 29g

ROASTED PORK LOIN WITH GRAINY MUSTARD SAUCE

Serves 8 / Prep time: 10 minutes / Cook time: 1 hour 10 minutes

This sauce is delicious; you might have to double the amount you make because eating it by the spoonful as a snack is a real treat. It is also stellar with barbecued beef tenderloin or a perfectly roasted lamb rack.

1 (2-pound) boneless pork loin roast
Pink Himalayan salt
Freshly ground black pepper
3 tablespoons extra-virgin olive oil

1½ cups heavy (whipping) cream
3 tablespoons grainy mustard, such as Pommery

1. Preheat the oven to 375°F.

2. Season the pork roast all over with salt and pepper.

3. In a large skillet over medium-high heat, heat the olive oil.

4. Brown the roast on all sides in the skillet, about 6 minutes in total, and place the roast in a baking dish.

5. Roast until a meat thermometer inserted in the thickest part of the roast reads 155°F, about 1 hour.

6. Approximately 15 minutes before the end of the roasting time, place a small saucepan over medium heat, and add the cream and mustard.

7. Stir the sauce until it simmers, then reduce the heat to low. Simmer the sauce until it is very rich and thick, about 5 minutes. Remove the pan from the heat and set aside.

8. Let the pork rest for 10 minutes before slicing, and serve with the sauce.

INGREDIENT TIP Look for Pommery mustard, which is slightly sweet and adds a lovely burst of flavor to this decadent sauce.

PER SERVING Calories: 368; Fat: 29g; Carbs: 2g; Net Carbs: 2g; Fiber: 0g; Protein: 25g

CARNITAS

ONE POT

Serves 2 / Prep time: 10 minutes / Cook time: 8 hours

Carnitas are easy to prepare and make ahead for quick meals later in the day. The key is letting the pork cook low and slow and infusing the meat with ingredients such as onions and garlic to enhance the flavor of the pork. These are especially tasty in Carnitas Nachos (page 220).

½ tablespoon chili powder

1 tablespoon extra-virgin olive oil

1 pound boneless pork butt roast

2 garlic cloves, minced

½ small onion, diced

Pinch pink Himalayan salt

Pinch freshly ground black pepper

Juice of 1 lime

1. With the crock insert in place, preheat the slow cooker to low.

2. In a small bowl, mix to combine the chili powder and olive oil, and rub it all over the pork.

3. Place the pork in the slow cooker, fat-side up.

4. Top the pork with the garlic, onion, salt, pepper, and lime juice.

5. Cover and cook on low for 8 hours.

6. Transfer the pork to a cutting board, shred the meat with two forks, and serve.

INGREDIENT TIP Save the juices from the slow cooker after cooking the carnitas so you can drizzle them on top before serving. Also use them to moisten leftover carnitas when reheating them in a skillet.

PER SERVING Calories: 446; Fat: 26g; Carbs: 6g; Net Carbs: 4g; Fiber: 2g; Protein: 45g

CARNITAS NACHOS

Serves 2 / Prep time: 5 minutes / Cook time: 10 minutes, plus 5 minute to rest

Pork-rind nachos are a terrific way to use slow-cooker Carnitas (page 219). You won't even miss traditional nachos after you taste these. Make the carnitas ahead, and you can whip up a batch of these in no time.

1 tablespoon extra-virgin olive oil, plus more for coating the dish

2 cups pork rinds

½ cup shredded cheese (Mexican blend works well)

1 cup Carnitas (page 219)

1 avocado, diced

2 tablespoons sour cream

1. Preheat the oven to 350°F. Coat a 9-by-13-inch baking dish with olive oil.

2. Put the pork rinds in the prepared baking dish, and top with the cheese.

3. Bake until the cheese has melted, about 5 minutes. Transfer to a cooling rack and let rest for 5 minutes.

4. In a medium skillet over high heat, heat the olive oil. Put the carnitas in the skillet, and add some of the reserved pan juices. Cook for a few minutes, until you get a nice crispy crust on the carnitas, then flip the carnitas to the other side and cook briefly.

5. Divide the heated pork rinds and cheese between two plates.

6. Top the pork rinds and cheese with the reheated carnitas, add the diced avocado and a dollop of sour cream to each, and serve hot.

INGREDIENT TIPS

- For more kick, use spicy pork rinds.
- Keep an eye on the cheese; it won't take very long to melt, and it will continue to melt after you bring the dish out of the oven.

PER SERVING Calories: 587; Fat: 51g; Carbs: 10g; Net Carbs: 5g; Fiber: 6g; Protein: 51g

PEPPERONI LOW-CARB TORTILLA PIZZA

Serves 2 / Prep time: 5 minutes / Cook time: 5 minutes

There are so many great ways to make a low-carb pizza, but this version has to be one of the quickest and the easiest. It's a perfect recipe for those evenings when you get home late.

2 tablespoons extra-virgin olive oil

1 large low-carb tortilla (such as Mission Whole Wheat Low-Carb Tortillas)

4 tablespoons low-sugar tomato sauce (such as Rao's)

1 cup shredded mozzarella cheese

2 teaspoons dried Italian seasoning

½ cup pepperoni

1. In a medium skillet over medium-high heat, heat the olive oil. Add the tortilla.

2. Spoon the tomato sauce onto the tortilla, spreading it out. Sprinkle on the cheese, Italian seasoning, and pepperoni. Work quickly so the tortilla doesn't burn.

3. Cook until the tortilla is crispy on the bottom, about 3 minutes. Transfer to a cutting board, and cut into slices. Put the slices on a serving plate and serve hot.

INGREDIENT TIP You can use your favorite low-carb tortilla for this recipe. The olive oil helps make it really crisp so it feels like a pizza.

VARIATIONS Since it's pizza, the possibilities are endless. Here are some favorite combinations:

- Skip the tomato sauce entirely: Top with just mozzarella cheese, pepperoni, pepperoncini, and Parmesan cheese.
- Try a take on pizza Margherita: tomato sauce, slices of fresh mozzarella cheese, thin tomato slices, and fresh basil leaves.

PER SERVING Calories: 547; Fat: 44g; Carbs: 17g; Net Carbs: 8g; Fiber: 9g; Protein: 27g

LAMB CHOPS WITH KALAMATA TAPENADE

Serves 4 / Prep time: 15 minutes / Cook time: 25 minutes, plus 10 minutes to rest

Lamb racks seem like the epitome of fine dining, perfectly cooked and cut into chops that are arranged in patterns with elegant bones pointing to the ceiling. Frenching the racks—removing the meat from the upper bones cleanly—is not difficult but can certainly be time consuming if you have never done it before. If you get the racks from your local butcher, you can always ask them to do the work for you to save valuable kitchen time.

FOR THE TAPENADE

1 cup pitted Kalamata olives

2 tablespoons chopped fresh parsley

2 tablespoons extra-virgin olive oil

2 teaspoons minced garlic

2 teaspoons freshly squeezed
   lemon juice

FOR THE LAMB CHOPS

2 (1-pound) racks French-cut lamb
   chops (8 bones each)

Pink Himalayan salt

Freshly ground black pepper

1 tablespoon extra-virgin olive oil

TO MAKE THE TAPENADE

1. Put the olives, parsley, olive oil, garlic, and lemon juice in a food processor and process until the mixture is puréed but still slightly chunky.

2. Transfer the tapenade to a container and store sealed in the refrigerator until needed.

TO MAKE THE LAMB CHOPS

1. Preheat the oven to 450°F.

2. Season the lamb racks with salt and pepper.

3. In a large ovenproof skillet over medium-high heat, heat the olive oil.

4. Pan sear the lamb racks on all sides until browned, about 5 minutes in total.

5. Arrange the racks upright in the skillet, with the bones interlaced, and roast in the oven until they reach your desired doneness, about 20 minutes for medium-rare or until the internal temperature reaches 125°F.

6. Let the lamb rest for 10 minutes, then cut the lamb racks into chops. Arrange 4 chops per person on the plate, top with the Kalamata tapenade, and serve.

SUBSTITUTION TIP Kalamata olives are grown in Greece and are a glorious purple-black color. Keep an eye out for unusual olives to try with this recipe, and try to avoid the standard canned black olives, which are often processed unripe fruit.

PER SERVING Calories: 348; Fat: 28g; Carbs: 2g; Net Carbs: 1g; Fiber: 1g; Protein: 21g

ONE
PAN

ROSEMARY-GARLIC LAMB RACKS

Serves 4 / Prep time: 10 minutes, plus 1 hour to marinate /
Cook time: 25 minutes, plus 10 minutes to rest

Lamb is not one of the most popular meat choices in North America, but it is consumed in many other countries as a staple food. Spring lamb is the best choice, although you can find lamb both fresh and frozen year-round in most grocery stores. If you are using frozen lamb, make sure it is completely thawed before adding the racks to the marinade.

¼ cup extra-virgin olive oil

2 tablespoons finely chopped
 fresh rosemary

2 teaspoons minced garlic

Pinch pink Himalayan salt

2 (1-pound) racks French-cut lamb
 chops (8 bones each)

1. In a small bowl, whisk together the olive oil, rosemary, garlic, and salt.

2. Place the racks in a resealable freezer bag, and pour the olive oil mixture into the bag. Massage the meat through the bag so it is coated with the marinade. Press the air out of the bag and seal it.

3. Marinate the lamb racks in the refrigerator for 1 to 2 hours.

4. Preheat the oven to 450°F.

5. Set a large ovenproof skillet over medium-high heat. Take the lamb racks out of the bag and sear them in the skillet on all sides, about 5 minutes in total.

6. Arrange the racks upright in the skillet, with the bones interlaced, and roast in the oven until they reach your desired doneness, about 20 minutes for medium-rare, or until the internal temperature reaches 125°F.

7. Let the lamb rest for 10 minutes, then cut the racks into chops.

8. Serve 4 chops per person.

PER SERVING Calories: 354; Fat: 30g; Carbs: 0g; Net Carbs: 0g; Fiber: 0g; Protein: 21g

LAMB LEG WITH SUN-DRIED TOMATO PESTO

Serves 8 / Prep time: 15 minutes, plus 10 minutes to rest / Cook time: 1 hour 10 minutes

Sun-dried tomatoes, especially those packed in seasoned olive oil, provide an intense burst of flavor and are perfect for pesto and sauces. The drying process removes the tomatoes' water content while retaining and amplifying most of the nutrients and the sweet taste of this popular fruit. Sun-dried tomatoes are an excellent source of iron, vitamin K, and protein.

FOR THE PESTO

1 cup sun-dried tomatoes packed in oil, drained

¼ cup pine nuts

2 tablespoons extra-virgin olive oil

2 tablespoons chopped fresh basil

2 teaspoons minced garlic

FOR THE LAMB LEG

1 (2-pound) lamb leg

Pink Himalayan salt

Freshly ground black pepper

2 tablespoons extra-virgin olive oil

TO MAKE THE PESTO

1. Place the sun-dried tomatoes, pine nuts, olive oil, basil, and garlic in a blender or food processor; process until smooth.

2. Set aside until needed.

TO MAKE THE LAMB LEG

1. Preheat the oven to 400°F.

2. Season the lamb leg all over with salt and pepper.

3. In a large ovenproof skillet over medium-high heat, heat the olive oil.

4. Sear the lamb on all sides until nicely browned, about 6 minutes in total.

5. Spread the sun-dried tomato pesto all over the lamb, and place the lamb on a baking sheet. Roast until the meat reaches your desired doneness, about 1 hour for medium.

6. Let the lamb rest for 10 minutes before slicing and serving.

PER SERVING Calories: 352; Fat: 29g; Carbs: 5g; Net Carbs: 3g; Fiber: 2g; Protein: 17g

CHAPTER NINE
DESSERTS & SWEET TREATS

◀ Strawberry-Lime Ice Pops, page 230

MINT-CHOCOLATE CHIP ICE CREAM

Serves 2 / Prep time: 10 minutes, plus 4 hours to freeze / Cook time: 30 minutes

There are many low-carbohydrate ice creams on the market these days, but nothing beats making your own. You don't have to have a fancy ice cream maker at home to make this ice cream.

½ tablespoon butter

1 tablespoon Swerve natural sweetener

10 tablespoons heavy (whipping) cream, divided

¼ teaspoon alcohol-free peppermint extract

2 tablespoons sugar-free chocolate chips

1. Put a medium metal bowl and your hand-mixer beaters in the freezer to chill.
2. In a small, heavy saucepan over medium heat, melt the butter. Whisk in the sweetener and 5 tablespoons of cream.
3. Turn the heat up to medium-high and bring the mixture to a boil, stirring constantly. Turn the heat down to low and simmer, stirring occasionally, for about 30 minutes. You want the mixture to be thick, so that it sticks to the back of a spoon.
4. Stir in the peppermint extract.
5. Pour the thickened mixture into a medium bowl and refrigerate to cool.
6. Remove the metal bowl and the mixer beaters from the freezer. Pour the remaining 5 tablespoons of cream into the bowl. With the electric beater, whip the cream until it is thick and fluffy and forms peaks. Don't overbeat, or the cream will turn to butter. Take the cream mixture out of the refrigerator.
7. Using a rubber scraper, gently fold the whipped cream into the cooled mixture.
8. Transfer the mixture to a small metal container that can go in the freezer (such as a mini loaf pan).
9. Mix in the chocolate chips, and cover the container with foil or plastic wrap.
10. Freeze the ice cream for 4 to 5 hours before serving, stirring it twice during that time.

SUBSTITUTION TIP If you don't care for peppermint extract, you can replace it with alcohol-free vanilla extract to make chocolate-chip ice cream.

PER SERVING Calories: 325; Fat: 33g; Carbs: 17g; Net Carbs: 4g; Fiber: 4g; Protein: 3g

BLUEBERRY-BLACKBERRY ICE POPS

Serves 2 / Prep time: 5 minutes, plus 2 hours to freeze

If they aren't already, ice pops are likely to become one of your favorite desserts. They are simple to make, so you can always have a keto-friendly alternative on hand to satisfy your sweet tooth. Once you become adept at making ice pops, you can get creative with different flavors. Here, blueberries and blackberries combine with coconut milk or cream for a sweet that's both creamy and refreshing. And the color is gorgeous!

½ (13.5-ounce) can coconut cream, ¾ cup unsweetened full-fat coconut milk, or ¾ cup heavy (whipping) cream

2 teaspoons Swerve natural sweetener or 2 drops liquid stevia
½ teaspoon alcohol-free vanilla extract
¼ cup mixed blueberries and blackberries (fresh or frozen)

1. In a food processor (or blender), mix together the coconut cream, sweetener, and vanilla.

2. Add the mixed berries, and pulse just a few times so the blueberries retain their texture.

3. Pour into ice pop molds and freeze for at least 2 hours before serving.

INGREDIENT TIP If you don't have both blueberries and blackberries, you can make this recipe with just one or the other.

PER SERVING Calories: 165; Fat: 17g; Carbs: 4g; Net Carbs: 2g; Fiber: 1g; Protein: 1g

STRAWBERRY-LIME ICE POPS

Serves 4 / Prep time: 5 minutes, plus 2 hours to freeze

The fresh, delicious flavors of this ice pop are reminiscent of a Mexican paleta. With the addition of lime juice, you have sweet, creamy, and sour flavors all in one delicious ice pop.

½ (13.5-ounce) can coconut cream, ¾ cup unsweetened full-fat coconut milk, or ¾ cup heavy (whipping) cream

2 teaspoons Swerve natural sweetener or 2 drops liquid stevia

1 tablespoon freshly squeezed lime juice

¼ cup hulled and sliced strawberries (fresh or frozen)

1. In a food processor (or blender), mix together the coconut cream, sweetener, and lime juice.
2. Add the strawberries, and pulse just a few times so the strawberries retain their texture.
3. Pour into ice pop molds, and freeze for at least 2 hours before serving.

INGREDIENT TIP You can also replace the strawberries with blackberries.

PER SERVING Calories: 166; Fat: 17g; Carbs: 5g; Net Carbs: 3g; Fiber: 1g; Protein: 1g

COFFEE ICE POPS

Serves 4 / Prep time: 5 minutes, plus 2 hours to freeze

Coffee is a staple for so many people on a keto diet. Why not freeze it into a convenient ice pop form? The mix of coffee and cream is extra fun with the addition of sugar-free chocolate chips.

2 cups brewed coffee, cold

¾ cup coconut cream, ¾ cup unsweetened full-fat coconut milk, or ¾ cup heavy (whipping) cream

2 teaspoons Swerve natural sweetener or 2 drops liquid stevia

2 tablespoons sugar-free chocolate chips

1. In a food processor (or blender), mix together the coffee, coconut cream, and sweetener until thoroughly blended.

2. Pour into ice pop molds, and drop a few chocolate chips into each mold.

3. Freeze for at least 2 hours before serving.

INGREDIENT TIP You can adjust the sweetness to your personal taste.

VARIATIONS You can add in your favorite sugar-free flavorings to customize the ice pops just as you would your coffee:

- Cinnamon
- Vanilla
- Chocolate protein powder

PER SERVING Calories: 105; Fat: 10g; Carbs: 7g; Net Carbs: 2g; Fiber: 2g; Protein: 1g

NO COOK

FUDGE ICE POPS

Serves 4 / Prep time: 5 minutes, plus 2 hours to freeze

These creamy ice pops are a perfect keto-friendly choice to satisfy your chocolate cravings.

½ (13.5-ounce) can coconut cream,
   ¾ cup unsweetened full-fat
   coconut milk, or ¾ cup heavy
   (whipping) cream
2 teaspoons Swerve natural sweetener
   or 2 drops liquid stevia

2 tablespoons unsweetened
   cocoa powder
2 tablespoons sugar-free
   chocolate chips

1. In a food processor (or blender), mix together the coconut cream, sweetener, and unsweetened cocoa powder.

2. Pour into ice pop molds, and drop chocolate chips into each mold.

3. Freeze for at least 2 hours before serving.

INGREDIENT TIP You can adjust the sweetness to your personal taste.

VARIATIONS Have fun playing with the mix-ins:
- You can add collagen powder to the mix for added health benefits.
- Choose the heavy (whipping) cream and add cream cheese. Fold in the chocolate chips at the end of the recipe.

PER SERVING Calories: 193; Fat: 20g; Carbs: 9g; Net Carbs: 3g; Fiber: 3g; Protein: 2g

VANILLA-ALMOND ICE POPS

Serves 8 / Prep time: 10 minutes, plus 4 hours to freeze / Cook time: 5 minutes

For children (and adults!), nothing is better than a sweet treat on a hot summer day. This is a more elegant ice pop that can be enjoyed after a leisurely barbecue with friends. It features simple vanilla and coconut flavoring, which can be enhanced with cut fruit if you want a little more texture to the pop.

2 cups almond milk

1 cup heavy (whipping) cream

1 vanilla bean, halved lengthwise

1 cup shredded unsweetened coconut

1. In a medium saucepan over medium heat, heat the almond milk, cream, and vanilla bean.

2. Bring the liquid to a simmer, and reduce the heat to low. Continue to simmer for 5 minutes.

3. Remove the saucepan from the heat, and let the liquid cool.

4. Take the vanilla bean out of the liquid, and use a knife to scrape the seeds out of the bean into the liquid.

5. Stir in the coconut, and divide the liquid among the ice pop molds.

6. Freeze until solid, about 4 hours, and enjoy.

PER SERVING Calories: 166; Fat: 15g; Carbs: 4g; Net Carbs: 2g; Fiber: 2g; Protein: 3g

ROOT BEER FLOAT

Serves 2 / Prep time: 5 minutes

With this keto-friendly root beer float, you won't miss the sugar, at all.

1 (12-ounce) can diet root beer
  (such as Zevia)

4 tablespoons heavy (whipping) cream

1 teaspoon alcohol-free vanilla extract

6 ice cubes

1. In a food processor (or blender), combine the root beer, cream, vanilla, and ice.

2. Blend well, pour into two tall glasses, and serve.

INGREDIENT TIP If you are looking for a boozy root beer float, you can add vanilla vodka or rum to this mix.

PER SERVING Calories: 56; Fat: 6g; Carbs: 3g; Net Carbs: 1g; Fiber: 0g; Protein: 1g

ORANGE CREAM FLOAT

Serves 2 / Prep time: 5 minutes

Orange is not a flavor you get to experience very often on the keto diet. But whenever you have a craving for orange goodness, look to this keto-friendly float, which calls for orange soda made with stevia. The citrusy tang and creamy texture are a nostalgic nod to many a child's favorite treat.

1 can diet orange soda (such as Zevia)

4 tablespoons heavy (whipping) cream

1 teaspoon alcohol-free vanilla extract

6 ice cubes

1. In a food processor (or blender), combine the orange soda, cream, vanilla, and ice.

2. Blend well, pour into two tall glasses, and serve.

INGREDIENT TIP If you're after a boozy orange cream treat, add vanilla vodka to this mix.

PER SERVING Calories: 56; Fat: 6g; Carbs: 3g; Net Carbs: 1g; Fiber: 0g; Protein: 1g

STRAWBERRY SHAKE

Serves 2 / Prep time: 10 minutes

This creamy delight offers the flavors of strawberry cheesecake, in the form of a shake. No baking or waiting for anything to set. Just whip it up—ready in minutes!

¾ cup heavy (whipping) cream

2 ounces cream cheese, at room temperature

1 tablespoon Swerve natural sweetener

¼ teaspoon alcohol-free vanilla extract

6 strawberries, sliced

6 ice cubes

1. In a food processor (or blender), combine the heavy cream, cream cheese, sweetener, and vanilla. Mix on high to fully blend.

2. Add the strawberries and ice, and blend until smooth.

3. Pour into two tall glasses and serve.

INGREDIENT TIP A little swirl of whipped cream is always a nice topping to any milkshake.

PER SERVING Calories: 407; Fat: 42g; Carbs: 13g; Net Carbs: 6g; Fiber: 1g; Protein: 4g

"FROSTY" CHOCOLATE SHAKE

Serves 2 / Prep time: 10 minutes, plus 1 hour to chill

This copycat keto-friendly recipe for the frozen dessert from Wendy's gets close to the real thing.

¾ cup heavy (whipping) cream

4 ounces unsweetened full-fat
coconut milk

1 tablespoon Swerve natural sweetener

¼ teaspoon alcohol-free vanilla extract

2 tablespoons unsweetened
cocoa powder

1. Pour the cream into a medium cold metal bowl, and with your hand mixer and cold beaters, beat the cream just until it forms peaks.

2. Slowly pour in the coconut milk, and gently stir it into the cream. Add the sweetener, vanilla, and cocoa powder, and beat until fully combined.

3. Pour into two tall glasses, and chill in the freezer for 1 hour before serving. Stir the shakes twice during this time.

INGREDIENT TIPS

- When you open the can of coconut milk, stir the contents to combine them.
- Almond milk will work if you don't have coconut milk.
- Chill the bowl and beaters in the freezer before making this recipe.

PER SERVING Calories: 444; Fat: 47g; Carbs: 15g; Net Carbs: 7g; Fiber: 2g; Protein: 4g

PUMPKIN SPICE FAT BOMBS

Serves 16 / Prep time: 10 minutes, plus 1 hour to chill

Pumpkin is a natural choice for desserts, especially those that also include warm spices reminiscent of holiday pumpkin pie. Like its vegetable counterpart, carrots, the bright orange flesh of pumpkin indicates it is a stellar source of beta-carotene. Pumpkin is also very high in vitamins A and C as well as potassium, making this pretty ingredient perfect for flushing toxins from your body and fighting cancer.

½ cup butter, at room temperature

½ cup cream cheese, at room temperature

⅓ cup pure pumpkin purée

3 tablespoons chopped almonds

4 drops liquid stevia

½ teaspoon ground cinnamon

¼ teaspoon ground nutmeg

1. Line an 8-by-8-inch pan with parchment paper and set aside.

2. In a small bowl, whisk together the butter and cream cheese until very smooth.

3. Add the pumpkin purée and whisk until blended.

4. Stir in the almonds, stevia, cinnamon, and nutmeg.

5. Spoon the pumpkin mixture into the pan. Use a spatula or the back of a spoon to spread it evenly in the pan, then place it in the freezer for about 1 hour.

6. Cut into 16 pieces and store the fat bombs in a tightly sealed container in the freezer until ready to serve, for up to 3 months.

STORAGE TIP Keep extras in your freezer in a zip-top bag for up to 3 months. They'll be ready any time you are craving a sweet treat.

PER SERVING (1 FAT BOMB) Calories: 87; Fat: 9g; Carbs: 1g; Net Carbs: 1g; Fiber: 0g; Protein: 1g

CREAMY BANANA FAT BOMBS

Serves 12 / Prep time: 10 minutes, plus 1 hour to chill

Banana-flavored desserts are a strange combination of exotic and comforting, as well as undeniably delicious. Fat bombs fall into savory or sweet categories, with these being on the sweeter side, but you can reduce the amount of sweetener if you want a less dessert-like experience. A sprinkling of shredded toasted coconut would top off these fat bombs beautifully.

1¼ cups cream cheese, at room temperature

¾ cup heavy (whipping) cream

1 tablespoon alcohol-free banana extract

6 drops liquid stevia

1. Line a baking sheet with parchment paper and set aside.

2. In a medium bowl, beat together the cream cheese, cream, banana extract, and stevia until smooth and very thick, about 5 minutes.

3. Gently spoon the mixture onto the baking sheet into 12 mounds, leaving some space between each mound, and place the baking sheet in the refrigerator until firm, about 1 hour.

4. Store the fat bombs in an airtight container in the refrigerator for up to 1 week.

PER SERVING (1 FAT BOMB) Calories: 134; Fat: 12g; Carbs: 1g; Net Carbs: 1g; Fiber: 0g; Protein: 3g

BLUEBERRY FAT BOMBS

Serves 12 / Prep time: 10 minutes, plus 3 hours to chill

The color of these fat bombs is a distinct blue, which you might find startling. Frozen unsweet-ened berries will work if fresh are not available or in season: Just thaw the frozen fruit first. If your area has wild blueberries, use these smaller berries because they have a significantly higher level of antioxidants than cultivated blueberries.

½ cup coconut oil, at room temperature

½ cup cream cheese, at room temperature

½ cup blueberries, mashed with a fork

6 drops liquid stevia

Pinch ground nutmeg

1. Line a mini muffin tin with paper liners and set aside.

2. In a medium bowl, stir together the coconut oil and cream cheese until well blended.

3. Stir in the blueberries, stevia, and nutmeg until combined.

4. Divide the blueberry mixture among the muffin cups, and place the tray in the freezer until set, about 3 hours.

5. Place the fat bombs in an airtight container and store in the freezer until you wish to eat them, for up to 3 months.

PER SERVING (1 FAT BOMB) Calories: 115; Fat: 12g; Carbs: 1g; Net Carbs: 1g; Fiber: 0g; Protein: 1g

SPICED-CHOCOLATE FAT BOMBS

Serves 12 / Prep time: 10 minutes, plus 15 minutes to chill / Cook time: 4 minutes

Good-quality cocoa powder is an acceptable ingredient on the keto diet, which means you can still enjoy a chocolate dessert and snack when you need a fix. Dark chocolate such as cocoa is very high in manganese, magnesium, copper, iron, and fiber as well as antioxidants, which fight free radicals in the body. Dark chocolate has been found to help lower blood pressure, reduce cholesterol, and improve cognitive function.

¾ cup coconut oil

¼ cup cocoa powder

¼ cup almond butter

⅛ teaspoon chili powder

3 drops liquid stevia

1. Line a mini muffin tin with paper liners and set aside.

2. In a small saucepan over low heat, heat the coconut oil, cocoa powder, almond butter, chili powder, and stevia until the coconut oil is melted, then whisk to blend.

3. Spoon the mixture into the muffin cups and place the tin in the refrigerator until the bombs are firm, about 15 minutes.

4. Transfer the cups to an airtight container and store the fat bombs in the freezer until you want to serve them, up to 3 weeks.

PER SERVING (1 FAT BOMB) Calories: 117; Fat: 12g; Carbs: 2g; Net Carbs: 2g; Fiber: 0g; Protein: 2g

LEMONADE FAT BOMBS

Serves 2 / Prep time: 10 minutes, plus 2 hours to freeze

If you love lemon, this fat bomb is for you. Let the ingredients sit on the counter for about 2 hours to come to room temperature before you start preparing this recipe—an important step to keep in mind for any fat bomb recipe.

½ lemon

4 ounces cream cheese, at room temperature

2 ounces butter, at room temperature

2 teaspoons Swerve natural sweetener or 2 drops liquid stevia

Pinch pink Himalayan salt

1. Zest the lemon half with a very fine grater into a small bowl. Squeeze the juice from the lemon half into the bowl with the zest.

2. In a medium bowl, combine the cream cheese and butter. Add the sweetener, lemon zest and juice, and salt. Using a hand mixer, beat until fully combined.

3. Spoon the mixture into small silicone cupcake molds or an ice cube tray. If you have neither, you can use cupcake paper liners fitted into the cups of a muffin tin.

4. Freeze for at least 2 hours, unmold, and eat!

PER SERVING (1 FAT BOMB) Calories: 404; Fat: 43g; Carbs: 8g; Net Carbs: 4g; Fiber: 1g; Protein: 4g

BERRY CHEESECAKE FAT BOMBS

Serves 2 / Prep time: 10 minutes, plus at least 2 hours to freeze

These fat bombs give you all the flavor of cheesecake in a small bite. You can use any berries you like; a combination of strawberries and blackberries works well. All ingredients should be room temperature—an important step for making successful fat bombs.

4 ounces cream cheese, at room temperature

4 tablespoons (½ stick) butter, at room temperature

2 teaspoons Swerve natural sweetener or 2 drops liquid stevia

1 teaspoon alcohol-free vanilla extract

¼ cup berries, fresh or frozen

1. In a medium bowl, use a hand mixer to beat the cream cheese, butter, sweetener, and vanilla.

2. In a small bowl, mash the berries thoroughly. Fold the berries into the cream cheese mixture using a rubber scraper. (If you put slices of berries in the cream cheese mixture without mashing them, they will freeze and have an off-putting texture.)

3. Spoon the cream cheese mixture into small silicone cupcake molds or an ice cube tray. If you have neither, you can use cupcake paper liners fitted into the cups of a muffin tin.

4. Freeze for at least 2 hours, unmold them, and eat!

PER SERVING (1 FAT BOMB) Calories: 414; Fat: 43g; Carbs: 9g; Net Carbs: 4g; Fiber: 1g; Protein: 4g

ONE POT

PEANUT BUTTER FAT BOMBS

Serves 2 / Prep time: 10 minutes, plus 30 minutes to freeze / Cook time: 1 minutes or less

If you're nuts for peanut butter, these fat bombs are an easy way to make yourself very happy. You can mix these up before you make dinner, and they will be ready in time for dessert: quick and easy. All ingredients should be at room temperature; this is important for any fat bomb recipe.

1 tablespoon butter, at room temperature

1 tablespoon coconut oil

2 tablespoons natural peanut butter or almond butter

2 teaspoons Swerve natural sweetener or 2 drops liquid stevia

1. In a microwave-safe medium bowl, melt the butter, coconut oil, and peanut butter in the microwave on 50 percent power. Mix in the sweetener.

2. Pour the mixture into small silicone cupcake molds or an ice cube tray. If you have neither, you can use cupcake liners fitted into the cups of a muffin tin.

3. Freeze for 30 minutes, unmold them, and eat! Keep some extras in your freezer so you can eat them anytime you are craving a sweet treat.

PER SERVING (1 FAT BOMB) Calories: 196; Fat: 20g; Carbs: 8g; Net Carbs: 3g; Fiber: 1g; Protein: 3g

STRAWBERRY CHEESECAKE MOUSSE

Serves 2 / Prep time: 10 minutes, plus 1 hour to chill

This is a super-easy dessert that any cheesecake-loving person will devour! It takes only 10 minutes to make and can easily be customized with different fruits.

4 ounces cream cheese, at room temperature

1 tablespoon heavy (whipping) cream

1 teaspoon Swerve natural sweetener or 1 drop liquid stevia

1 teaspoon alcohol-free vanilla extract

4 strawberries, sliced (fresh or frozen)

1. Break up the cream cheese block into smaller pieces and distribute evenly in a food processor (or blender). Add the cream, sweetener, and vanilla.

2. Mix together on high. Stop the mixer twice, and stir and scrape down the sides of the bowl with a small rubber scraper to make sure everything is mixed well.

3. Add the strawberries to the food processor, and mix until combined.

4. Divide the strawberry cheesecake mixture between two small dishes, and chill for 1 hour before serving.

INGREDIENT TIP The heavy whipping cream helps thin out the cream cheese a bit. If it still seems too thick when you are mixing, mix in a little more cream.

VARIATIONS

- You can use blackberries instead of strawberries, about ¼ cup.
- At winter holidays, instead of strawberries, add 3 ounces of pumpkin purée to this mixture along with 1 teaspoon of pumpkin pie spice.

PER SERVING Calories: 221; Fat: 21g; Carbs: 11g; Net Carbs: 4g; Fiber: 1g; Protein: 4g

CHOCOLATE MOUSSE

Serves 2 / Prep time: 10 minutes, plus 1 hour to chill

This dessert is rich, chocolatey, and super indulgent. It is packed with fats and bursting with creamy, chocolatey flavor.

1½ tablespoons heavy (whipping) cream

¼ cup butter, at room temperature

1 tablespoon unsweetened cocoa powder

¼ cup cream cheese, at room temperature

1 tablespoon Swerve natural sweetener

1. In a medium chilled bowl, use a whisk or fork to whip the cream. Refrigerate to keep cold.

2. In a separate medium bowl, use a hand mixer to beat the butter, cocoa powder, cream cheese, and sweetener until thoroughly combined.

3. Take the whipped cream out of the refrigerator. Gently fold the whipped cream into the chocolate mixture with a rubber scraper.

4. Divide the pudding between two dessert bowls.

5. Cover and chill for 1 hour before serving.

COOKING TIP For making the whipping cream, leave a clean medium metal bowl in the freezer for a couple of hours before using it. If using beaters, you can also put those in the freezer to chill for a few minutes before whipping the cream.

VARIATIONS Chocolate pairs well with a variety of flavors and textures:
- Fresh raspberries are delicious on top of this mousse.
- For extra-high-quality fat, add ¼ of an avocado to this mix. The avocado adds a smooth creaminess.

PER SERVING Calories: 460; Fat: 50g; Carbs: 10g; Net Carbs: 4g; Fiber: 1g; Protein: 4g

PEANUT BUTTER MOUSSE

Serves 4 / Prep time: 10 minutes, plus 30 minutes to chill

Peanut butter is always a handy, delicious sandwich spread, but it is used in many types of dishes all over the world. Moreover, it is very healthy. Eating peanut butter, even in this scrumptious dessert, can reduce your risk of cancer and heart disease and help lower choles-terol levels. Natural peanut butter is very high in unsaturated fats, protein, fiber, and folate.

1 cup heavy (whipping) cream

¼ cup natural peanut butter

1 teaspoon alcohol-free vanilla extract

4 drops liquid stevia

1. In a medium bowl, beat together the cream, peanut butter, vanilla, and stevia until firm peaks form, about 5 minutes.

2. Spoon the mousse into 4 bowls, and place in the refrigerator to chill for 30 minutes.

3. Serve.

PER SERVING Calories: 280; Fat: 28g; Carbs: 4g; Net Carbs: 3g; Fiber: 1g; Protein: 6g

CHOCOLATE-AVOCADO PUDDING

Serves 2 / Prep time: 5 minutes, plus 30 minutes to chill

Chocolate-and-avocado creations can be a bit tricky to pull off, but when they do come out right, they are delicious, like this pudding recipe.

1 ripe medium avocado, cut into chunks

2 ounces cream cheese, at room temperature

1 tablespoon Swerve natural sweetener

4 tablespoons unsweetened cocoa powder

¼ teaspoon alcohol-free vanilla extract

Pinch pink Himalayan salt

1. In a food processor (or blender), combine the avocado with the cream cheese, sweetener, cocoa powder, vanilla, and salt. Blend until completely smooth.

2. Pour into two small dessert bowls, and chill for 30 minutes before serving.

INGREDIENT TIP If you have an extra-large avocado, only use half. You don't want the avocado flavor to be too overwhelming.

PER SERVING Calories: 281; Fat: 27g; Carbs: 27g; Net Carbs: 12g; Fiber: 10g; Protein: 8g

RASPBERRY CHEESECAKE

Serves 12 / Prep time: 10 minutes / Cook time: 25 to 30 minutes

Cheesecake is a sublime dessert experience: tart, sweet, and infinitely velvety on the tongue. This is a crust-free cheesecake featuring plump, ripe raspberries and a distinct vanilla undertone. You can use any type of berry, sliced peaches or plums, or even a tablespoon of cocoa powder to create gorgeous variations. Your imagination is the limit when you have a perfect cheesecake base to use in your experiments.

⅔ cup coconut oil, melted

½ cup cream cheese, at room temperature

6 large eggs

3 tablespoons granulated sweetener

1 teaspoon alcohol-free vanilla extract

½ teaspoon baking powder

¾ cup raspberries

1. Preheat the oven to 350°F. Line an 8-by-8-inch baking dish with parchment paper and set aside.

2. In a large bowl, beat together the coconut oil and cream cheese until smooth.

3. Beat in the eggs, scraping down the sides of the bowl at least once.

4. Beat in the sweetener, vanilla, and baking powder until smooth.

5. Spoon the batter into the baking dish, and use a spatula to smooth out the top. Scatter the raspberries on top.

6. Bake until the center is firm, about 25 to 30 minutes.

7. Allow the cheesecake to cool completely before cutting into 12 squares and serving.

SUBSTITUTION TIP Any type of berry is delicious in this luscious treat, such as blueberries, strawberries, or blackberries. Whenever possible for your recipes, use seasonal local fruit for the best flavor and color.

PER SERVING (1 SQUARE) Calories: 176; Fat: 18g; Carbs: 3g; Net Carbs: 2g; Fiber: 1g; Protein: 6g

ONE PAN

CRUSTLESS CHEESECAKE BITES

Serves 4 / Prep time: 10 minutes, plus 3 hours to chill / Cook time: 30 minutes

If you love cheesecake, take heart: It is so easy to make keto-friendly cheesecake! These make perfect bite-size desserts for family dinners or for a take-along to a dinner party.

4 ounces cream cheese, at room temperature

¼ cup sour cream

2 large eggs

⅓ cup Swerve natural sweetener

¼ teaspoon alcohol-free vanilla extract

1. Preheat the oven to 350°F.
2. In a medium mixing bowl, use a hand mixer to beat the cream cheese, sour cream, eggs, sweetener, and vanilla until well mixed.
3. Place silicone liners (or cupcake paper liners) in the cups of a muffin tin.
4. Pour the cheesecake batter into the liners, and bake for 30 minutes.
5. Refrigerate until completely cooled before serving, about 3 hours.

INGREDIENT TIP It is much easier to mix the cream cheese when you allow it to come to room temperature.

STORAGE TIP Store extra cheesecake bites in a zip-top bag in the freezer for up to 3 months.

VARIATIONS
- Add lemon zest for a delicious burst of flavor.
- For a keto-friendly version of key lime cheesecake, add ½ teaspoon of sugar-free lime Jello mix and ½ teaspoon of freshly squeezed lime juice to this recipe.

PER SERVING Calories: 169; Fat: 15g; Carbs: 18g; Net Carbs: 2g; Fiber: 0g; Protein: 5g

PUMPKIN CRUSTLESS CHEESECAKE BITES

Serves 4 / Prep time: 10 minutes, plus 3 hours to chill / Cook time: 30 minutes

These bites have classic cheesecake flavor with a pumpkin twist. They're perfect for fall, when you're craving all things pumpkin, but equally delicious any time of the year.

4 ounces pumpkin purée

4 ounces cream cheese, at room temperature

2 large eggs

⅓ cup Swerve natural sweetener

2 teaspoons pumpkin pie spice

1. Preheat the oven to 350°F.

2. In a medium mixing bowl, use a hand mixer to mix the pumpkin purée, cream cheese, eggs, sweetener, and pumpkin pie spice until thoroughly combined.

3. Place silicone liners (or cupcake paper liners) into the cups of a muffin tin.

4. Pour the batter into the liners, and bake for 30 minutes.

5. Refrigerate until completely cooled before serving, about 3 hours.

INGREDIENT TIP You'll want to use pure pumpkin for this recipe, not pumpkin pie mix, which has added sugar.

STORAGE TIP Put leftover cheesecake bites in a zip-top plastic bag and store in the freezer for up to 3 months.

PER SERVING Calories: 156; Fat: 12g; Carbs: 21g; Net Carbs: 4g; Fiber: 1g; Protein: 5g

BERRY-PECAN MASCARPONE BOWL

Serves 2 / Prep time: 5 minutes

A lot of people enjoy this dish for breakfast when it's made with cottage cheese. But with mascarpone, a touch of sweetener, and a small handful of keto-friendly chocolate chips, you'll be in dessert heaven.

1 cup chopped pecans

1 teaspoon Swerve natural sweetener or 1 drop liquid stevia

¼ cup mascarpone

30 sugar-free dark-chocolate chips

6 strawberries, sliced

1. Divide the pecans between two dessert bowls.
2. In a small bowl, mix the sweetener into the mascarpone cheese. Top the nuts with a dollop of the sweetened mascarpone.
3. Sprinkle in the chocolate chips, top each dish with the strawberries, and serve.

SUBSTITUTION TIP You could also use ricotta cheese instead of mascarpone.

PER SERVING Calories: 462; Fat: 47g; Carbs: 15g; Net Carbs: 6g; Fiber: 7g; Protein: 6g

CHOCOLATE-COCONUT TREATS

Makes 16 treats / Prep time: 10 minutes, plus 30 minutes to chill / Cook time: 3 minutes

Chocolate and coconut are a flawless combination often found in candy bars and many desserts. Here is a keto-friendly version you'll love.

⅓ cup coconut oil

¼ cup unsweetened cocoa powder

4 drops liquid stevia

Pinch pink Himalayan salt

¼ cup shredded unsweetened coconut

1. Line a 6-by-6-inch baking dish with parchment paper and set aside.

2. In a small saucepan over low heat, stir together the coconut oil, cocoa, stevia, and salt for about 3 minutes.

3. Stir in the coconut, and press the mixture into the baking dish.

4. Place the baking dish in the refrigerator until the mixture is hard, about 30 minutes.

5. Cut into 16 pieces, and store the treats in an airtight container in a cool place.

PREP TIPS For a more elegant presentation, try these ideas:

- Spoon the hot mixture into candy molds instead of a baking dish. Pop the molds in the refrigerator for 30 minutes, or until firm, and pop the treats out into a container.
- Omit the coconut in step 3 and roll the semihardened chocolate mixture into balls instead of spreading it in a pan. Then roll the balls in the shredded coconut and place the treats in the freezer to firm up completely.

PER SERVING (1 TREAT) Calories: 43; Fat: 5g; Carbs: 1g; Net Carbs: 1g; Fiber: 0g; Protein: 1g

ALMOND BUTTER FUDGE

Makes 36 pieces / Prep time: 10 minutes, plus 2 hours to chill

Fudge should be smooth and dense with no grittiness or graininess. Since you won't be using granulated sugar for this treat, the chances of getting the wrong texture are greatly reduced. Almond butter is a stellar source of protein, vitamin E, iron, manganese, and fiber.

1 cup coconut oil, at room temperature

1 cup almond butter

¼ cup heavy (whipping) cream

10 drops liquid stevia

Pinch pink Himalayan salt

1. Line a 6-by-6-inch baking dish with parchment paper and set aside.
2. In a medium bowl, whisk together the coconut oil, almond butter, cream, stevia, and salt until very smooth.
3. Spoon the mixture into the baking dish, and smooth the top with a spatula.
4. Place the dish in the refrigerator until the fudge is firm, about 2 hours.
5. Cut into 36 pieces, and store the fudge in an airtight container in the freezer for up to 2 weeks.

SUBSTITUTION TIP If you aren't a fan of almond butter, peanut butter or cashew butter would also be delicious and create the same tempting results.

PER SERVING (2 PIECES OF FUDGE) Calories: 204; Fat: 22g; Carbs: 3g; Net Carbs: 2g; Fiber: 1g; Protein: 3g

NUTTY SHORTBREAD COOKIES

Makes 18 cookies / Prep time: 10 minutes, plus 30 minutes to chill / Cook time: 10 minutes

Traditional shortbread has very few ingredients and is intensely buttery, slightly crumbly, and not too sweet. The nuts used here in place of flour create the desired texture and add a complex, pleasing flavor. These cookies will continue to cook on the baking sheets after you take them out of the oven, so don't forget to transfer them to wire racks quickly to avoid overbrowning.

½ cup butter, at room temperature, plus more for greasing the baking sheet

½ cup granulated sweetener, such as Swerve

1 teaspoon alcohol-free vanilla extract

1½ cups almond flour

½ cup ground hazelnuts

Pinch pink Himalayan salt

1. In a medium bowl, cream together the butter, sweetener, and vanilla until well blended.

2. Stir in the almond four, ground hazelnuts, and salt until a firm dough is formed.

3. Roll the dough into a 2-inch cylinder, and wrap it in plastic wrap. Place the dough in the refrigerator for at least 30 minutes, until firm.

4. Preheat the oven to 350°F. Line a baking sheet with parchment paper and lightly grease the paper with butter; set aside.

5. Unwrap the chilled cylinder, slice the dough into 18 cookies, and place the cookies on the baking sheet.

6. Bake the cookies until firm and lightly browned, about 10 minutes.

7. Allow the cookies to cool on the baking sheet for 5 minutes, then transfer them to a wire rack to cool completely.

PREP TIP It is less expensive to purchase whole nuts and then grind them in a food processor or blender than to buy a preground product. Make sure you don't process the nuts in the appliance too long, though, or you'll end up with nut butter.

PER SERVING (1 COOKIE) Calories: 105; Fat: 10g; Carbs: 2g; Net Carbs: 1g; Fiber: 1g; Protein: 3g

ANUT BUTTER COOKIES

15 cookies / Prep time: 5 minutes / Cook time: 10 minutes, plus 10 minutes to cool

If you like peanut butter, you will love these cookies. They are very simple, using just three ingredients, and they taste just like the full-sugar version.

1 cup natural crunchy peanut butter

½ cup Swerve natural sweetener

1 large egg

1. Preheat the oven to 350°F. Line a baking sheet with a silicone baking mat or parchment paper.

2. In a medium bowl, use a hand mixer to mix together the peanut butter, sweetener, and egg.

3. Roll up the batter into small balls, about 1 inch in diameter.

4. Spread out the cookie-dough balls on the prepared pan. Press each dough ball down with the tines of a fork, then repeat to make a crisscross pattern.

5. Bake for about 12 minutes, or until golden.

6. Let the cookies cool for 10 minutes on the lined pan before serving. If you try to move them too soon, they will crumble.

7. Store leftover cookies covered in the refrigerator for up to 5 days.

INGREDIENT TIP You can use creamy peanut butter, but the texture of the cookies will be different.

PER COOKIE Calories: 98; Fat: 8g; Carbs: 10g; Net Carbs: 3g; Fiber: 1g; Protein: 4g

DARK-CHOCOLATE STRAWBERRY BARK

Serves 2 / Prep time: 10 minutes, plus 2 hours to chill / Cook time: 1 minute

When the craving for some dark chocolate hits you, try this treat—reminiscent of chocolate-covered strawberries, but in bark form, and with a little crunch.

½ (2.8-ounce) keto-friendly
   chocolate bar
1 tablespoon heavy (whipping) cream

2 tablespoons salted almonds
1 fresh strawberry, sliced

1. Line a baking sheet with parchment paper.

2. Break up the chocolate bar half into small pieces, and put them in a microwave-safe bowl with the cream.

3. Heat in the microwave for 45 seconds at 50 percent power. Stir the chocolate, and cook for 20 seconds more at 50 percent power. Stir again, making sure the mixture is fully melted and combined. If not, microwave for another 20 seconds.

4. Pour the chocolate mixture onto the parchment paper, and spread it in a thin, uniform layer.

5. Sprinkle on the almonds, then add the strawberry slices.

6. Refrigerate until hardened, about 2 hours.

7. Once the bark is nice and hard, break it up into smaller pieces to nibble on. Yum!

8. The bark will keep for up to 4 days in a sealed container in the refrigerator.

SUBSTITUTION TIP For another delicious option, substitute macadamia nuts for the almonds in this dessert.

PER SERVING Calories: 111; Fat: 10g; Carbs: 9g; Net Carbs: 4g; Fiber: 5g; Protein: 3g

14-DAY KETO INTRO MEAL PLAN

The meal plans provided on the following pages are meant to give you a jump-start in your keto diet. Having a road map makes it easier to succeed. These meal plans include meals for every part of the day, premade shopping lists, and macronutrient and calorie counts for each meal. They even account for leftovers. These meals plans will make starting your keto lifestyle much easier and more enjoyable! You can also use other recipes to create your own meal plans or swap out recipes in the meal plans provided.

Each day's meals provide anywhere from 1,600 to 1,850 calories. If you don't know how many calories you should be eating, be sure to check out an online keto macro calculator (see page 272). If you need to eat more calories than are provided in the meal plan, you can always add more of an ingredient or oil when you cook.

Please note: If you have any allergies or aversions to any of the ingredients, be sure to change them out.

WEEK 1 MEAL PLAN

MONDAY

Breakfast: Nut Medley Granola (page 55)

Snack: Bacon-Cheese Deviled Eggs (2) (page 90, see variation)

Lunch: Chicken-Avocado Lettuce Wraps (page 94)

Snack: Creamy Cinnamon Smoothie (page 53)

Dinner: Lamb Leg with Sun-Dried Tomato Pesto (page 225) and Cheesy Mashed Cauliflower (page 107)

Per Day

Calories: 1,840; Fat: 152g; Protein: 79g; Carbs: 39g; Fiber: 14g; Net Carbs: 25g

Fat 74% • Protein 20% • Carbs 6%

TUESDAY

Breakfast: Peanut Butter Cup Smoothie (page 49)

Snack: Walnut Herb-Crusted Goat Cheese (page 84)

Lunch: Cauliflower-Cheddar Soup (page 126)

Snack: Bacon-Cheese Deviled Eggs (2) (page 90)

Dinner: Lamb Leg with Sun-Dried Tomato Pesto (leftovers) (page 225) and Sautéed Crispy Zucchini (page 116)

Per Day

Calories: 1,725; Fat: 139g; Protein: 87g; Carbs: 26g; Fiber: 10g; Net Carbs: 16g

Fat 74% • Protein 21% • Carbs 5%

WEDNESDAY

Breakfast: Avocado and Eggs (page 59)

Snack: Spinach-Blueberry Smoothie (page 52)

Lunch: Cauliflower Cheddar Soup (leftovers) (page 126)

Snack: Nutty Shortbread Cookies (page 255)

Dinner: Baked Coconut Haddock (page 167) and Brussels Sprouts Casserole (page 105)

Per Day

Calories: 1,607; Fat: 123g; Protein: 77g; Carbs: 34g; Fiber: 17g; Net Carbs: 17g

Fat 77% • Protein 19% • Carbs 4%

THURSDAY

Breakfast: Lemon-Cashew Smoothie (page 51)

Snack: Almond Butter Fudge (2) (page 254)

Lunch: BLT Salad (page 130)

Snack: Bacon-Pepper Fat Bombs (page 82)

Dinner: Roasted Pork Loin with Grainy Mustard Sauce (page 218) and Golden Rosti (page 119)

Per Day

Calories: 1,637; Fat: 137g; Protein: 79g; Carbs: 26g; Fiber: 6g; Net Carbs: 20g

Fat 75% • Protein 20% • Carbs 5%

FRIDAY

Breakfast: Berry Green Smoothie
(page 50)

Snack: Bacon-Pepper Fat Bombs (2)
(page 82)

Lunch: Roasted Pork Loin with Grainy
Mustard Sauce (leftovers) (page 218)

Snack: Vanilla-Almond Ice Pops
(page 233)

Dinner: Turkey Meatloaf (page 188) and
Golden Rosti (leftovers) (page 119)

Per Day

Calories: 1,635; Fat: 134g; Protein: 85g;
Carbs: 21g; Fiber: 7g; Net Carbs: 14g

Fat 74% • Protein 21% • Carbs 5%

SATURDAY

Breakfast: Breakfast Bake (page 58)

Snack: Creamy Cinnamon Smoothie
(page 53)

Lunch: Turkey Meatloaf (leftovers)
(page 188)

Snack: Nutty Shortbread Cookies
(page 255)

Dinner: Cheesy Garlic Salmon (page 160)
and Garlicky Green Beans (page 114)

Per Day

Calories: 1,633; Fat: 137g; Protein: 81g;
Carbs: 19g; Fiber: 5g; Net Carbs: 14g

Fat 76% • Protein 20% • Carbs 4%

SUNDAY

Breakfast: Nut Medley Granola (page 55)

Snack: Smoked Salmon Fat Bombs
(page 83)

Lunch: Breakfast Bake (leftovers)
(page 58)

Snack: Almond Butter Fudge (2)
(page 254)

Dinner: Chicken Bacon Burgers (page 173)
and Portobello Mushroom Pizzas
(page 100)

Per Day

Calories: 1,712; Fat: 143g; Protein: 79g;
Carbs: 27g; Fiber: 13g; Net Carbs: 14g

Fat 75% • Protein 20% • Carbs 5%

WEEK 1 SHOPPING LIST

MEAT AND SEAFOOD

Bacon (44 slices)

Chicken breast, 1 boneless (6 ounces)

Chicken, ground (1 pound)

Haddock fillets, 4 (5 ounces each)

Lamb leg (2 pounds)

Pork loin roast, boneless (2 pounds)

Salmon fillets, 4 (5 ounces each)

Salmon, smoked (2 ounces)

Sausage, preservative-free or homemade
   (1 pound)

Turkey, ground (1½ pounds)

DAIRY, DAIRY ALTERNATIVES, AND EGGS

Almond milk (2 cups)

Asiago cheese (½ cup)

Butter (2 cups)

Cashew milk, unsweetened (1 cup)

Cheddar cheese, shredded (2¼ cups)

Coconut cream (¾ cup)

Coconut milk (7 cups)

Cream cheese (5 ounces)

Eggs, large (20)

Goat cheese (12 ounces)

Heavy (whipping) cream (5⅓ cups)

Mozzarella cheese, shredded (1 cup)

Parmesan cheese (1 cup)

Swiss cheese (1¼ cups)

PRODUCE

Acorn squash (1)

Avocados (4)

Basil, fresh (1 bunch)

Blueberries (1 pint)

Boston lettuce (2 heads)

Brussels sprouts (1 pound)

Cauliflower (2)

Celeriac (1)

English cucumber (1)

Garlic cloves (12)

Green beans (1 pound)

Kale (2 ounces)

Lemons (2)

Mint sprigs, fresh (1 bunch)

Onion, sweet (1)

Oregano, fresh (1 bunch)

Parsley, fresh (1 bunch)

Portobello mushrooms (4)

Raspberries (1 pint)

Spaghetti squash (1)

Spinach (1 cup)

Thyme, fresh (1 bunch)

Tomato (2)

Zucchini (4)

CANNED AND BOTTLED ITEMS

Almond butter (2 cups)

Chicken stock (4 cups)

Coconut oil (2 cups)

Dijon mustard (½ teaspoon)

Grainy mustard (3 tablespoons)

Mayonnaise (⅔ cup)

Olive oil, extra-virgin (1 cup plus
   2 tablespoons)

Red wine vinegar (2 tablespoons)

Stevia, liquid (30 drops)

Sun-dried tomatoes packed in oil (1 cup)

Vanilla extract, alcohol-free (2 teaspoons)

PANTRY ITEMS

Almonds, ground (1¾ cup)

Almonds, sliced (1 cup)

Black pepper, freshly ground

Cinnamon, ground (3 teaspoons)

Coconut, shredded unsweetened (4 cups)

Hazelnuts, ground (¾ cup)

Nutmeg, ground (1 teaspoon)

Peanut butter (2 tablespoons)

Pine nuts (¼ cup)

Protein powder, chocolate (2 tablespoons)

Protein powder, plain (4 tablespoons)

Protein powder, vanilla (8 tablespoons)

Pumpkin seeds, raw (½ cup)

Pink Himalayan salt

Sesame seeds (1 teaspoon)

Sunflower seeds, raw (1¼ cups)

Sweetener, granulated (⅔ cup)

Vanilla bean (2)

Walnuts, chopped (10 ounces)

WEEK 2 MEAL PLAN

MONDAY

Breakfast: Berry Green Smoothie
(page 50)

Snack: Nutty Shortbread Cookies
(page 255)

Lunch: Chicken-Avocado Lettuce Wraps
(page 94)

Snack: Crispy Parmesan Crackers
(page 85)

Dinner: Baked Coconut Haddock
(page 167) and Brussels Sprouts
Casserole (page 105)

Per Day

Calories: 1,622; Fat: 126g; Protein: 88g;
Carbs: 34g; Fiber: 15g; Net Carbs: 19g

Fat 70% • Protein 22% • Carbs 8%

TUESDAY

Breakfast: Nut Medley Granola (page 55)

Snack: Vanilla-Almond Ice Pops
(page 233)

Lunch: Crab Salad–Stuffed Avocado
(page 95)

Snack: Chocolate-Coconut Treats (2)
(page 253)

Dinner: Lamb Leg with Sun-Dried Tomato
Pesto (page 225) and Brussels Sprouts
Casserole (leftover) (page 105)

Per Day

Calories: 1,606; Fat: 130g; Protein: 77g;
Carbs: 35g; Fiber: 17g; Net Carbs: 18g

Fat 73% • Protein 20% • Carbs 7%

WEDNESDAY

Breakfast: Peanut Butter Cup Smoothie
(page 49)

Snack: Crispy Parmesan Crackers
(page 85)

Lunch: BLT Salad (page 130)

Snack: Smoked Salmon Fat Bombs
(page 83)

Dinner: Lamb Leg with Sun-Dried Tomato
Pesto (leftovers) (page 225) and Cheesy
Mashed Cauliflower (page 107)

Per Day

Calories: 1,604; Fat: 130g; Protein: 86g;
Carbs: 23g; Fiber: 9g; Net Carbs: 14g

Fat 73% • Protein 21% • Carbs 6%

THURSDAY

Breakfast: Avocado and Eggs (page 59)

Snack: Almond Butter Fudge (2)
(page 254)

Lunch: Cauliflower-Cheddar Soup
(page 126)

Snack: Berry Green Smoothie (page 50)

Dinner: Herb Butter Scallops (page 153)
and Pesto Zucchini Noodles (page 118)

Per Day

Calories: 1,720; Fat: 140g; Protein: 83g;
Carbs: 32g; Fiber: 13g; Net Carbs: 19g

Fat 73% • Protein 20% • Carbs 7%

FRIDAY

Breakfast: Lemon-Cashew Smoothie (page 51)

Snack: Peanut Butter Mousse (page 247)

Lunch: Cauliflower-Cheddar Soup (leftovers) (page 126)

Snack: Chocolate-Coconut Treats (page 253)

Dinner: Roasted Pork Loin with Grainy Mustard Sauce (page 218) and Mushrooms with Camembert (page 102)

Per Day

Calories: 1,707; Fat: 139g; Protein: 84g; Carbs: 30g; Fiber: 7g; Net Carbs: 23g

Fat 73% • Protein 20% • Carbs 7%

SATURDAY

Breakfast: Breakfast Bake (page 58)

Snack: Queso Dip (page 92)

Lunch: Roasted Pork Loin with Grainy Mustard Sauce (leftovers) (page 218)

Snack: Almond Butter Fudge (3) (page 254)

Dinner: Lemon-Butter Chicken (page 172) and Sautéed Asparagus with Walnuts (page 103)

Per Day

Calories: 1,651; Fat: 142g; Protein: 75g; Carbs: 20g; Fiber: 5g; Net Carbs: 14g

Fat 76% • Protein 20% • Carbs 4%

SUNDAY

Breakfast: Nut Medley Granola (page 55)

Snack: Chicken-Avocado Lettuce Wraps (page 94)

Lunch: Breakfast Bake (leftovers) (page 58)

Snack: Raspberry Cheesecake (page 249) with ¼ cup whipped cream

Dinner: Turkey Meatloaf (page 188) and Creamed Spinach (page 121)

Per Day

Calories: 1,697; Fat: 140g; Protein: 71g; Carbs: 31g; Fiber: 13g; Net Carbs: 18g

Fat 74% • Protein 20% • Carbs 6%

WEEK 2 SHOPPING LIST

MEAT AND SEAFOOD

Bacon (14 slices)

Chicken breast, 2 boneless (6 ounces each)

Chicken thighs, bone-in, skin-on (4)

Dungeness crabmeat (4½ ounces)

Haddock fillets, 4 (5 ounces each)

Lamb leg (2 pounds)

Pork loin roast, boneless (2 pounds)

Sausage, preservative-free or homemade
  (1 pound)

Sea scallops (1 pound)

Turkey, ground (1½ pounds)

DAIRY, DAIRY ALTERNATIVES, AND EGGS

Almond milk (2 cups)

Butter (1¼ cups)

Camembert cheese (4 ounces)

Cashew milk, unsweetened (1 cup)

Cheddar cheese (13 ounces)

Coconut cream (¾ cup)

Coconut milk (½ cup)

Cream cheese (1¾ cups)

Eggs, large (20)

Goat cheese (2 ounces)

Heavy (whipping) cream (6⅓ cups)

Parmesan cheese (10 ounces)

Swiss cheese (4 ounces)

PRODUCE

Asparagus (¾ pound)

Avocados (4)

Basil, fresh (1 bunch)

Bell pepper, red (1)

Boston lettuce (2 heads)

Brussels sprouts (1 pound)

Button mushrooms (1 pound)

Cauliflower (2)

Cilantro (1 bunch)

English cucumber (1)

Garlic cloves (10)

Jalapeño pepper (1)

Kale (1 bunch)

Lemons (3)

Onions, sweet (2)

Oregano, fresh (1 bunch)

Parsley, fresh (1 bunch)

Raspberries (2 pints)

Scallion (1)

Spaghetti squash (1)

Spinach (3 ounces)

Thyme, fresh (1 bunch)

Tomato (1)

Zucchini (4)

CANNED AND BOTTLED ITEMS

Almond butter (2 cups)

Chicken stock (4¾ cups)

Coconut oil (1¾ cups)

Grainy mustard (3 tablespoons)

Mayonnaise (⅓ cup)

Olive oil, extra-virgin (½ cup plus
  6 tablespoons)

Red wine vinegar (2 tablespoons)

Stevia, liquid (18 drops)

Sun-dried tomatoes packed in oil (1 cup)

Vanilla extract, alcohol-free (2 teaspoons)

PANTRY ITEMS

Almond flour (1½ cups)

Almonds, sliced (1 cup)

Baking powder (½ teaspoon)

Black pepper, freshly ground

Cayenne pepper (¼ teaspoon)

Cinnamon, ground (1 teaspoon)

Cocoa powder (¼ cup)

Coconut, shredded unsweetened (3¼ cups)

Hazelnuts, ground (¼ cup)

Nutmeg, ground (1 teaspoon)

Nutritional yeast (2 teaspoons)

Onion powder (½ teaspoon)

Peanut butter (6 tablespoons)

Pine nuts (¼ cup)

Protein powder, chocolate (2 tablespoons)

Protein powder, plain (2 tablespoons)

Protein powder, vanilla (2 tablespoons)

Pumpkin seeds (½ cup)

Pink Himalayan salt

Sesame seeds (1 teaspoon)

Sunflower seeds (1 cup)

Sweetener, granulated (¼ cup)

Walnuts, chopped (1 cup)

ADVICE FOR GOING OUT TO EAT

Getting rid of all culinary temptations is great for eating at home, but what happens when you go out to eat? Staying on a low-carb diet might seem difficult at first, but it can be easy with these few tips and a little bit of practice!

BREAKFAST

Skip the bagels, pancakes, Belgian waffles, French toast, or anything of the like. Opt for an omelet or a few eggs with a side of sausage or ham. Skip the toast and hash browns.

LUNCH

Get a salad with lots of meat. Try a Cobb, chicken Caesar, or garden salad with chicken on top. Use plenty of extra-virgin olive oil and pink Himalayan salt (electrolytes). You'll feel great afterward and have plenty of energy to last you until dinner. Carbs are why people get sleepy after lunch. Don't be a victim!

DINNER

When ordering a burger, ask to have it wrapped in lettuce. If the restaurant staff are unable to do that, just ask for no bun. If the server brings the bun, take the patty and anything else off the bun and put it to the side. Skip the ketchup as well—it's full of sugar. Try mayo, mustard, red pepper sauce, Sriracha, or any other low-carb sauce.

At Italian restaurants, skip the pasta and pizza, and order the protein-based dinners. Make sure to request salad or any other low-carb alternatives instead of the usual high-carb sides. If all else fails, just eat the topping off of the pizza and avoid the crust.

With Mexican cuisine, try to get your food in a bowl instead of in a burrito wrap or tortilla. Don't get rice or beans; instead, get extra sour cream and guacamole.

SIDES

French fries, steak fries, mashed potatoes, baked potatoes, rice, beans, corn on the cob, banana bread, and any other high-carb sides can be replaced with salad, asparagus, broccoli, green beans, or other low-carb vegetables. Most restaurants have some sort of salad for you to choose from. Make sure to always ask and double-check with the waiter or staff.

DRINKS AND ALCOHOL

Instead of juice or soda, stick to water, tea, and coffee. Use heavy cream or half-and-half instead of milk.

In addition to fat, carbs, and protein, alcohol is also a macronutrient. It provides 7 calories per gram, the second most after fat, which provides 9 calories per gram. It is burned by the body before all the other macronutrients. If you drink too much alcohol, you will slow down your fat-burning process and impede your weight loss, if that is your goal.

If you're ordering alcohol, stay away from any cocktails, as they're all loaded with sugar. Dry or semidry wine has about 3 grams of carbs per glass, and low-carb beers such as Michelob Ultra and Modelo have 3 to 4 grams of carbs per bottle. All pure spirits—vodka, Cognac, brandy, bourbon, whisky, rum, tequila, and gin—contain zero carbs. As always, drink in moderation, stay safe, and enjoy!

MEASUREMENT CONVERSIONS

VOLUME EQUIVALENTS (LIQUID)

US STANDARD	US STANDARD (OUNCES)	METRIC (APPROXIMATE)
2 tablespoons	1 fl. oz.	30 mL
¼ cup	2 fl. oz.	60 mL
½ cup	4 fl. oz.	120 mL
1 cup	8 fl. oz.	240 mL
1½ cups	12 fl. oz.	355 mL
2 cups or 1 pint	16 fl. oz.	475 mL
4 cups or 1 quart	32 fl. oz.	1 L
1 gallon	128 fl. oz.	4 L

OVEN TEMPERATURES

FAHRENHEIT (F)	CELSIUS (C) (APPROXIMATE)
250°F	120°C
300°F	150°C
325°F	165°C
350°F	180°C
375°F	190°C
400°F	200°C
425°F	220°C
450°F	230°C

VOLUME EQUIVALENTS (DRY)

US STANDARD	METRIC (APPROXIMATE)
¼ teaspoon	1 mL
½ teaspoon	2 mL
1 teaspoon	5 mL
1 tablespoon	15 mL
¼ cup	59 mL
⅓ cup	79 mL
½ cup	118 mL
1 cup	235 mL

WEIGHT EQUIVALENTS

US STANDARD	METRIC (APPROXIMATE)
½ ounce	15 g
1 ounce	30 g
2 ounces	60 g
4 ounces	115 g
8 ounces	225 g
12 ounces	340 g
16 ounces or 1 pound	455 g

RESOURCES

BOOKS

Givens, Sara. *Ketogenic Diet Mistakes: You Wish You Knew*. Amazon Books, 2014. If you hit a weight-loss plateau or are running into any issues, this book can help you break through and reach your goals.

Moore, Jimmy, and Eric Westman. *Keto Clarity: Your Definitive Guide to the Benefits of a Low-Carb, High-Fat Diet*. Las Vegas: Victory Belt Publishing, 2014. A great read and further look into the science behind the keto diet and benefits from eating that diet.

Wilson, Jacob, and Ryan Lowery. *The Ketogenic Bible: The Authoritative Guide to Ketosis*. Las Vegas: Victory Belt Publishing, 2017. This book is an excellent resource for a deep dive into the science of keto and ketosis.

WEBSITES AND BLOGS

ketointhecity.com Keto in the City is a beginner-friendly blog that features keto FAQs, interviews, and many recipes.

dietdoctor.com Diet Doctor is a low-carb–focused site that provides articles and recipes as well as instructional videos and support.

ketodietapp.com Keto Diet App is a keto-only blog and a great resource for science-backed articles and recipes. It also has an app for mobile devices which includes recipes, articles, meal planning, and progress tracking.

tasteaholics.com Tasteaholics is a keto-centric website and resource that provides science-backed articles and recipes.

reddit.com/r/keto A large community with hundreds of thousands of users, who discuss progress, share cravings, and support each other.

ONLINE TOOLS AND APPS

Keto Macro Calculators

tasteaholics.com/keto-calculator The simplest and most straightforward.

keto-calculator.ankerl.com The most detailed and complex.

ketogains.com/ketogains-calculator A simple calculator with no charts and only numbers.

ruled.me In addition to the calculator, includes meal plans, recipes, and more.

Apps

MyFitnessPal A diet and exercise journal that provides meal tracking, calorie and macronutrient tracking, automatic calculation of meal nutrition, exercise tracking and caloric spend, and much more.

Carb Manager An app that includes carb counters, carb management tools, meal plans, an extensive database of low-carb recipes, and more.

REFERENCES

Allen, B. G., S. K. Bhatia, J. M. Buatti, K. E. Brandt, et al. "Ketogenic Diets Enhance Oxidative Stress and Radio-Chemo-Therapy Responses in Lung Cancer Xenografts." *Clinical Cancer Research* 19, no. 14 (July 2013): 3905–13. doi:10.1158/1078-0432.

Allen, Bryan G., Sudershan K. Bhatia, Carryn M. Anderson, Julie M. Eichenberger-Gilmore, et al. "Ketogenic Diets as an Adjuvant Cancer Therapy: History and Potential Mechanism." *Redox Biology* vol. 2 (2014): 963–70. doi:10.1016/j.redox.2014.08.002.

American Diabetes Association. "Statistics About Diabetes." www.diabetes.org /diabetes-basics/statistics/.

Aude, Y., A. S., Agatston, F. Lopez-Jimenez, et al. "The National Cholesterol Education Program Diet vs a Diet Lower in Carbohydrates and Higher in Protein and Monounsaturated Fat: A Randomized Trial." *JAMA Internal Medicine* 164, no. 19 (2004): 2141–46. doi: 10.1001/archinte.164.19.2141.

Brehm, Bonnie J., Randy J. Seeley, Stephen R. Daniels, and David A. D'Alessio. "A Randomized Trial Comparing a Very Low Carbohydrate Diet and a Calorie-Restricted Low Fat Diet on Body Weight and Cardiovascular Risk Factors in Healthy Women." *The Journal of Clinical Endocrinology & Metabolism* 88, no. 4 (January 2009). doi: 10.1210/jc.2002-021480.

Brinkworth, Grant D., Manny Noakes, Jonathan D. Buckley, Jennifer B. Keogh, and Peter M. Clifton. "Long-Term Effects of a Very-Low-Carbohydrate Weight Loss Diet Compared with an Isocaloric Low-Fat Diet after 12 Mo." *The American Journal of Clinical Nutrition* 90, no. 1 (July 2009): 23–32. doi:10.3945 /ajcn.2008.27326.

Centers for Disease Control and Prevention, National Center for Health Statistics. "Dietary Intake for Adults Aged 20 and Over." 2016. www.cdc.gov/nchs /fastats/diet.htm.

Chowdhury, R., S. Warnakula, S. Kunutsor, F. Crowe, H. A. Ward, et al. "Association of Dietary, Circulating, and Supplement Fatty Acids with Coronary Risk: A Systematic Review and Meta-Analysis." *Annals of Internal Medicine* 160 (2014): 398–406. doi:10.7326/M13-1788.

Daly, M. E., R. Paisey, R. Paisey, B. A. Millward, et al. "Short-Term Effects of Severe Dietary Carbohydrate-Restriction Advice in Type 2 Diabetes—a Randomized Controlled Trial." *Diabetic Medicine* 23, no. 1 (January 2006): 15–20. doi:10.1111/j.1464-5491.2005.01760.x.

Davis, C., and E. Saltos. "Dietary Recommendations and How They Have Changed Over Time," Agriculture Information Bulletin No. (AIB-750) 494 pp, *U.S. Department of Agriculture*, May 1999: 36-44. www.ers.usda.gov//media/91022/aib750b_1_.pdf.

De Lau, L. M., M. Bornebroek, J. C. Witteman, A. Hofman, et al. "Dietary Fatty Acids and the Risk of Parkinson Disease: The Rotterdam Study." *Neurology* 64, no. 12 (June 2005): 2040–45. doi:10.1212/01.WNL.0000166038.67153.9F.

Freeman, J. M., E. P. Vining, D. J. Pillas, P. L. Pyzik, et al. "The Efficacy of the Ketogenic Diet-1998: A Prospective Evaluation of Intervention in 150 Children." *Pediatrics* 102, no. 6 (December 1998): 1358–63. www.ncbi.nlm.nih.gov/pubmed/9832569/.

Fryar, C. D., M. D. Carroll, and C. L. Ogden. "Prevalence of Overweight, Obesity, and Extreme Obesity Among Adults: United States, 1960–1962 Through 2011–2012." Centers for Disease Control and Prevention, September 2014. www.cdc.gov/nchs/data/hestat/obesity_adult_11_12/obesity_adult_11_12.htm#table2.

Hemingway, C., J. M. Freeman, D. J. Pillas, and P. L. Pyzik. "The Ketogenic Diet: A 3- to 6-Year Follow-Up of 150 Children Enrolled Prospectively. *Pediatrics* 108, no. 4 (October 2001): 898–905. www.ncbi.nlm.nih.gov/pubmed/11581442/.

Henderson, S. T. "High Carbohydrate Diets and Alzheimer's Disease." *Medical Hypotheses* 62, no. 5 (2014): 689–700. doi:10.1016/j.mehy.2003.11.028.

Neal, E. G., H. Chaffe, R. H. Schwartz, M. S. Lawson, et al. "The Ketogenic Diet for the Treatment of Childhood Epilepsy: A Randomised Controlled Trial." *Lancet Neurology* 7, no. 6 (June 2008): 500–06. doi:10.1016/S1474-4422(08)70092-9.

Otto, C., U. Kaemmerer, B. Illert, B. Muehling, et al. "Growth of Human Gastric Cancer Cells in Nude Mice Is Delayed by a Ketogenic Diet Supplemented with Omega-3 Fatty Acids and Medium-Chain Triglycerides." *BMC Cancer* 8 (April 2008): 122. doi:10.1186/1471-2407-8-122.

Paoli, Antonio, Antonino Bianco, Ernesto Damiani, and Gerardo Basco. "Ketogenic Diet in Neuromuscular and Neurodegenerative Diseases." *Biomed Research International* 474296 (2014). doi:10.1155/2014/474296.

Samaha, Frederick F., Nayyar Iqbal, Prakash Seshadri, Kathryn L. Chicano, et al. "A Low-Carbohydrate as Compared with a Low-Fat Diet in Severe Obesity." *The New England Journal of Medicine* 348 (May 2003): 2075–81. doi:10.1056 /NEJMoa022637.

Siri-Tarino, P. W., Q. Sun, F. B. Hu, and R. M. Krauss. "Meta-Analysis of Prospective Cohort Studies Evaluating the Association of Saturated Fat with Cardiovascular Disease." *American Journal of Clinical Nutrition* 91, no. 3 (March 2010): 535–46. doi:10.3945/ajcn.2009.27725.

Sondike, Stephen B., Nancy Copperman, and Marc S. Jacobson. "Effects of a Low-Carbohydrate Diet on Weight Loss and Cardiovascular Risk Factor in Overweight Adolescents." *The Journal of Pediatrics* 142, no. 3 (March 2003): 253–58. doi: 10.1067/mpd.2003.4.

Tetzloff, W., F. Dauchy, S. Medimagh, D. Carr, A. Bärr. "Tolerance to Subchronic, High-Dose Ingestion of Erythritol in Human Volunteers." *Regulatory Toxicology and Pharmacology* 24, no, 2 (October 1996): S286–95. doi:10.1006/rtph.1996.0110.

Vanitallie, T. B., C. Nonas, A. Di Rocco, K. Boyar, S. B. Heymsfield. "Treatment of Parkinson Disease with Diet-Induced Hyperketonemia: A Feasibility Study." *Neurology* 64, no. 4 (February 2005): 728–30. doi:10.1212/01. WNL.0000152046.11390.45.

Volek, J. S., S. D. Phinney, C. E. Forsythe, et al. "Carbohydrate Restriction Has a More Favorable Impact on the Metabolic Syndrome than a Low Fat Diet." *Lipids* 44, no. 4 (2009): 297. doi:10.1007/s11745-008-3274-2.

Volek, J. S., M. J. Sharman, A. L. Gómez, D. A. Judelson, et al. "Comparison of Energy-Restricted Very Low-Carbohydrate and Low-Fat Diets on Weight Loss and Body Composition in Overweight Men and Women." *Nutrition & Metabolism* 1 (2004): 13. doi: 10.1186/1743-7075-1-13.

Westman, Eric C., William S. Yancy, John C. Mavropoulos, Megan Marquart, and Jennifer R. McDuffie. "The Effect of a Low-Carbohydrate, Ketogenic Diet versus a Low-Glycemic Index Diet on Glycemic Control in Type 2 Diabetes Mellitus." *Nutrition & Metabolism* 5 (2008): 36. doi:10.1186/1743-7075-5-36.

Zuccoli, G., N. Marcello, A. Pisanello, F. Servadei, et al. "Metabolic Management of Glioblastoma Multiforme Using Standard Therapy Together with a Restricted Ketogenic Diet: Case Report." *Nutrition & Metabolism* 7 (2010): 33. doi:10.1186/1743-7075-7-33.

RECIPE INDEX

INDEX

V

Vegetables, 12. *See also* specific

W

Walnuts
  Chicken-Avocado Lettuce Wraps, 94
  Nut Medley Granola, 55
  Nut-Stuffed Pork Chops, 217
  Sautéed Asparagus with Walnuts, 103
  Walnut Herb-Crusted Goat Cheese, 84
Weight loss, 2
Wraps. *See* Sandwiches and wraps

Z

Zesters, 17
Zucchini
  Baked Zucchini Gratin, 117
  Crunchy Pork Rind Zucchini Sticks, 87
  Pesto Zucchini Noodles, 118
  Sautéed Crispy Zucchini, 116